Praise for
Deena Katz on Practice Management
for Financial Advisers, Planners, and Wealth Managers
by Deena B. Katz

"Physician heal thyself is a long-standing adage in the medical community, but the same spirit applies to all professions. How many fine planners run poor businesses simply because they don't apply the same energies to their practice as they do to their clients. Thankfully, **Deena Katz has made yet another valuable contribution to the profession. This book outlines step-by-step how you can make your practice an efficient, profitable, and highly professional endeavor**."

> DON PHILLIPS
> Managing Director
> Morningstar, Inc.

"**An indispensable resource for any financial planner** who wants good ideas and insights on how to make a practice more successful—and it also gives some real perspective on what success is."

> JANET G. McCALLEN, CAE
> Executive Director
> Financial Planning Association

"I am very impressed with Deena's writing style and her ability to share her understanding of this business in such an entertaining and honest way. **This book is a no-nonsense guide for anyone contemplating entering this business—or for that matter, anyone already in business who wants to be more efficient**! As I teach financial planning candidates, Deena's book absolutely will be required reading. **What a contribution Deena has made to this profession**."

> PATRICIA P. HOULIHAN, CFP
> Chair, CFP Board of Standards
> Chair, International CFP Council

"**Every financial planner in practice, anywhere in the world, should read this book.** The chapter on the 'Concierge Service' is worth many times the price on its own."

DAVID S. NORTON, CFP
Former president, Institute of Financial Planning
United Kingdom

"**This volume belongs on every financial planner's bookshelf.** The book is filled with ideas, techniques and resources of benefit to the experienced planner and novice alike .... **The finest practice management volume available to financial planners today.**"

Journal of Financial Planning

"The book is like a hard-copy chat room for the exchange of valuable ideas on how to make your business a success. **The checklists, agenda outlines, and forms make it an indispensable reference work for any financial advisor. Whether you are an investment consultant, financial planner, or wealth manager, there is something for you.**"

The Journal of Investment Consulting

"Deena Katz covers all the bases—from articulating the company's values to selecting the right software. Reading her book is like sitting down with an old friend for a cup of coffee. Her style is warm and **her dedication to outstanding client service makes her advice relevant to any service business.**"

Morningstar.com

"**Deena has done it again! Another must-have for the financial adviser/wealth manager's library**. Valuable for improving both the thought process and the practice of wealth management."

DAVID H. DIESSLIN, MBA, CFP
Founder
Diesslin & Associates, Inc.

DEENA KATZ
ON PRACTICE
MANAGEMENT

Also available from
Bloomberg Press

*The Financial Planner's Guide to Moving Your Practice Online:
Creating Your Internet Presence and Growing Your Business*
by Douglas H. Durrie

*Deena Katz's Tools and Templates for Your Practice:
for Financial Advisers, Planners, and Wealth Managers*
by Deena B. Katz

Best Practices for Financial Advisors
by Mary Rowland

Protecting Your Practice
by Katherine Vessenes, in cooperation with the
International Association for Financial Planning

A complete list of our titles is available at
www.bloomberg.com/books

BLOOMBERG® WEALTH MANAGER magazine is the premiere
professional information resource for independent financial planners and
investment advisers who are serving clients of high net worth.
See wealth.bloomberg.com or call 1-800-681-7727.

BLOOMBERG PROFESSIONAL LIBRARY

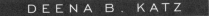

DEENA B. KATZ

DEENA KATZ
ON PRACTICE MANAGEMENT

FOR FINANCIAL ADVISERS,
PLANNERS, AND WEALTH MANAGERS

With a Foreword by Ross Levin

BLOOMBERG PRESS

PRINCETON

Books are available for bulk purchases at special discounts. Special editions or book excerpts can also be created to specifications. For information, please write: Special Markets Department, Bloomberg Press.

This publication contains the author's opinions and is designed to provide accurate and authoritative information. It is sold with the understanding that the author, publisher, and Bloomberg L.P. are not engaged in rendering legal, accounting, invest-ment-planning, or other professional advice. The reader should seek the services of a qualified professional for such advice; the author, publisher, and Bloomberg L.P. cannot be held responsible for any loss incurred as a result of specific investments or planning decisions made by the reader.

First edition published 1999
 3 5 7 9 10 8 6 4 2

Katz, Deena B., 1950–
     Deena Katz on practice management for financial advisers, planners, and wealth managers / Deena B. Katz ; foreword by Ross Levin.
       p.   cm. – (Bloomberg professional library)
     Includes bibliographical references.
     ISBN 1-57660-070-X
     1. Business enterprises – Finance–Handbooks, manuals, etc.
   2. Financial planners–Handbooks, manuals, etc.   I. Title.
   II. Title: Practice management for financial advisers, planners, and wealth managers. III. Series.
   HG4011.K38 1999
   658.15–dc21   99-23252
                                                                 CIP

Acquired and edited by Jared Kieling

To Harold

(You know why)

CONTENTS

Acknowledgments

I AM VERY LUCKY. In the past twenty-three years in financial services, I have met some extraordinary people. They have shared information, thoughts, whims, and visions with great generosity. They have challenged, infuriated, entertained, and delighted me. Many have become treasured lifetime friends. I'd like to take this opportunity to express my deep gratitude for their contributions to my life, as well as their contributions to this book. With deepest thanks to:

◆ Mary Rowland, one of the best financial writers I know, who suggested I write this book, recommended me to Bloomberg, then publicly announced it, so I couldn't get cold feet

◆ Jared Kieling, a terrific editor, who thankfully has mastered the delicate balance of critique and nurture

◆ The Alpha Group:

Mark Balasa, CPA, CFP, Balasa & Hoffman, Inc.; Schaumburg, Illinois

Eleanor Blayney, CFP, Sullivan, Bruyette, Speros & Blayney, Inc.; McLean, Virginia

James L. Budros, CFP, Budros & Ruhlin, Inc.; Columbus, Ohio

David H. Bugen, CFP, Bugen Stuart Korn & Cordaro, Inc.; Chatham, New Jersey

Ram Kolluri, CFP, GlobalValue Investors, Inc.; Princeton, New Jersey

Ross Levin, CFP, Accredited Investors, Inc.; Edina, Minnesota

Peggy M. Ruhlin, CPA/PFS, CFP, Budros & Ruhlin, Inc.; Columbus, Ohio

Louis P. Stanasolovich, CFP, Legend Financial Advisors, Inc.; Pittsburgh, Pennsylvania

Gregory Sullivan, CPA/PFS, CFP, Sullivan, Bruyette, Speros & Blayney, Inc.; McLean, Virginia

John W. Ueleke, CFP, Legacy Wealth Management; Memphis, Tennessee

Robert Winfield, CFP, Legacy Financial Advisors; Memphis, Tennessee

◆ Rick Adkins, III, CFP, ChFC, The Arkansas Financial Group, Inc.; Little Rock, Arkansas

- Shaun Anderson, Investec Investment Management Services; Sandton, South Africa
- Marco Bauer, Bauer & Thomson; Johannesburg, South Africa
- John Blankinship Jr., CFP, Blankinship & Foster; Del Mar, California
- Norman Boone, CFP, Boone Financial Advisors, Inc.; San Francisco, California
- Paul Brady, CFP, Brady & Associates; Sydney, Australia
- Thomas A. Bray, The Legacy Trust Company; Overland Park, Kansas
- James Bruyette, CPA, CFP, Sullivan Bruyette Speros & Blayney, Inc.; McLean, Virginia
- Cynthia L. Conger, CPA/PFS, CFP, The Arkansas Financial Group, Inc.; Little Rock, Arkansas
- Stan B. Corey, Jr., ChFC, CFP, Great Falls Financial Services; Great Falls, Virginia
- Karla Curtis, Vice President, PIE Technologies; Midlothian, Virginia
- Robert Curtis, President, PIE Technologies; Midlothian, Virginia
- Kathleen Day, CFP, CFA, Kathleen Day & Associates; Miami, Florida
- David H. Diesslin, CFP, Diesslin & Associates; Fort Worth, Texas
- Roy T. Diliberto, CLU, ChFC, CFP, RTD Financial Advisors, Inc.; Philadelphia, Pennsylvania
- Charles Fitzgerald, CFP, Certified Financial Group; Maitland, Florida
- Roger Gibson, CFP, CFA, Gibson Capital Management; Pittsburgh, Pennsylvania
- Randi K. Grant, CPA/PFS, CFP, Morrison, Brown, Argiz & Company; Miami, Florida
- John W. Guy, CFP, Wealth Planning & Management, LLC; Indianapolis, Indiana
- Charles D. Haines, Jr., CFP, Haines Financial Advisors; Birmingham, Alabama

- Lynn Hopewell, CFP, The Monitor Group, Inc.; Fairfax, Virginia
- William B. Howard, Jr., ChFC, CFP, William Howard & Co. Financial Advisors, Inc.; Memphis, Tennessee
- Diana Kahn, CFP, The Financial Pharmacist; Miami, Florida
- The Katz Family: Isadore, Ernest, and especially, Burt
- Sharon Kayfetz, CFP, Personal Financial Consultants, Inc.; San Ramon, California
- Joseph J. Kopczynski, CFP, ChFC, Universal Advisory Services, Inc.; Albuquerque, New Mexico
- Judith W. Lau, CFP, Lau and Associates, Ltd.; Wilmington, Delaware
- Jeffrey R. Lauterbach, American Guaranty & Trust Company; Wilmington, Delaware
- Robert Levitt, CFP, CFA, Levitt Novakoff & Co., LLC; Boca Raton, Florida
- Julie Lord, FIFP, CFP, Cavendish Financial Management Ltd.; Cardiff, United Kingdom
- Warren J. Mackensen CFP, ProTracker Software, Inc.; Hampton, New Hampshire
- Gary Mockler, Kessel Feinstein; Benmore, South Africa
- Ed Morrow, CLU, ChFC, CFP, RFC, Financial Planning Consultants; Middleton, Ohio
- Wes McMaster, CFP, Financial Planning Association of Australia; Hobart, Tasmania, Australia
- Rick Medina, President, and Ernesto Quant, Netrus; Miami, Florida
- Jerry Neill, CFP, Neill & Associates; Kansas City, Missouri
- Madeline I. Noveck, CFP, Novos Planning Associates, Inc.; New York, New York
- David S. Norton, CFP, Norton Partners; Bristol,United Kingdom
- Moira O'Shaughnessy, The Financial Planning Corporation; Southport, United Kingdom
- Jennifer A. Patterson, CFP, CIMC, VP, Financial Division, First Bermuda Financial Services; Hamilton, Bermuda
- Mark Ralphs, The Financial Planning Corporation; Southport, United Kingdom

- Judy Shine, CFP, Shine Investment Advisory Services, Inc.; Englewood, Colorado
- Roger Smothers, MS, Global Financial Services; Binghamton, New York
- Karen Spero, CFP, Spero-Smith Investment Advisers; Cleveland, Ohio
- Susan Spraker, CFP, Spraker, Fitzgerald & Tamayo, LLC; Maitland, Florida
- David Strege, CFP, CFA, Syverson, Strege, Sandager & Co.; West Des Moines, Iowa
- Ron Tamayo, CFP, Spraker, Fitzgerald & Tamayo, LLC; Maitland, Florida
- Mark C. Tibergien, Moss Adams Advisory Services; Seattle, Washington
- Benjamin A. Tobias, CFP, CPA, PFS, Tobias Financial Advisors; Plantation, Florida
- Lewis J. Walker, CFP, CIMC, Walker Capital Management Corporation; Norcross, Georgia
- Lewis Wallensky CFP, Lewis Wallensky Assoc., Inc.; Los Angeles, California
- Stewart H. Welch, III, CFP, AEP, The Welch Group, LLC; Birmingham, Alabama
- My extraordinary staff, my biggest critics and best buddies: Mena C. Bielow, Lane M. Jones, Deana L. Kelly, Esmè J. Market, Matthew A. McGrath, Robert E. Sambor, Veronica M. Vilchez Paguaga, Tammi E. Wells, F. Scott Wells, and particularly to Jennifer A. Arbeene, my indispensable assistant
- My partner, Peter Brown, whose support is better than suspenders and a belt
- My sister, Sharon Mort and brother, Robert Boone, who have taken permanent residence in my corner
- My Mom, Gladys Rhinehart Boone, who taught me that I could do anything I put my mind to, except become a Chicago Bears linebacker
- And finally, my partner, husband, friend, confidant, and bashert, Harold Evensky, who completes and amplifies me.

BY ROSS LEVIN, CFP

FOREWORD

I HAVE BEEN A FINANCIAL PLANNER for sixteen years and have had my share of successes. They have not been without an inordinate number of struggles. I came into financial planning with reasonable skills technically, and a tremendous entrepreneurial drive. What I didn't come into financial planning with was any sense of what it would take to create an environment that could facilitate my success.

I love and have always loved being a financial planner. I cannot say that I have always loved having a financial planning company. Where in the vast reading I had done regarding modern portfolio theory had I ever come across keeping my staff excited and fulfilled? As I tried to master the nuances of the tax code, how was I also to search for the right office technology?

The struggles that I faced in being a planner only partially involved finding and serving clients (although that was no cakewalk). Most of the problems I faced were how to run a financial planning business. I can't tell you how many steps backwards I had taken in either working with people whose values were not congruent with my own or in trying to make staffing decisions based on how comfortable I was in the interview.

The only way that I could build my practice in a manner that rewarded me personally and professionally was to talk to people in the field. Fortunately, one of the people I could most easily lean on was Deena Katz.

If I had had Deena's book as a resource when I started my practice, I would have accelerated my success by years. What is the value of that?

I remember a couple of years ago I was having some internal office problems. We had worked with a consultant, but were still having difficulty articulating a philosophy for our office and then executing it. I realized that while we had already spent thousands of dollars on a local consultant, the person I really needed to talk to was Deena.

In a fifteen-minute phone call, Deena helped me get to some of the core issues I was facing and provided pragmatic, useful solutions for changing them. My practice was changed forever for the better, and I am eternally grateful. She now has spent time sharing some of those pearls in this book, and the industry should be eternally grateful.

Golfer Chi Chi Rodriguez told the story about a man who drives his car through a red light. His passenger asks, "Why?" The man replies, "Because my brother does it." This happens again at the next red light. Again the passenger asks and is given the same answer. The driver then gets to a green light and slams on the brakes and looks to his left and then to his right. The passenger again asks, "Why?" The driver says, "Because my brother might be coming."

Over the years, I have developed a set of habits, some of which have been quite helpful, others that have impeded my progress. In reading Deena's book, I was able to quickly identify some of the areas that I need to change and how to change them.

Deena believes that "we manage our client's lives, not their money." To me this is the core value that we all need to encompass in the work that we do. Deena's book gives us a step-by-step guide in setting up a practice to facilitate this.

Some of the statements in the book are pithy—"We can't make you rich, but we won't make you poor"; some are profound—"We need to improve the quality of our client's lives"; and some are mischievous—". . . .provide such value to our clients that they cheerfully pay our fees and recommend us to their friends."

Deena takes us through the creating of the business plan, to determining how to find an appropriate business partner, to how to compensate staff. Her chapter on "Killing the Sacred Cows" is particularly useful. It essentially gives us the template to help reinvent ourselves. This chapter alone will make your practice more profitable and more importantly, more fulfilling.

I especially enjoy the fact that this book is not just based on the information stored in Deena's capacious mind, but it has distilled opinion from some of the people I have always respected in this business. The book has the feel of sharing a cup of coffee with some of the most creative and successful financial planners in the world, who are unselfishly discussing their hits and their misses. I wish I could have written this.

I have had the good fortune of meeting many quality people in my years of service to the financial planning industry. As I continue to reflect on how I can leave a legacy to a career that has meant so much to me, I somewhat jealously recognize that with this fine book, Deena has left hers.

INTRODUCTION
ON PRACTICE MANAGEMENT

Business excellence begins with how high
you set your standards.

— L E O B . H E L Z E L ,

Author of *A Goal is a Dream with a Deadline*

What's in This for You?

MY PARTNERS AND I have been offering financial advice

for over twenty years. Our business has grown and suc-

ceeded despite years of "tried and died" ideas. Many of

our peers have had similar experiences. As I conducted

my interviews for this book it became obvious that there

is no universal model for structuring financial planning

practices. Over the years, we've all invented our own business styles, refining as we learned from each other. Nevertheless, significant principles emerged, such as the need to focus on the delivery of intangibles (e.g., service) instead of performance, and the critical importance of organizational structure and operational systematization. These basic principles are integral to every successful practice I've seen. This book is a compilation of principles that emerged during more than 1,000 hours of interviews and networking with some of the most creative and successful practitioners in our field, plus from my own experiences.

I wrote the book to help you improve your bottom line. *On Practice Management* is not an academic treatise, nor is it a substitute for the texts on business management that I recommend in Chapter 15. Consider it a hand-held consulting firm, with advice from experts who know our profession very well. Recognizing that advisers practice in all types of environments and have businesses at varying levels of maturity, I've made sure that the book has a wide scope and that it addresses all stages of a successful business's development. Let me offer you three examples.

FOGGING A MIRROR

WHEN I STARTED in this business, if a prospect fogged a mirror, I took him as a client. My partner Harold Evensky would stop people on the street and offer them lunch if they would listen to him talk about bonds. He once even held a seminar for two drunks in a bar. (There is no truth to the rumor that he was one of the drunks.)

My practice grew in spite of my taking on clients who did not add to my bottom line. To get new clients, I often agreed to prepare special reports or take on unusual responsibilities that consumed a great deal of time. I spent hours driving to visit prospects, giving away free advice to gain their confidence, and taking on relationships with people I didn't particularly like. As my practice matured, I realized I needed to identify an appropriate client profile and say no to those who did not exhibit it. Even more difficult, I had to scrutinize current client relationships, eliminate special, unproductive, and time-consuming activities, and graduate from my practice those clients who just didn't fit.

I am not alone. Years ago I attended an ICFP retreat in Ft. Collins, Colorado. The dean of the conference was

Lewis J. Walker, CFP, of Walker Capital Management Corporation in Norcross, Georgia. Unwittingly, Lew changed my life. Lew and the other conference organizers put on a skit about the day in the life of a financial planner. The planner's day began with a visit by some prospects. After a grueling three-hour conference, they thanked him politely and announced they were going to invest with a cousin who had a hot limited partnership. We all laughed and agreed that this was a common experience, but it really triggered my thinking.

That afternoon I wrote a complete description of my client base, developing a profile of the clients with whom I liked working. I then devised a detailed client qualification sheet and returned home with new resolve to screen prospects thoroughly, taking only those who fit my written description. I literally stuttered the first time I refused an inappropriate client relationship. They wanted to work with me, and I said no! After a few weeks, I discovered that I had more time to identify the desirable clients, establishing rewarding relationships that are with me today. I know now that with forethought and a willingness to take a leap of faith, a practice can be positioned for growth without the painful wrong turns that many of us made fifteen years ago. If you haven't yet made the mistake of building a practice based on "mirror foggers," heeding the advice in this book will be worth the price of admission. If you have, there are plenty of ideas here to help you get back on track.

Obviously, there are practical issues to consider when

screening out clients. Unless you are moving from a well-established practice such as accounting or law, or unless you have sufficient financial stability to sustain you for several years while you build a practice, it would not be in your interest to refuse client relationships arbitrarily. I do recognize that it is difficult to spread ideals on a cracker. Nevertheless, you'll see how it is possible to be more discerning and to eliminate unfruitful client relationships from the beginning.

This book is also for seasoned advisers with mature practices that need a facelift. In recent years, we've often found ourselves managing staff instead of managing relationships. We worry about staff and client retention, practice monetization, and exit strategies. Growth leads to our becoming overworked and overwhelmed. The good news is that it's still not too late to change our ways and our client base.

PUTTING A FACE TO THE MONEY

A FEW YEARS AGO, Jean-Marie Eveillard of SoGen Funds visited Miami to speak at a seminar for the American Association of Individual Investors. My partners and I took him to dinner after the meeting. I thought Jean-Marie would like to know what confidence I had in his management style, so I proceeded to tell him about my brother, a Salvation Army minister. My brother owned a trailer that he and his wife used for vacations. One night during a storm a tree fell on it, demolishing it. The insurance company gave my brother $5,000, more money than he had ever accumulated. He called me and asked where he should invest it. I recommended SoGen International Fund. When I finished telling the story, Jean-Marie stood up, simultaneously slamming his fists down on the dinner table. "I wish you hadn't told me that," he said. "Now you've put a face to the money." This singular moment was the biggest "ah-ha" in my professional life. It clarified for me the difference between the services of a portfolio manager and what financial consultants do; we put a face to the money. We manage the quality of our clients' lives, not just their dollars.

There's a great deal of talk these days about what we call ourselves. "Financial Planner" seemed just right until the media started equating financial planning with brainless sales. Remember the April 1988 issue of *Forbes* magazine? On the cover was a picture of a monkey dressed in a three-piece business suit. The title was: "Anyone Can Call Himself a Financial Planner." After that public ridicule, many of us wanted to be called anything but. We tried using Financial Consultant, Investment Adviser, Investment Consultant, and Financial Adviser—anything that would give us more credibility.

Times have changed. The public has come to recognize that there is value in the financial planning process, and practitioners who place the client's interest first are in demand.

Whatever you call yourself, if you're successful, you care about your clients. You put a face to the money. You are concerned with your client's holistic interim and long-term goals. You don't have to maximize return, because you are more concerned about your clients achieving those goals. If you are just managing clients' assets independent of their financial goals and objectives, then all you really have to offer is performance. If you are touting performance as your value as a planner, then you are attempting to deliver something over which you ultimately have no control. All markets are volatile. For example, from 1973 to 1974 your client would have asked why he was paying you, as you both watched his portfolio fall 40 or 50 percent. The antidote for this, you'll see, is to know what you do for a living and know how to express it to the world.

BUYING THE FUTURE

YEARS AGO A FRIEND OF MINE from Chicago was contemplating buying a boat. He asked me to join him in his search. After weeks of research and study, he chose a twenty-one-foot sailing sloop. It was a beautiful boat. As we sailed back to the dock after our first afternoon on Lake Michigan he took me aside. "I've made a serious mistake," he said. "This boat is just right for today, but tomorrow, it will be too small." There is a powerful lesson in this for us. In planning your practice, always aim for the future, not the present. This book will help keep you focused on a more successful tomorrow.

The financial advisory business is evolving rapidly—the financial services supermarket is already a reality. If you perceive that your value is strictly designing asset allocation strategies and providing performance, your competition will be every distribution center with services on sale at every corner. Your clients can already visit Wal-Mart to buy groceries, furniture, and financial products, and they can diversify their portfolios buying AAdvantage mutual funds on their next American Airlines flight.

If, on the other hand, you carve out a niche offering various levels of planning, support, and counseling; putting the interest of your client first; and providing a holistic service, you will have little real competition. You will be the future. Now is the time to devise programs and systems to demonstrate real value to your clients. That perception of value will keep them as clients in good times and bad. The time to fix the roof is while the sun is shining.

Yesterday, a breathing client was all I needed. Today I re-evaluate my client profile every day. Had I spent more time planning for my future business, my current client base would be different, and so would my bottom line.

WHAT I'M GOING TO DELIVER

I HAVE DIVIDED THE TEXT into six areas of interest. Section One is concerned with the philosophical and organizational design of a financial planning business, with chapters specifically addressing mission and vision statements, business styles, and contingency and succession concerns.

Section Two focuses on people, beginning with a discussion of partnerships and the selection of good staff. I also discuss ways of successfully managing and retaining key employees.

Section Three, on the office environment, is not confined to the design of the workplace. It also outlines technological hardware and software solutions for improving practice efficiency, including systematizing your office procedures.

I have called Section Four "The Growing" because it addresses the issues advisers face in this competitive world, such as challenging some sacred business practices that can stymie your growth. This section also offers advice about public relations and making the transition from commissions to fee-and-commissions or to fee-only.

Section Five relates to issues about the client, with practical advice for hiring, firing, and refusing client relationships to ensure that your practice can grow effectively. This section also outlines strategies for retailing your best client retention, including managing their expectations through the review process, regular communications, and a unique service style we refer to as Concierge Service.

The final section is devoted entirely to resources. Knowing what the experts are using, and why, is the best shortcut there is. I have included a list of Web sites, books, software, organizations, companies, magazines— everything that my network of successful practitioners think we "gotta have" to enhance our businesses.

That's it, except for two final words.

Enjoy. Grow.

SECTION

ONE

THE
BUSINESS

SUCCESSFUL ENTREPRENEURS constanly re-evaluate and refine current practices. Moving water never stagnates. This section is concerned with firming up the foundation of your practice by re-examining your core values, mission, and vision. It will discuss the importance of selecting your business model and will provide recommendations related to managing business crises and planning for succession.

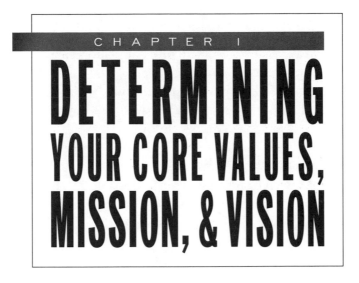

CHAPTER I

DETERMINING YOUR CORE VALUES, MISSION, & VISION

To be a good leader, you have to have a clear set
of values you implant in the company.

— HERB KELLEHER,

Chairman of Southwest Airlines

PSYCHOLOGICAL STUDIES INDICATE that people devel-

op their attitudes toward money at a relatively early age.

This process is rarely scientific and almost never rational.

Isadore Katz, a business genius and financial success,

who was also my mentor and father-in-law, inadvertently

taught me an important lesson about determining value. Isadore loved the stock market. Well into his eighties he would sit by the pool with *The Wall Street Journal* in one hand and a small radio dispensing market reports in the other.

When he reached his mid-seventies, Isadore's driving skills had begun to fade and his sons persuaded him to buy a limousine. Daily, his driver would take him downtown to his club to play cards with his pals, then drive him home again in the evening. One day, his driver was sick. Isadore's youngest son called to tell his dad to take a taxi to the club since his chauffeur would not be available. "I'll take the bus," Isadore told his son, "I'm not going to pay that kind of money for a cab just to go downtown."

In a time-pressured world, people will pay for all sorts of services including personal chefs, exercise trainers, dog walkers, and house sitters. There is even a scooper service in California called Tidy Lawn ("We pick up where your dog left off.").

There is no practical way to determine, much less control, how people assign value to various services. What matters is that you value what you do, because if you don't believe that your advice or service is desirable, prospects won't either. How you feel about your work is transmitted immediately to people.

One of my first clients was a United Airlines captain. At the time, United pilots were entertaining the possibility of a strike, since negotiations for their new contract were not going well. At one of our appointments I remarked that considering the responsibility pilots have in the air, I'd give pilots any salary increase they wanted and not bat an eye. Surprisingly, my client didn't agree. "The money I make is already obscene," he remarked. "I'm just a glorified bus driver."

In one statement, my view of him as a professional was altered by his own perception of himself. My client went on to explain that when he started flying commercially, he was working in a 727 cockpit with a copilot and engineer, all three of them busy virtually every minute of a flight. He had recently been promoted to captain of a 737. This cockpit was more automated and required only two people. With fewer activities, he often felt like a glorified bus driver.

Consider how technology affects how you see yourself and your value to your clients. In my earlier days of practice, there wasn't much financial planning software, no performance database, and no optimizers. We had to scramble for information on mutual funds, fund managers, and fund performance. We relied heavily on marketing material and anything we could glean from a prospectus. When I prepared a review, I literally sat with copies of my client's nine mutual fund statements and typed relevant information onto a single sheet so I could provide a consolidated report. We couldn't handle many clients because the data gathering and report preparation took forever. We were in the publishing business, not the planning business. Compared to those days, my practice activities today are a breeze. There is no doubt that the personal computer and companies like Schwab and Morningstar have put advisers like me in business. But, by themselves, they won't keep me in business.

I asked financial adviser Eleanor Blayney of Sullivan, Bruyette, Speros and Blayney (SBSB), for her perception of her value to clients. "I know I add a great deal to their lives, but in the back of my mind I keep thinking, what am I missing? Why should I be paid so well for this? It's fun and it's easy." The ease of preparing physical reports leads us to forget how hard we worked (and continue to work) to acquire our specialized knowledge and skills. Our value to clients is not derived from the easily prepared reports. Our value is reflected in our clients' success in meeting their goals, assisted by our knowledge and skills. Vladimir Horowitz made playing the piano look effortless. What his audience actually heard, and paid for, was his expertise, training, and talent sharpened by the endless hours he spent practicing.

We Need to Express Our Value to Clients in Benefits, Not Features

MORE THAN ONE ADVISER I know describes his value in the statement, "My clients sleep well at night." Telling our clients we design well-balanced (deadly dull and boring) portfolios is less effective than telling them that if they follow our advice they will sleep soundly.

That's why you shouldn't give clients the impression that performance is the value you add to their lives. In fact, if you believe in asset allocation and diversification, you guarantee that your clients' returns underperform the hot market of the moment. Diversification requires including asset classes that are poorly correlated. The possibility of making a killing is what your client gives up to sleep well at night. On the other hand—here comes the benefit—when a single market is depressed, diversification will buoy returns. Stated as a value to the client, you help them avoid getting battered in the market. We tell prospects, "We can't make you rich, but we won't make you poor. Our job is to help you enjoy life and sleep well at night." In our firm, we demonstrate our value by keeping our clients from chasing returns in bull markets and from bailing out in bear markets. All of our interaction and communication with clients revolves around managing their expectations. I think this is such an important issue that I have devoted Chapter 14 to it.

John Guy, Wealth Planning & Management in Indianapolis, Indiana, has an interesting perspective on the value of an adviser. "My guess is that over the course of a long-term relationship, a financial adviser is likely to render at least one piece of immensely valuable advice. The advice usually arises from coincidence, even when the adviser understands investment markets and the client's personal situation. Usually, the value of advice is not recognized at the time it is delivered. Instead, it is recognized months or years later." (*Thoughtful Wealth Planning & Management*, Vol. 2, No. 2, October 1998.)

In 1997–98, market volatility was unprecedented. The Dow was down 500 points one day, up 300 the next. The first time this happened, we called our clients and then followed up with a soothing letter. After several incidents of this, many of our clients suggested we save the postage. "I know you're doing your best work, now," one of my clients told me, "but why don't you concentrate on some of your newer clients? I've already been on this roller-coaster ride and it doesn't make me sick to my stomach anymore."

Not every prospect will find value in your services. Like Isadore, they may be unwilling to pay for services that they believe they can get elsewhere "for free." "Why should I pay you," they ask, "when I can get all this information on the Internet and do it myself at a discount broker?" When you encounter these people, and it appears that you are not speaking the same language, move on. I'm fascinated to hear advisers tell me about their "conversion ratio." Conversion should not be a part of your job description. If you are presenting yourself and your business effectively, prospects either understand your philosophy and appreciate your value, or they do not. To me, conversion presupposes resistance. Clients I've successfully "converted" were never satisfactory relationships for me.

Most Advisers Spend Little Time Defining Themselves and Building Their Practices

THE CLEARER THE ADVISER is about what he does, the better he is able to explain it to a prospect. It helped me to sit down, enumerate my ideal client in detail, and describe what I could do for that client. This thinking process became the basis for developing my core values, mission and vision statements, and ultimately, our company philosophy.

In speaking with other advisers, I discovered that we have no consistent way of developing these essential components of our business. In fact, many used different names for the same idea. For example: core belief, core value, and core purpose all seemed to describe the same fundamental concept. Because I often refer to "building a practice," I thought a building analogy would be useful in clarifying how successful practices are developed. Therefore, the following are, in priority order, descriptions of the four statements that I believe must be in place in order to "construct" successful practices.

1 One thing. There is a huge range of services and products one might offer in a financial planning business. In order to be successful, you must determine at the outset the unique service you propose to provide. What will set you apart from everyone else? For what will you be known? I refer to this as your *one thing*. In building a practice, this is your preliminary survey, the staking out with words the idea that describes your *one thing*.

2 Core values. What fundamental beliefs underlie the philosophy and policies of your company? Your firm's core values are analogous to the foundation of your practice, a largely unseen but essential underpinning.

3 Mission statement. Once you have determined your one thing and your core values, you must describe how you wish your practice to look. Analogous to the plans for a building, a mission statement provides the basis for the design of your company.

4 Vision statement. If a mission statement is analogous to a building's blueprints, a vision statement is the equivalent of an architectural rendering of the completed practice. The vision statement describes what the practice will look like once the practice is successfully established.

One Thing

MY PARTNERS Harold Evensky and Peter Brown began their partnership in 1985, five years before I joined them. When I arrived, there were eight advisers with the planning practice and twenty registered representatives with our broker-dealer, which Harold and Peter had started in order to eat while they waited for financial planning to earn them a living.

If you had asked them individually to describe their client base, their assessments would have been as diverse as the descriptions of blindfolded men feeling different parts of an elephant. Although we suspected we shared the same basic philosophy, we had never formally shared it with each other. So we never expressed it uniformly to our clients. We assumed that having a common name, one brochure, and similar work product was enough. Consequently, we had a practice of people who had their own enterprises. We were not a business. We shared the same vague image of the future, but we weren't sure how to bring that vision into focus.

One evening after a lengthy "reorganization" meeting, Peter, Harold, and I went to see the movie *City Slickers*. In the film, Billy Crystal's character discusses the meaning of life with an old cowboy. "The secret of life," says the cowboy, "is *one thing*." "What is that *one thing?*" asks Billy. "That's for you to find out," says the old cowboy. Another "ah-ha" for me. We hadn't figured out what our *one thing* was. As a result, we hadn't been able to communicate it to our advisers and staff, much less to our prospects and clients.

Starting (or reviving) your own practice begins with finding out what your *one thing* is, then explaining it to those around you. The financial planning industry today is made up of specialties. Even if you are a comprehensive planner, that too is now a specialty, much the same as family practice is for a physician. These days my partners and I call ourselves wealth managers. To me, this is a specialty within financial planning, describing our holistic approach to our investment advisory services that I'll explain in more detail in the next chapter.

Joe Kopczynski, President of Universal Advisory Services, Inc., in Albuquerque, New Mexico, says his *one thing* is comprehensive planning—not conventional comprehensive planning, either. He has negotiated leases, mortgages, and even HMO contracts for his physician clients. "It all comes down to trust. Clients who trust you want you to help them in many other aspects of their lives, not just the financial part." Joe says he grew up in corporate America where people are taught to stay professional by keeping at arm's length from colleagues and clients. "That just doesn't make sense to me. It's vital to have trust and accountability at all levels. For that, you've got to roll up your sleeves and get involved." Joe uses a family office as a model for the services and relationships he develops with clients. His model includes far more servicing than a conventional planning practice, with business consulting and personal mentoring. Joe's *one thing* is to become the primary guide for all aspects of his clients' personal and business planning.

Dave Diesslin, of Diesslin & Associates in Ft. Worth, Texas, is also a comprehensive planner. His *one thing* is instilling confidence. "We know that we add value and that we communicate well. Our clients have confidence in our ability to support them and confidence in the role we fulfill in their lives."

As I interviewed practitioners around the world, most described their *one thing* in such terms as engendering trust and confidence, maintaining personal relationships, or providing superior personal service to their clients. Some expressed their *one thing* in terms of actions, specifically offering special services. No one suggested that producing fancy reports or voluminous analyses was the key to their success.

When Charlie Haines from Birmingham, Alabama, reviewed his client base, he made a startling discovery. The demographics and buoyant economy of the past few years had produced a group of successful and unhappy people. "I've got to address that situation, so now we require that all our clients spend two hours with a family therapist who discusses issues of money, preparation for retirement, and wealth transfers." Charlie finds that using a professional helps facilitate the planning process and his relationship with his clients. "Sometime between the retirement planning meeting and the estate planning meeting, we tell our clients, 'We want to get your reaction to the first chapter of the rest of your life. We would like to have a family therapist at that meeting, since she is more skilled at facilitating these discussions than we are.'" No one has turned them down.

Although Charlie feels it is essential to deal with the psychological and behavioral aspects of a client's life, he warns that there is a big danger in our industry to overstep our bounds. Planners by nature are "counseling-oriented financial nerds. Unless we are trained as counselors or therapists, we shouldn't attempt to function like them. We wouldn't dream of practicing as an attorney unless we have a JD. We need to treat professional counseling in the same manner."

Our *one thing* is expressed in the tagline my firm uses under our company name: "A Lifestyle Company." This line describes the unique function that we believe we have in our clients' lives. We plan, and assist our clients, to help them achieve their chosen lifestyle. This line also describes our relationship with our partners and staff. We measure our success not by the money we make, but by the quality of life enjoyed by everyone who works with us or for us.

Core Values

WHEN YOU'VE FIGURED OUT the *one thing* that defines you and your organization, you must develop from it the foundation on which you build your business practices. I refer to these fundamentals as core values. Core values simply state your permanent personal and business principles. We've expanded our *one thing* into these simple bullet points:

◆ **Teamwork.** Working together for common goals
◆ **Quality in Execution.** Do it once; do it well

◆ **Ethics.** Honesty and professionalism

◆ **Critical review.** Unrelenting pursuit of excellence

◆ **Enjoyment.** Supplying the resources and physical environment that bring out the best in people

Everyone in our office has a copy of our core values. These are internal and not shared with clients, but we use them constantly as a compass and a reality check. Many of the planners I spoke with share the same attitudes about these statements. I've included two here to give you a sense of how unique, yet similar, firms' core values can be.

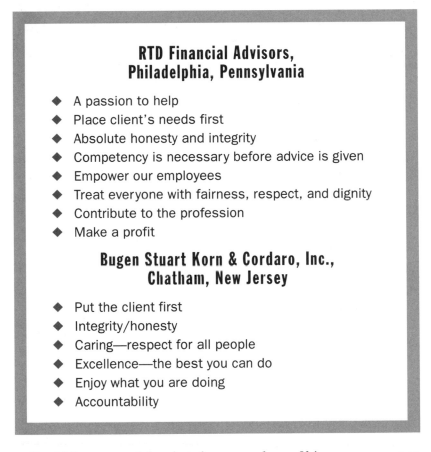

RTD Financial Advisors, Philadelphia, Pennsylvania

◆ A passion to help
◆ Place client's needs first
◆ Absolute honesty and integrity
◆ Competency is necessary before advice is given
◆ Empower our employees
◆ Treat everyone with fairness, respect, and dignity
◆ Contribute to the profession
◆ Make a profit

Bugen Stuart Korn & Cordaro, Inc., Chatham, New Jersey

◆ Put the client first
◆ Integrity/honesty
◆ Caring—respect for all people
◆ Excellence—the best you can do
◆ Enjoy what you are doing
◆ Accountability

David Bugen explains that the core values of his company are so integral to their practice that they make every important decision in the context of their core values. For example, David told me,

"Before we place our investment policy in the hands of our clients, we always ask ourselves, 'Is this the best we can do?'"

Mission Statements

AFTER YOU HAVE DEVELOPED your *one thing* into core values, you will need to devise a mission statement. Your mission statement ensures that everyone in your practice is focused on the same goals. It should be just long enough to express your position, but not so long as to be tedious. As with your core values, every significant business decision you make should be consistent with your mission. Joe Kopczynski said it very well when he told me, "it's extremely important for those of us who manage other people's money to understand who we are, to make sure we don't deviate from who we are and who we've told the client we are."

In military terms, the mission is to accomplish some goal, usually to overtake a target. Your mission statement is a broad plan of action to help you overtake your target market.

I wrote my first mission statement alone: "To provide financial education, direction, and planning for women who have previously left financial decisions to their spouses or who are in a life transition and require guidance to empowerment." Writing it clarified the goals for my practice and gave me a sense of direction, much like a financial plan does for our clients. At the time I started my practice, I enjoyed working with women clients. Some were widows, some divorced, and some business owners. When thinking about the commonality of this diverse group, I described it as "women in transition." My ideal client was a woman, age fifty and older, who needed education, constant handholding, and emotional support. This was a woman who had never played an active part in her family's financial decisions, but was abruptly left with these responsibilities through divorce or widowhood. Because of my background in social work, education, and finance, I felt uniquely qualified to provide this type of advice.

When my partners and I formed our new company, we wrote our *one thing* as, "We are financial planners with a unique expertise in the area of investment planning for conservative clients." We referred to this as "wealth management." We then prepared a new mission statement. "We are financial planners and we want to make a comfortable income doing what we like while helping our clients get where they want to go." Okay, we weren't very sophisticated, but it was a start. It is important for everyone involved in your practice to understand why you are in business (the *one thing*), what your fundamental beliefs are (core values), and what you are trying to accomplish (the mission statement). Use these statements as your reality checks, especially when you find opportunities to engage in activities that may seem peripheral to your primary business.

Roy Diliberto has distilled his *one thing* and mission into one brief statement that defines the purpose of his company: "Improve the quality of our clients' lives." Every challenge Roy meets is measured against this statement. Roy tells about one of his clients who experienced moments of literal paralysis thinking about the chaos that the year 2000 could bring. "He envisioned deteriorating markets and recession. He wasn't sleeping nights. He just wanted us to move everything to cash. I thought about it, then went back to our core purpose: to improve the quality of our clients' lives. If I move his money to cash, will it improve the quality of his life? Absolutely, he will sleep nights. Will it improve his portfolio? No, but he already has enough to accomplish his primary goals. Improving his portfolio is not consistent with our mission. We moved him to cash."

During our reorganization stages, we determined that we did not want to have a large practice with many advisers. Coincidentally, around this time, the media began a campaign to educate the consumer about fee-only planning. My Uncle Walt always advised, "if you see a right hook coming, lean into it, it will lessen the blow." If the media were going to strike a blow for "fee-only," we'd be crazy not to lean into it. We decided we were going to be fee-only and our "one thing" would be to provide fee-only holistic investment planning. This meant two very big changes. One, we needed to sell our broker-dealer. Two, we needed to take on clients with more assets to manage so we could afford to provide fee-only planning. To accomplish these goals, we realized that we needed to "grow down." Not everyone attached to our broker-dealer shared our fee-only vision. Similarly, we met with the advisers in our planning practice to determine who wished to make the leap to fee-only with us.

We are not opposed to other forms of compensation. The fee-only approach simply works best for our practice. I am not suggesting that you adopt this style. Instead, you need to be clear about your *one thing*, then adapt your compensation structure to it.

At our first company retreat, we redesigned our initial mission statement. It was a powerful team-building effort with all the partners and staff contributing ideas. Each year we revisit it to ensure that it still communicates our purpose. We use our mission statement as our strategic planning guide. As we set our goals for each year, we measure them against this mission statement. For years, our mission statement read:

> EBK seeks to be the preeminent provider of fee-only wealth management services to individuals, qualified and public plans, nonprofits, foundations, and trusts with financial assets of two to fifty million dollars.

It was a comprehensive affirmation of what we want to be when we grow up and what we are trying to accomplish for our staff, our clients, and ourselves.

Today, our mission statement reads:

> EBK seeks to be an internationally recognized boutique financial adviser and consultant firm to thoughtful, conservative delegators who influence or control significant investable assets, by providing education, expertise, assurance, personal service, and trust.

Whether you write your mission statement alone at the kitchen table, or craft it during a company retreat, it should still answer several questions:

◆ Who do you want to be?
◆ What do you expect to do?
◆ For whom will you do it?
◆ What needs will you fulfill?

Here are three mission statements from some of the best planners around the world. All describe planning firms, yet each description is unique, reflecting the nature of each practice.

Norton Partners of Bristol, United Kingdom

TO PROVIDE AN excellent financial planning and tax service to our clients, to be recognized as true professionals in our field, to enjoy what we are doing and to provide such value to our clients that they cheerfully pay our fees and recommend us to their friends.

Blankinship & Foster, Del Mar, California

TO PROVIDE OUR CLIENTS with the best financial planning and investment management advice and services available.

To work with integrity, candor, and imagination with our clients, their advisers and our employees.

To help each of our employees attain his or her best level of achievement and professional satisfaction.

To set a standard of excellence in our profession reflecting the importance of our work and assisting tomorrow's planners and investment advisers to achieve the highest public regard.

Sullivan, Bruyette, Speros & Blayney, McLean, Virginia

AT SULLIVAN, BRUYETTE, Speros and Blayney, Inc., our mission is to be indispensable in helping our clients make smart financial decisions through uncompromising integrity, trust, and personalized service.

I particularly like the "cheerfully pay our fees" that Norton Partners uses. David Norton confides that he frequently tells prospects, "We're not cheap, but we're good; take your choice." This is an interesting positioning statement. Russ Alan Prince, who has done a great deal of work analyzing high net worth individuals, suggests exactly this statement in his book, *Cultivating the Affluent*, "Certainly the knowledge that the cost of services is not a major factor in selecting an investment manager is valuable; it indicates that financial providers will succeed with the affluent by marketing themselves as good, not cheap." (Russ Alan Prince and Karen Maru File, New York: Institutional Investor, Inc., 1995.)

Eleanor Blayney says that the essence of the Sullivan, Bruyette, Speros and Blayney mission statement is for them to be indispensable to their clients. SBSB's partners frequently visit this statement and make business changes as they continually recalibrate their view of how to be "indispensable." SBSB provides tax planning as well as financial planning and asset management services. Since SBSB devised their first mission statement, it hasn't changed much, and they have now written one for each of the service areas of their business.

"It [the mission statement] seemed corny at first, but it grows on you once you begin to understand the different ways you can interpret it," Eleanor confides. "We want our staff to feel its importance, so at our annual retreat we make new employees sing the mission statement to the tune of their alma mater fight song."

Blankinship & Foster in Del Mar, California, includes their mission statement on their brochure. "We want prospects to know immediately what they may expect from us," Jack Blankinship says. Their mission statement addresses the clients and their other advisers, as well as the profession as a whole.

Good mission statements are universal. They do not necessarily need to reflect your business specifically. See if you can guess what company the following mission statement belongs to:

◆ To be a premier and progressive growth company, with a balanced approach toward people, quality, and profitability.

◆ To be focused, sensitive, and responsive to our employees, customers, and our environment.

◆ To empower our team to exceed customer expectations—to become customer obsessed.

◆ To enhance a high level of excellence, innovation, integrity, and ethics.

◆ To attract, develop, and retain a superior team.

◆ To enhance long-term shareholder growth.

It is essential that the mission statement become an integral part of your business practices. It should serve as your benchmark to gauge progress, as well as function as your reality check when you have decisions to make. Look at the mystery mission statement. Did you guess whose statement it is? It's from Chili's Restaurants.

Samuel Goldwyn, well-known movie mogul, had a single statement hanging on the wall behind his desk. When anyone came in to pitch a new movie idea, recommend a new actor, or ask for changes in a script, he'd listen intently, then turn around to read the line: "Will it sell tickets?" Goldwyn knew he wasn't in the movie business; he knew he was in the business of selling tickets. Each decision he made needed to reflect that belief.

The Vision Statement

AS IF ALL THESE STATEMENTS about who you are and what you do aren't enough, I am going to ask you to consider one more, the vision statement. At one of our retreats, an adviser asked, "We think we know what we want to be when we grow up, but where are we really going?" We have found it invaluable to supplement our mission statement with a vision that indicates what we expect to happen as a consequence of the mission. The vision statement should be specific and goal oriented. "By 2002, EBK will have global presence with strategic alliance relationships with Certified Financial Planner practitioners in at least four major countries. We will control over one billion in assets with less than 3 percent turnover." It may be ambitious, but it is our unique vision.

It is vital that your staff be a part of the development of your mission and vision. Eleanor Blayney admits that those who were involved in the drafting of theirs feel differently about it than those who were not. Retreats are great opportunities for drafting or refining these statements. I'll discuss them in Chapter 6.

Philosophy Statement

WHILE I BELIEVE it is imperative for a successful practice to have in place the four ideas I've just discussed—*one thing*, core values, mission, and vision—there is an optional statement that you might find useful. We refer to this as our philosophy statement. In this, we outline our basic approach to the advice and service we've developed in advising others about their money. While the prior four statements are primarily used internally in our firm, we have

Evensky, Brown & Katz Philosophy

THE ENTIRE STAFF of Evensky, Brown & Katz participates, at different levels, in the development of our philosophy. All members of the firm are committed to its consistent implementation.

WE ARE COMMITTED TO THE FINANCIAL PLANNING PROCESS

◆ **Goal setting.** We believe that our clients must set their own goals. It is our responsibility to educate them in the process and to assist them to define, quantify, and prioritize their goals.

◆ **Rule of thumb planning.** We believe that "rule of thumb" planning (such as retirement income should equal 80 percent of pre-retirement income) is an incompetent and unprofessional method in planning for a client's financial independence.

◆ **Cash flow.** We believe that our clients need total return, not dividends or interest. The traditional concept of an "income" portfolio is archaic and places unnecessary and inappropriate restrictions on portfolio design

◆ **Capital needs analysis assumptions.** We believe that "conservative" assumptions are a dangerous myth. As an example, if we should be "conservative" and not include any social security income for a client in our retirement planning calculation, the result might well be the projection of a significant shortfall in the resources necessary for retirement. That, in turn, could lead to a recommendation that the client either significantly reduces his or her current standard of living, delay retirement, and/or invest more aggressively. The point is, a "conservative" assumption might well result in an inappropriate and aggressive solution. We believe in making intelligent assumptions not relying on fundamentally unsound, "conservative" defaults.

WE ARE COMMITTED TO PROFESSIONALISM

◆ All of our advisers are either CFP licensees or in the process of becoming CFP licensees and are expected to be active participants in our professional organizations. Continuing education is mandatory for all our professional staff.

WE ARE COMMITTED TO OUR CLIENTS' INDIVIDUAL NEEDS

◆ Our primary allegiance is to our client. If commitment on the part of the client is not forthcoming, we will not agree to an engagement.

WE ARE COMMITTED TO A FUNDAMENTAL INVESTMENT PHILOSOPHY THAT INCLUDES THE FOLLOWING ELEMENTS

◆ **Risk and return.** We believe in appropriate measures of risk and return.

◆ **Efficient market hypothesis.** We believe in the weak form.

◆ **Value over growth.** We believe in Fama French research.

◆ **Active vs. passive.** We believe it is not either/or; we use both.

◆ **Asset allocation.** We believe that the portfolio policy is the primary determinant of the variability of long-term portfolio performance.

◆ **Optimization.** We believe that mathematical optimization is the appropriate method for designing a strategic asset allocation model. However, we also believe that an optimizer is simply a tool, to be used by a knowledgeable adviser.

◆ **Arithmetic vs. geometric returns.** We believe in using geometric returns for historical analysis and future estimates.

◆ **Time diversification.** We believe that the concept of time diversification is appropriate in its conclusion that the relative risk of increasing equity exposure decreases as the time horizon of the goal increases.

WE ARE COMMITTED TO CUSTOMIZED INVESTMENT IMPLEMENTATION

◆ **Policy.** We believe that an investment policy should be written and should be customized to the needs of our client. It should describe our client's goals and discuss his risk tolerance.

◆ **Managers.** We believe that professional money managers will provide results far superior to a client's or wealth manager's direct security selection and management. With rare exception, separate account management (including wrap accounts) is inefficient and expensive.

◆ **Ongoing management.** We believe that there should be a regular review of a client's situation to determine if he is continuing to move toward achieving his goals.

WE ACCEPT FIDUCIARY RESPONSIBILITY

◆ We believe that we are uniquely qualified to integrate the skills and talents of financial planning with investment skills, knowledge, and technology previously available only to large institutional clients, for the benefit of our clients.

Accredited Investors Philosophy Statement

ROSS LEVIN'S PHILOSOPHY statement reflects both Ross's personality and his business style. Ross explained that he and his staff spent the better part of last year creating and revising their philosophy statement. Today, it is a compilation of their mission, core values, and philosophy.

Ross's prospects receive a copy of his philosophy statement prior to their first visit so there is no misunderstanding of what they believe or how they will work with them. This is their first step in managing client expectations.

We believe in comprehensive professional financial planning. Our purpose is to help you determine what is important to you and bring congruity between your actions and your values. Our expectation is to build a committed relationship with you over your lifetime.

We believe:

◆ Financial planning involves maximizing your wealth. At Accredited Investors, Inc., we define wealth as integrating all of your resources—**financial, emotional, physical, and spiritual.**

◆ We help you strike a healthy balance between all of your resources throughout your life via **Life Planning.**

◆ The level of communication between us will determine success. Financial planning is personal, so we often ask that you share with us some of the many things that you don't share with anyone but your family.

reproduced our philosophy statement as a special issue of our newsletter, *In$ites*, and we share it with prospects and clients. Although I have included an edited copy of our philosophy statement in this chapter, you can find the full text in my partner Harold Evensky's book, *Wealth Management* (New York: McGraw-Hill, 1997).

◆ We believe in integrating the five key areas of financial planning—**Asset Protection, Disability and Income Planning, Debt Management, Asset Management, and Estate Management**. We believe all of these areas are integral for achieving your personal financial success.

◆ We do not believe in timing the market. We believe that if your time horizon is greater than three years, you should accept some of the volatility risks of the stock market. For those needs that occur in less than three years, you should not accept this risk.

◆ We believe that if we make mistakes, we must correct them. But first, we must know of them. Please talk to us so that we may do so.

◆ We believe that a competent and fulfilled staff is critical to execute our mission. We treat our staff with respect and ask that you would as well.

◆ We believe that we should like and trust each other. If that ever stops happening, we believe our relationship needs to be reevaluated.

◆ We believe that you should be as involved in your plan as we are. This means that we will often ask you for help in gathering information or talking with other advisers who may have this information.

◆ We believe in the value of synergy. A competent, healthy communication and exchange of ideas between all related advisers is essential to achieving the desired success for you.

Get Busy

BY NOW, YOU SHOULD have enough material to design, develop, or just renew your own core values, mission, and vision statements. Start with your *one thing* and work from there. A good building is never built until the architect blends the dream with the details.

CHAPTER 2

DESIGNING THE BUSINESS

Most importantly, to successfully develop a serious business,

you need a process, a practice, by which to obtain that

information and, once obtained, a method with which to put

that information to use in your business productively.

— MICHAEL GERBER , *The E-Myth*

FINANCIAL PLANNING PRACTICES have largely evolved from

a sales model originally developed in the late 1960s. At

that time some stockbrokers and insurance agents began

to recognize the need to address a broad spectrum of

financial issues for their clients. For these forward-looking advisers, it was clear that clients' needs were interrelated and interdependent. And from a business perspective, planning for clients ultimately resulted in selling financial products. In the early 1970s a group of advisers originated the Certified Financial Planner designation based on a six-step planning process. This disciplined approach gave birth to the comprehensive financial plan.

My first financial plan was 103 pages. I figured it was my responsibility to tell the client everything about herself and her financial life that I could. My client looked at the plan, flipped through it and exclaimed, "Oh my goodness, you published!" It took me fifteen years and many more clients to realize that a financial plan is not for the client, it's for me. I want to know as much as I can about my clients so I can guide them in making intelligent decisions. I need to understand what motivates them to spend, save, work, and play so that I can help them achieve their life goals, whatever they are.

As the financial planning profession matured, so did our practices. I found myself doing more modular plans, such as college funding, retirement planning, and investment planning. What clients wanted, I realized, were answers to very specific questions. How can I pay for my child's college education? When can I retire? How can I expand my investments? These I could answer without requiring them to pay me to do a full-blown plan that discussed their property-casualty and disability needs.

In the late 1980s, the planning community discovered asset management. What the clients *really* wanted to know, we reasoned, was how to *invest their money*. Many planners embraced asset management like a long-lost relative. Companies like Schwab, Fidelity, and Jack White put us in business by allowing us to consolidate positions, download trading activity, and produce our own performance reports. A roaring bull market made us look brilliant. Business for planners never looked better.

In the late 1990s many of us became concerned that if we abandoned the financial planning aspects of our practices, we were betting the farm on market performance. Further, to the extent we believe in and utilize asset allocation and diversification principles in our practices, we guarantee that our client's performance will never be as good as any one well-performing asset class. The answer is what I call holistic planning. I've described that as comprehensive planning without killing any trees. We just don't print the 103 pages anymore. "Plans," says Ross Levin, "should be process driven, not paper driven."

For example, when I was producing comprehensive plans, I took the responsibility for sending out the client's property-casualty to be reviewed by an agent who specialized in property and casualty. I did evaluations and wrote extensive reports on disability and life insurance needs. Today, I identify the risk exposures and direct the client to knowledgeable insurance agents. My plans now hover between ten and fifteen pages, and the meat is in the action plan section.

The most important part of my professional service is not anything written on paper. It's the counseling, the coaching, the listening, and the caring, as well as the knowledgeable and intelligent planning that I wrap into my relationship with the client. The responsibility I take for maintaining and improving the quality of their lives is what they value and pay me for.

Don't get me wrong. I am not suggesting that a planner does not have to possess the technical capabilities. I am saying that an adviser must be able to synthesize complex and sophisticated concepts and communicate them effectively to clients, while maintaining an environment of caring and trust.

As the financial planning profession has matured, many planners have added more client services to their service mix, until ultimately a service model has developed as an alternative to the traditional sales model. This service model, even in cases where its compensation is commission based, promotes a client-centered relationship rather than a product-centered one. Structurally, the service model tends to fit more with entrepreneurial practices.

The most recent trend is the increasing participation of advisers from related financial fields, such as banking, brokering, accounting, and law. The result is the emergence of what I'll call the "professional model." This model incorporates the attributes of a service orientation with the traditional attributes of a professional relationship (e.g., credentialed professionals, confidentiality, fiduciary relationship, fee-based compensation, and structurally independent practices that do not represent any one financial institution or product). Steve Moeller, of American Business Visions, maintains that the financial adviser of the future will practice "comprehensive wealth management" ("When Clients Move Center Stage," *Dow Jones Investment Advisor*, April 1998) consulting on financial, tax, and estate planning, counseling, teaching, and providing business advice and investment management services.

Today, practices based on sales, service, and professional models are all viable alternatives. The trend is clear, however. The market is increasingly deserting sales-based practices for service and professional alternatives. "No longer is our business about products, or sales of products—our business is about advice, delivered in a way that cannot be duplicated by computers or toll-free phone numbers," says Lew Walker. "Information is not knowledge, judgment, or empathy." The market you serve and your personal business style should determine the choice of a practice model. But it pays to know the pros and cons of each model before you choose.

Compensation Structures

THE MEDIA HAVE FUELED the differences between the sales and service models and the professional model by suggesting to the public that the only competent adviser is one who has no conflict of interest. They frequently suggest that advisers compensated by commissions or a combination of fees and commission cannot act in the client's best interest. This controversy regarding fees and commissions has existed for twenty years among advisers. I believe that all advisers have conflicts. We would be less than truthful if we did not admit it. For example, I choose to use Schwab as a third-party custodial partner, for the convenience of back office operations. There are other discount brokers and they may be even less expensive for my clients. This is surely a conflict. The clients who want to work with me are expected to have a relationship with Schwab as well. To my mind, the measure of who is a professional, giving quality advice, is one of competence, value of services delivered, disclosure, and ethics, not compensation. However, the marketing reality is that there is a certain professionalism that the public associates with fee-only planning, and this is a perception that someone accepting commissions must overcome.

How Do You Charge for Your Services?

RECENTLY, BOB VERES, editor of the monthly publication *Inside Information*, suggested that fee advisers should think about lowering their assets-under-management fees to twenty or thirty basis points, then charging a separate fee for their financial planning work. This unbundling would let the clients know what they are paying for. Those that do not want or need the planning don't pay for it.

Our services are bundled with the asset management fee. We refer to it as a retainer. Many fee planners I've interviewed also use this method and would not be comfortable changing. "I roll it all up into an asset management fee. I don't want a client to do so much self-diagnosis," says Charlie Haines. Charlie is concerned, as are many advisers, that clients will not want to pay outright for the financial planning services, skimping on the important planning aspects.

I once had an attorney who used one of those little meters attached to his phone that kept track of the time for each call. He charged me for every fifteen minute increment, whether we were on the phone, in his office, whatever. I thought long and hard each time I needed to pick up the phone for a quick question, which discouraged me from calling. I would have much preferred if he had just charged a retainer. I think this nickel and diming a client is a barrier to maintaining a good relationship.

Joe Kopczynski charges a fee based on net worth. He feels that basing the fee on performance is sending the wrong message to the client. He admits many clients balk at this. One prospect told him, "I made my million dollars and you had nothing to do with it. Why should I pay you for that?" Most of his clients warm to the arrangement, though, when Joe tells them that he's responsible for helping them preserve that million.

"In one day," says Joe Kopczynski, "I might scout out a new building my client wants to buy, help secure a mortgage for another, and negotiate fees with an HMO for a third. Most of my clients are doctors so I have become an expert at supporting them and their unique needs." Joe has cultivated a relationship with a local bank so that when his clients need mortgages, he can provide the personal financial information, then personally escort them to the bank to complete the deal, making the whole process relatively painless.

Joe's expertise in negotiating HMO contracts has become notorious in his town of Albuquerque, New Mexico. "Doctors want to spend their time with their patients, not battling with other providers. To me and my clients, this is what comprehensive planning means."

The Sales Model

THE COMMISSION-BASED SALES MODEL generally works well for a middle income market whose net worth is under $250,000. I am constantly amazed at the media touting fee-only planning for the general public. Frankly, we can't charge enough for our time to satisfy this market on a fee-only basis. Lew Wallensky, of Lewis Wallensky Associates in Los Angeles, in an interview with *Investment Adviser* magazine, said it best, "Do you know what I call financial planners who say, 'Talk to me anytime about anything'? I call them poor." Moreover, someone with a net worth of less than $250,000 may find it difficult to pay an annual ongoing fee.

Practitioners utilizing this model are typically employees or agents of major financial services firms. Compensation structure is based on commissions and fee income from the proprietary offerings of their corporate partner. These advisers generally serve large numbers of clients. The critical business decision is the establishment of a strong corporate relationship, because most of the practitioner's income will be determined by the sale of products selected by the corporate partner.

This structure has many advantages—minimal start-up costs, strong marketing, compliance procedures, back office support, and minimal requirements for management of support staff. These advantages come with many disadvantages—including a lack of control over the allocation of resources, limited product choice, and, most important, the inability to independently represent the client's interest. This structure is best suited to a practitioner with significant sales skills who wishes to serve a large, relatively unsophisticated, middle income market.

The Service Model

PRACTITIONERS FOLLOWING THIS MODEL are generally independent entrepreneurs. They typically maintain a relationship with a financial services firm that provides services related to commission-based products. The service model has a number of attributes in common with the sales model. Advisers must have securities and insurance licenses. They also must have a corporate relationship, usually a broker-dealer. The primary differences are an increased flexibility in the choice of the compensation structure offered to clients (i.e., both fee and commission) and fewer restrictions with regard to the product available to their clients. Because of the higher level of personal service, these practices are more restricted in the numbers of clients an individual practitioner can manage.

The most successful practitioners utilizing this model have in common a number of attributes: They are client (as opposed to product) oriented and they follow the financial planning process in determining their product recommendations. In order to position themselves for marketing purposes as well as to expand their professional competence, most have or work toward obtaining recognized credentials such as the CFP license and the ChFC.

Most service-based practices are composed of practitioners who move from the large organization or who start as a sole practitioner associated with a less restrictive broker-dealer. Don't kid yourself. Even if you work with a broker-dealer, you are a sole practitioner. You are expected to develop a book of business, and although you may have supervision and support, you are essentially building a raft of relationships that depend very much upon you. The best part about this arrangement is that you probably have a great deal of flexibility in the way you work. You develop your own style and philosophy. You may add support staff, but the cost burden and practice success is solely dependent upon you and your personality. You can make decisions without having to run them by another person.

This structure is best suited for a practitioner who wants to serve a limited market (e.g., 200–500 clients) of middle and upper-middle income clients and for those who wish to transition in the future to the professional model.

The Professional Model

THE ATTRIBUTES of the professional model generally include a fee-only (or migration towards fee-only) practice committed to the financial planning process. The firm's professionals are credentialed (often with multiple credentials) and consider themselves to be acting in a fiduciary capacity. The practice typically prides itself on its total independence (no mandatory affiliations), sophisticated and customized planning and implementation, and commitment to confidentiality.

This is the profile of the practice often touted by the media, and its model is very client oriented and service intensive. It is not economically feasible for practitioners serving the general market. It is most appropriate for a client base consisting of clients with very high incomes and/or a significant net worth.

Many planners I've talked with who provide holistic professional planning feel the need to limit their client base to a range between 80 and 150. Judy Shine of Shine Investment Advisory Services in Englewood, Colorado, emphatically states that she will take no more than 100 clients. Her intensive involvement with her clients prevents her handling any more than that. "I am staying small by choice. I am not interested in being over-burdened with managing a huge staff, nor am I interested in having clients that I don't know and like very well."

While the sole practitioner management structure is common for service and professional practices, the growth of such solo practices will be limited. One solution is to expand the entrepreneurial base via partnership. This is an extremely important decision, so I have devoted Chapter 4 to it.

Business Plans

ONCE YOU'VE DETERMINED the business model of your practice (or it already exists), it's time to develop a business plan. I don't believe in cumbersome business plans. There are plenty of books, software programs, and other resources available to help you prepare a business plan. I prefer to use a simple model of my own. Whatever you use, it is important to have a plan and refer to it frequently. If not financial planners, who would understand the value of good planning? Perhaps the most important parts of the plan are the five-year vision, the six-month action plan, and the twelve-month budget. Almost all successful planners I know have business plans, some more elaborate than others.

Creating the Business Plan

START WITH THE BASICS. Who you are, why you are in business, who your target market is, and what you provide for them. If you went through the process of developing core values and a mission statement, you will already have thought these through. The first section of the plan should include:

◆ Charter date and revision dates of business plan
◆ Charter (formal name of company)
◆ Mission Statement (what do you want to be?)
◆ Services and products
◆ Types of clients
◆ Where business operates

The next section of the business plan, under the heading, Long-Term Objectives and Strategies, should include your five-year plan. What is your ultimate goal for this company? What will this company be when it grows up? What is your vision?

Then consider operational issues:

◆ What will your fee structure be?
◆ Will you use a third-party provider?
◆ Will you have a relationship with a broker-dealer?
◆ Will you use individual stocks, bonds, and/or mutual funds? What due diligence will you institute in the selection of these investment vehicles?

◆ What are your regulatory and legal considerations?
◆ What services will you be providing?
◆ What are your personnel requirements?

Next, tackle your marketing plan. How will you reach your ideal client? At this stage you do not have to detail your entire marketing strategy. Frankly, marketing strategies require a plan of their own. In this section, state whether you will do seminars, cultivate spheres of influence, use direct mailing tactics, etc. Also state who will be responsible for marketing and whether additional personnel are required.

Once your five-year vision plan is developed, prepare a shorter-term action plan. I find it easier to accomplish things if I break them down into near-term goals, so I suggest devising a six-month action plan. In that section discuss where you will concentrate your efforts during the next six months. Will it be external, for example, marketing, or will it be internal, such as developing systems or training personnel. Be specific and create benchmarks to check your progress.

Finally, you will want to address your twelve-month budget. What is your expected budget for the year? Project your income and estimate how many new clients you expect to gain. What new expenditures do you expect? When you have completed your one-year projections, follow the same procedures to develop projections for your five-year plan. Quantify these plans by developing, for example:

◆ Expected new income
◆ Expected number of new clients
◆ Expected salaries
◆ Expected additional expenditures for software, advertising
◆ Budget summary

Business Structure— Not-So-Usual Suspects

THE DISCUSSION SO FAR has made the implicit assumption that a practitioner has settled on a legal structure that will be similar to that of the typical planning office (i.e., a simple corporation, partnership, or sole-proprietorship). While most practitioners will opt to follow the traditional path, others may wish to consider creative alternative structures, some of which I've included here.

The Trust Company

TOM BRAY, of The Legacy Trust Company in Overland, Kansas, described his company as a "plain vanilla RIA, with Schwab, no-load funds, and doing the big book, you know, comprehensive financial planning." That was before Tom's company became a trust company. Tom works with middle to upper-middle income clients who, in his estimation, will one day need dynasty trusts to handle all the assets they will acquire over their lifetimes. Tom was interested in providing a range of services for middle America—a family office, of sorts, for the little guys. He also knew that if this group continues to grow their assets, he would also need to provide for multigenerational transfers. Conventional custodial arrangements cannot facilitate this as well as a trust company can.

A trust company is a departure from the traditional financial planning or asset management business. It has several advantages, including the ability to capture all of the client's assets through custodial accounts, trust accounts, and agency (individual) accounts. There are three major considerations to be addressed prior to opening a trust company: accepting fiduciary responsibility, meeting significant capital requirements, and engaging in highly regulated activities. For example, Tom explains that bank examiners will visit annually, provide a list of items they need to see, examine them, and then leave. The job of maintaining the structural legal requirements is made easier by his administration software, Sunguard, one of the few proprietary trust software programs available that's efficient and user friendly.

On the downside, operating a trust company is much more expensive than running a conventional financial planning office. The software is proprietary, specialized, and costly. There are increased accounting costs, since a trust company must file audited financials. Additionally, trust companies require specialized, increased insurance coverage.

You don't have to open your own trust company to have specialized trust services, however. Jeffrey Lauterbach of Sentinel Management Company in Wilmington, Delaware, provides trust company support to advisers. He maintains that while advisers need the flexibility of a trust company, the development of the practice on this business model is divergent from the original purpose of a planning practice. "It's like everything else: you probably should concentrate on what you do best, and use support systems when you can. Trust services are a tool."

Strategic Alliances
and Co-Advisory Relationships

THE ONLY COMMODITIES advisers ultimately have are their time and knowledge. You might take a tip from major corporations that have increasingly been using strategic alliances to leverage their resources. A strategic alliance is a formal business arrangement, usually between two or more complementary organizations. We have a co-advisory relationship with a regional bank and two CPA firms.

The bank has selected us as their investment arm, using our model portfolios for their high net worth clients. The CPA firms work in tandem with us to provide full financial planning services to their clients, offering financial, retirement, estate planning, and tax advice, but utilizing our planning and investment expertise and support. This may entail our meeting with their larger clients, or simply providing back office services and reporting.

According to research by management consultants Bain & Co., of the top twenty-five management tools and strategies utilized by major corporations, strategic alliances rank 6th, behind strategic planning, development of mission and vision statements, and customer satisfaction measurements (Darrell K. Rigby, "What's Today's Special at the Consultant's Café," *Fortune*, Vol. 138, No. 5, September 7, 1998; pp. 162–63.) According to their 1997 survey, developing strategic alliances was among 1997 favorites. We can use the same technique and leverage our time by taking on strategic alliances (or super-client relationships) with banks, accountants, and law firms. This allows the practice to grow, but does not increase the time the adviser needs to make available for face-to-face meetings. In effect, the practice takes on a $10 million or possibly a $100 million client. Additionally, these relationships allow the adviser to increase leverage with vendors, to have more clout with providers, and to have increased resources for more research and more specialized staff.

If you are considering such an arrangement, the services you provide to another organization can range from designing the portfolio models and making recommendations to providing full back office support. Whatever you decide, systematize all activities as much as possible to ensure that you have the control you need to accomplish the tasks. Remember, you still have responsibility for the clients, even if you don't see them personally.

Unless you are working with a federally chartered bank, your co-adviser will need to become a registered investment adviser. The ADV Part II of both firms must explain the relationship. Shared clients will need to receive copies of ADVs from both entities and sign a disclosure statement that acknowledges the relationship between the co-adviser and the activities to be performed by each.

The co-advisory contract should outline the function of each entity, determine the fee structure, and provide for recourse and termination if the relationship is not working.

You will want to standardize your forms and procedures to ensure consistency in the client relationships. Our co-advisors, for example, are trained to use our proprietary risk-coaching questionnaire as part of their education process with each client. In this way, we know that aspects of risk have been evaluated and discussed by our co-advisers in the format we would use.

The box that appears on pages 54–55 is an example of one we provide to organizations seeking a co-advisory relationship with us.

Consider your fee structure carefully. If you are still required to meet directly with clients, your fee should reflect this. However, if you are providing only investment expertise and reporting, your fees can be lower.

The structure of these relationships can be complicated. Be sure to get competent legal advice, and as with any partnership arrangement, plan for termination if it doesn't work.

Your Style Is You

YOUR BUSINESS SHOULD BE comfortable and consistent with your personality and style, a reflection of you. Clients gravitate to advisers with whom they find empathy and trust. If you're not comfortable with how you've structured your business, they won't be either.

EBK Wealth Management Consulting
CPA Planning Firm
Wealth Management Services

CO-ADVISORY

◆ An Immediate "Start-Up" Program

◆ A professional relationship with the principals of a nationally recognized Wealth Management practice—not a wrap or referral arrangement

◆ A customized and flexible Wealth Management program

◆ Access to low institutional service fees and institutional management costs

SERVICES

◆ START UP

Assistance in establishing required state and federal registrations

On-site consulting and training on:

Portfolio management software (Centerpiece, SchwabLink, HOMER)

Back Office operations (Schwab, SEI)

Client Relationships (Agreements, Risk Coaching, Investment Models and Policies)

EBK Client Education Seminar

Joint CPA/EBK Client meetings

◆ ONGOING
- Assistance with Client Policy preparation
- Client Portfolio Implementation
- Client Quarterlies (for Schwab clients)
- Immediate access to client accounts via Schwab Link
- Marketing, PR, consultation, and use of EBK "name"
- Access to EBK transaction costs and managers
- Access to EBK SEI models
- Updating of all materials

◆ MATERIALS
- Client Policy & Investment Management agreements
- Risk Coaching documentation
- Client Education program
- Investment Policy Format

◆ ONE TIME CONTRACT FEE
- $XXXX (includes first quarter)

◆ ANNUAL FEE

First $XX Million	XXbp
Next XX Million	XXbp
Next XXX Million	XXbp
Over XXX Million	XXbp

Minimum Schwab account $500,000
Minimum SEI Account $150,000

CONTINGENCY & SUCCESSION

One of the most difficult problems that confronts any commander who has committed his forces in accordance with a well-developed plan is to alter this in the light of changing circumstances.

— S U N   T Z U , *The Art of War*

IT'S THE SHOEMAKER'S CHILDREN, they say, who go barefoot. Most advisers avoid thinking about retirement, death, or the chance that they or their partner will become disabled. Struggling to acquire and retain clients always seems to take precedence. I am not going to cover business succession planning techniques and mechanics in this chapter. You're a planner; I assume you know the basics. I want to explore the effect of a traumatic personal event on your practice and clients and to suggest how to make some practice contingency plans to be implemented in times of crisis. I also want to discuss some of the issues you must address when considering the transfer of your business. First, I'd like to share with you the experience of a few friends who have actually faced these issues.

Crisis Planning for Death

I MET ANDREW WRAY about ten years ago at an ICFP retreat. At the time, Andrew was a planner in Memphis with a small, successful practice and one partner, Bill Howard. Andrew and Bill met when they were taking courses for the CFP exam and had practiced together since 1985. They were best friends. The clients were all considered clients of the firm, but they primarily had a relationship with either Andrew or Bill. One Saturday evening, while working late, Andrew, then only forty-nine, suffered a heart attack and died at his desk. Andrew's son discovered his body when he went to the office because his dad had not returned home or responded to his worried family's phone calls. By Saturday morning, Andrew's death had affected not only his family, but Bill's life, and the lives of all their clients.

All of us in the planning community were stunned. Andrew was young. Andrew was presumably in good health. Andrew was gone. My partner Harold and I, along with many other advisers, offered help to Bill. Unfortunately, we did not know how we could be of assistance.

Bill, shocked and grieving, recognized immediately that the clients would also feel the tremendous loss. He began to make phone calls to each of them. He felt it was imperative to inform them of Andrew's death before they heard it anywhere else. So while Andrew's family was making preparations for the funeral, Bill was talking with the clients, assuring them of the business continuity and ongoing professional support. In the subsequent weeks, Bill met with each of Andrew's clients. He was pleased to find that for the most part, they were not concerned about the company's stability. Naturally, they were upset. In many cases, the grief for the loss of Andrew helped forge stronger relationships with Bill.

As Bill provided care for his clients, he was personally grieving for his friend and partner. He was also personally worried about his responsibilities to the staff. He and Andrew had just signed a new five-year lease and hired four additional staff people. Andrew had carried the primary responsibility for running the office. Bill had never been interested in that aspect of the practice. Now he had to take over under the worst circumstances. Bill had to keep the staff together, make the clients feel comfortable and confident, and finally, try to take care of himself.

The firm's staff was also suffering from grief and shock. Within one year, three left, compounding the chaos. Bill confides that systemization, coupled with his own tenacity, kept the business going. Two years after Andrew's death, Bill changed the name of the company. He felt this was necessary in order to focus on the future and keep the business growing. In hindsight, Bill said he probably should have done that sooner, but didn't want to seem disrespectful to Andrew's memory.

Disability Crisis

IT'S PRUDENT TO CONSIDER the possibilities of a partner dying. It is also important to consider the possibility of a partner suffering a disability or illness that might keep him or her from working for many months or years. This requires an entirely different type of contingency planning, because at some point you expect the partner to return. Consequently, it is necessary to also consider what that re-entry might be like.

A few years ago, John Ueleke of Legacy Wealth Management in Memphis, Tennessee, was diagnosed with a rare cancer. As part of his treatment plan, he had to move to Houston for several months. John told me, "When your practice gets large enough, and your staff consists of more than just you and a couple of support people, you have to think not only of your clients, but also of the employees who rely upon you for their livelihood. I realized that I had to make plans not just for my clients, but for the management of the business, too. I needed to do this so I could focus on myself, and getting better."

In the few days before John had to leave for Houston, he and his partners Bob Winfield, Dick Vosburg, and Sarah Haizlip worked out a new business plan. They used this as an opportunity to restructure their practice, making some changes they'd been thinking about in the past few months anyway. They began by developing a client strategy delivery worksheet, listing who was currently responsible for delivery of services to each client. They also reviewed the nature of their relationship with all of their clients. They listed client personality traits and familiarized each other with the nature of the engagement and client's personal circumstances. Based on this information and knowledge of their own personality style, they then assigned a primary partner, a primary assistant, and a backup partner.

They also felt it was important to be upfront with the clients about John's illness. Together they wrote a letter, explaining what they knew about John's condition and how they planned to redistribute the workload. John explains, "This brought an additional benefit. I was able to elicit support from my clients. Through this experience I have learned that we rely on our clients not only for financial sustenance, but for personal and spiritual support as well."

In preparation for this book, I discussed contingency plans with many successful planners, including Bill Howard, John Ueleke, and Bob Winfield. I've divided their suggestions into three parts: an action plan for now, a contingency plan for during a crisis, and one for after a crisis.

An Action Plan for Now

◆ **Draft a buy-sell agreement and fund it if required.** Many planners told me that in the early years, there seemed no reason to have a buy-sell agreement. The company wasn't worth much and was often burdened with debt from the start-up costs. Unfortunately, those same planners told me that by the time the company was making a nice profit, the partners were so preoccupied with growth, they never got around to revisiting the need for that agreement.

◆ **Get your business insurance planning in order.** Maintain and continually update all pertinent information including types and amounts of coverage, beneficiary designations, deductibles and exclusions, premium payments, renewal dates and contact phone numbers (including pager numbers), plus mail and e-mail addresses.

◆ **Get your personal risk management planning in order.** This includes disability and life insurance as well as property and casualty coverage. For example, when hurricane Andrew devastated much of South Florida in 1992, my partners and I were able to concentrate on the problems caused to our business (e.g., property damage and long-term power disruptions) and the problems faced by our clients, because our own personal insurance was adequate to cover the costs of quickly rectifying the damage to our own property. There were a few less-prepared planners who suffered significant business disruption because they had to spend so much time resolving their personal recovery problems.

◆ **Get your personal estate planning documents in order.** The quality of your personal estate planning will have a significant impact on your partner(s) and staff should you die while still active in the business.

◆ **You may be emotionally at risk to the family of a deceased partner.** If the family does not understand the business arrangements you and your partner have devised, they may have unrealistic expectations about the amount due them. You and your partner should consider discussing the rationale of your arrangement with those who may be beneficiaries. If you are not comfortable having the discussions prior to a crisis, consider writing a letter or making a videotape explaining your decisions, so that it will be available when needed.

◆ **Develop and document a contingency plan** for keeping your staff, clients, and partner's family informed of important activities and practice changes during the period of crisis.

◆ **Systematize your office activities and, based on this, prepare a crisis action plan.** No matter what the crisis, certain activities must be completed. If your contingency planning indicates that you will be required to bring in outside help (e.g., accounting support, computer consultation, personal counseling), determine and document in advance the type and sources of this assistance. Maintain a list of time-sensitive activities and a list of who will handle these activities during a crisis.

◆ **Maintain a comprehensive inventory of important documents** (e.g., property and casualty insurance policies, corporate records) and where to find them.

◆ **Establish a comprehensive computer backup system** (see Chapter 7). List where backups are stored and who has responsibility for the archiving system.

◆ **In addition to your client list, maintain a comprehensive and continually updated list of other important contacts,** such as your attorneys, bankers, accountants, property, casualty and health insurers, etc. Include a notation of when and how they should be contacted (phone, letter, or e-mail) and who will be responsible for the contact.

◆ **Clearly define the managing partner's responsibilities and plan for short-term coverage** of these responsibilities in the event of his absence.

◆ **Prepare a "re-entry plan"** in cases where a partner may return after a prolonged absence. Include how responsibilities will be redistributed and how long this assimilation will take.

During a Crisis

◆ **Implement the action plan.** This is *not* the time to rethink your strategies. Follow the plan.

◆ **Immediately contact clients personally** and assure them that you and your partner(s) had developed a comprehensive contingency plan and it is being implemented.

◆ **Take care of yourself emotionally.** Do not assume that you are Superman or Wonderwoman. You are human. Get a counselor or therapist to help you work through the emotional trauma you are experiencing.

◆ **Take care of your employees.** Consider counseling for your key employees.

◆ **Implement the contingency plan strategy** for keeping staff, clients, and your partner's family informed.

After the Crisis

◆ **Review with your staff, clients, and personal advisers** how well your crisis plan worked. Make adjustments and document them.

◆ **If the crisis was due to the death of a key person or partner,** review the business plan to establish new goals and objectives for the business.

◆ **Revisit all legal documents** to ensure that they reflect the nature and intention of the current owners or partners.

John Ueleke summed up your responsibilities to your company best: "When your business gets to a certain size, you realize that many people are depending upon its continuance. Never forget that you are not in this alone. You owe it to your clients, your staff, and your partners to see that your company will survive."

Business Succession

AS PLANNING PRACTICES MATURE, the decision of whether you want your business to outlive you becomes more pressing. To me, this decision differentiates a practice from a business. A practice is based on a personality. If that personality leaves, the practice dissolves. A business is dependent on structure, philosophy, and continuity; it does not rely upon any one personality.

The Loyola University American Family business survey of 1995 on small business succession revealed that 50 percent of all CEOs are within five years of retirement. Furthermore, over 70 percent had not yet identified a successor.

Greg Sullivan, of Sullivan, Bruyette, Speros & Blayney, and his partners have prepared for their succession by grooming younger people to move into key positions. This takes considerable time and training, but ensures continuity with clients. The partners and planners at SBSB work as a team to meet the clients' needs. Jim Bruyette explained that their decision to become somewhat dispensable within the client relationships is bittersweet. "One of my favorite clients called not long ago and I picked up the call. After a few moments of small talk, the client explained that he had actually asked for my associate, Mark. 'I need some advice,' he said, 'I can just talk it over with Mark.' Although that's the idea, I didn't feel particularly wanted or needed."

Eleanor Blayney confided that she likes the idea that her practice will survive her. "I envision one day, fifty years from now, two SBSB planners will walk through our office, looking at the picture of our founding partners. One will ask the other, 'Who was this Eleanor Blayney, anyway?'"

It's a good idea to consider your own plans for retirement before you commit to an exit strategy. Judy Lau, CFP, of Lau & Associates in Wilmington, Delaware, is a sole practitioner. Judy always thought that she'd sell her company to another planner one day and just retire. Recently she began to reconsider the ultimate disposition of her business. "If I retired, I would only want to play 50 percent of the time. I would need something else to do, so I probably would do volunteer work. The more I thought about this, the crazier it seemed. Let's see, I am going to stop doing something that I really love and for which I am very well paid, so that I can play half the time. In my spare time, I will work for a volunteer organization where I will have no control, no respect, no pay, and no appreciation. What's wrong with this picture?" Judy finally decided that she would hire someone with a high level of skills to work with her now to share the workload. This will allow her to take more time away from her office. Eventually her younger partner will assume ownership.

Outright Sale

IF YOU ARE NOT PLANNING to groom a successor, you may be thinking of an outright sale to someone already in the business. Loyola University's business survey found that only 40 percent of owners had determined the value of their businesses. If your business were a major asset, wouldn't you want to be aware of its worth so you could know how it would fit with your future plans?

In preparation for this book, I spoke with Mark Tibergien, of Moss Adams LLP in Seattle, Washington. Mark's expertise is valuing and facilitating the transfer of financial service companies. I asked Mark for some hints for financial advisers planning a sale as their exit strategy. Here is his "Dos and Don'ts" list:

◆ **Don't overestimate the value of your practice.** It's a buyer's market. You know what that can do to the price.

◆ **Do consider other issues besides price.** Mark reports that in his experience, only 30 percent of the deals are consummated. The failure of the rest is due to terms, contrary cultures, or differences in philosophy.

◆ **Do get a professional valuation.** If you are counting on the sale of your business for retirement, you definitely need a valuation to incorporate into your capital needs calculation. "Ask yourself, 'Can I afford to retire without including the value of my business?' You must perform the same analysis for yourself that you'd do for any financial planning client. As a rule, you shouldn't count on your business as a retirement bailout; merely your bonus," says Mark.

◆ **Don't overestimate the goodwill aspect of your business.** There is no correlation between goodwill and the number of years you have been in this business. Goodwill is that intangible that keeps clients coming to you. Your participation (or lack of it) in the new business may have a significant impact on the goodwill factor.

◆ **Do start your planning early.** Know the elements of valuation and manage your practice with that in mind.

◆ **Don't compare your business to others and anticipate the same terms.** Businesses are unique; valuations are unique; transfers are unique.

◆ **Don't confuse your business with asset managers.** When Michael Price sold Heine Securities to Franklin Templeton in 1996 for $800 million, we were all extraordinarily impressed with the purchase price. But remember, there is a great difference between asset managers and asset gatherers.

It is important to remember that the value of your business is realized every day in the form of high income. The more your practice is dependent upon you, the less attractive it is to a buyer. The more closely your company resembles a commercial enterprise, the more likely you will have something to transfer. A prospective buyer will be interested in your client demographics, your philosophy with regard to investments, and the nature of the income (e.g., if the income is largely dependent upon investment performance and market performance). He will also be interested in the level of service, operations, and the standardization you've instituted in your business.

Valuation

NATURALLY, IT IS POSSIBLE that you might consider the sale of your practice to someone who is not in this profession. This may be a

Consider planner Shari's practice. . .

SHE HAS A GOOD THING going and

    grosses annually $500,000

Based on conversations with friends she

    expects 4x gross or $2,000,000

Now, in order to generate net profit, the firm has some expenses. I'd calculate the firm's net income as follows:

Revenue	$500,000
Less:	
Direct expenses (including fair compensation for Shari)	
Operating expenses	
Taxes	
In a well-run practice these run about 80% of gross	
	($400,000)
New Profit	$100,000

Comparing the net profit of $100,000 to the projected sales price of $2,000,000 suggests a 5 percent capitalization rate. Mark concludes "that's about the return on a U.S. Treasury bond. Why on earth would anyone want to invest in a planner's business for a return that's about the same as a Treasury?"

much more difficult hurdle. During my interview with Mark, he walked me through an important reality check that I want to share with you.

There are two popular methods for valuing a company. One uses a multiple of the gross; the other uses a multiple of the net profit. The problem with using the gross figure is that the cost of realizing that income is not factored in. Mark suggests that planners thinking in terms of gross numbers may be living in a world of unrealistic expectations. He explained it this way:

Bottom line—to increase the value of your business, follow these four tenets from Mark Tibergien:

1 Maximize cash flow. Pay yourself a reasonable salary and watch your expenses.

2 Minimize risk. Ensure the operation of your business is not entirely dependent upon you.

3 Manage growth. Prepare for growth; don't let it surprise you.

4 Enhance transferability. Systematize your operations.

Don't Wait—Plan Now

STAN COREY of Great Falls Financial Services in Great Falls, Virginia, has been concerned with succession planning for some time now. "I am a sole practitioner. I have long dialogues with my clients about their own future plans, but I haven't had much to say to them about mine. Recently, I have discussed this with other planners in my area. We have agreed to formulate some succession plans among us. We will agree in advance on who is willing to pay for our clients if we retire or die."

Warren Mackensen of Hampton, New Hampshire, has the same idea. In his relationship manager software, ProTracker, he has built a field for an adviser to track relationships with other advisers who can take over during a crisis, or retirement. "We provide a description of our clients online. If someone is interested, we agree on terms and that's it. It's a good idea for small firms."

It is clear that no matter what size of business it is, you must think about its future, and yours. When you review a client's financial activities, you don't hesitate to discuss gaps in his risk exposures, e.g., no disability, no life insurance, no estate plan. Yet, many of the advisers I've interviewed in the past months have neglected to follow their own advice. Don't procrastinate. As your business grows, you will have less time to devote to your own planning. Do it now.

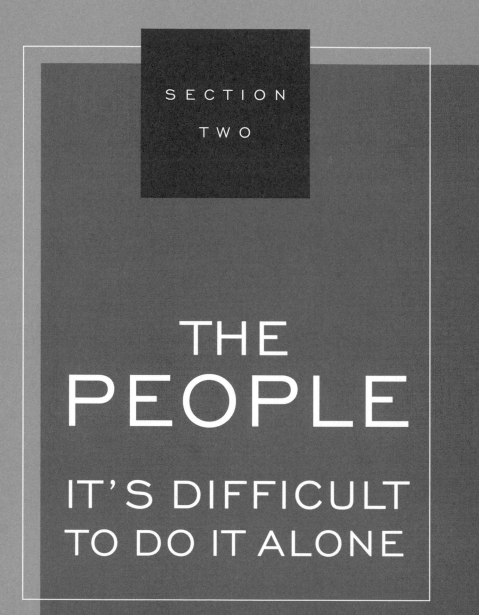

SECTION
TWO

THE
PEOPLE

IT'S DIFFICULT
TO DO IT ALONE

ONE OF THE PROBLEMS with managing a practice is the need for competent assistance. Forming a great staff is extremely difficult. As the practice matures, many advisers consider taking on partners and new staffing is required. Who you need to hire depends upon how you want to grow. Working out scenarios in advance avoids wasted time, money, and energy. This section discusses the value of strategic planning for selecting a partner plus hiring and retaining good staff.

CHAPTER 4

ADDING A PARTNER FOR FUN & PROFIT

*I choose to work with every single person I work with. That
ends up being the most important factor. I don't interact with
people I don't like or admire. That's the key. It's like marrying.*

— WARREN BUFFET

A YOUNG PLANNER STOPPED ME a few years ago at the

IAFP Success Forum in Minneapolis and told me he was

thinking about going on his own. He had spent the past

five years working with a medium-sized regional planning

practice, but now wanted ownership and more flexibility. He also wanted a partner. When I asked him why, he replied that he was nervous about making this leap and wanted someone who could share the responsibilities and work load. "I think I found him," he said. "He's a broker and has a pretty good business going, too, but he really doesn't do planning. He told me that although he's not interested in financial planning, he wouldn't mind having a partner who was."

At some point in their careers, many practitioners entertain the idea of taking on a partner. As with my friend in Minneapolis, this thought may crop up when considering a redefinition of your practice, or it may occur during a growth spurt when it seems impossible to keep up with new business and still maintain old relationships. Taking on additional personnel propels you into managing staff and focusing your attention away from clients. "If I only had a partner," you think. What you probably have in mind is cloning yourself.

Dr. Meredith Belbin, a British expert in management, spent nine years researching the effectiveness of management teams. His book, *Management Teams* (Butterworth-Heinemann Publishers, a division of Reed Educational and Professional Publishing, Ltd., Oxford, 1996), offers some invaluable advice for building partnerships. Dr. Belbin's research dealt with the formation of high-powered management teams, known as Apollo Teams. Based on the assumption that the most effective team would be one comprised of the most effective people, he established all-star partnerships, composed of clever, critical thinking individuals. Contrary to expectations, the Apollo Teams performed their tasks much less successfully than teams composed of less extraordinary but more complementary members. The problem was that the Apollo individuals all had the same aspirations and wanted to perform the same functions within the organization. They spent most of the time trying to persuade their partners to adopt their ideas. They were miserably ineffective teams. So much for cloning yourself.

Why a Partnership?

IT IS IMPORTANT TO DETERMINE why you really want a partner. I suspect my friend in Minneapolis was insecure about going on his own. The idea of having a partner seemed to fortify him. Unfortunately, a teddy bear is a better solution for insecurity, and a lot less expensive. Be sure you know why you want a partner. Ask yourself these key questions:

◆ **What can I contribute to a partnership?** Remember the old Groucho Marx story? He said he wouldn't want to belong to any club that would have him as a member. Why would someone want to partner with you? What strengths do you have that would enhance those of a partner? Both of you should see the collaboration as in your mutual interests.

◆ **What are the talents missing in my practice that can be best provided by another individual?** Ross Levin of Accredited Investors in Minneapolis admits that he is no administrator and is thankful to have a partner who is not only an excellent administrator but who also enjoys administration as much as Ross loves planning.

◆ **Do I really need to share ownership, or can I accomplish my goal by delegating authority to key employees?** Don't assume that a partnership is the only answer to your problems. New senior staff may add the necessary depth to your practice, without the added burden that a partner may bring.

◆ **Would an affiliation with another practitioner, sharing overhead and resources, be a better alternative?** To some, this may be the best of all worlds; your business remains autonomous, but you have access to resources and support when you need them. There are, however, some not-so-obvious drawbacks to an affiliation. If you operate as separate corporations but under one trade name, you run the risk of accepting liability for the actions of your affiliate. The world sees you as partners, and that is a risk you should not accept lightly.

◆ **How will work responsibilities be divided?** Probably one of the best partnerships I know is that of Jim Budros and Peggy Ruhlin, of Budros & Ruhlin, Inc., in Columbus, Ohio. All of their clients are clients of the firm and meet with the partners interchangeably. Peggy explains that she and Jim have very different work styles and specialties. This enhances the client relationship because they each have a different emphasis or focus when they meet with clients. Peggy usually handles the administrative activities, although Jim covered seamlessly for Peggy while she committed much of her time to meeting her responsibilities as President of the IAFP.

◆ **What new ideas or activities would the partnership bring to this practice? Do the advantages outweigh the disadvantages? Is the relationship in both your interests?** If you are joining forces with an experienced adviser, most likely he or she will be bringing a mature skill set to the mix. It may appear wonderful on the surface, but be sure that those skills are ones you want to bring into the practice. One adviser I know merged his practice with another planner who provided tax preparation as part of her practice. It was decided that the tax work would be integrated into the new entity and offered to all clients. My friend did not realize the impact that offering tax preparation would have on the business. It was a time-consuming activity, one that he felt they were not sufficiently paid for. More importantly, this new service caused some ill will among his existing referral sources, who were largely CPAs.

◆ **Would bringing in a partner improve your bottom line or just expand the workload?** Paul Brady of Australia suggests that it is necessary to analyze the impact of one or even two or three partners with respect to the expected profit. Often times it looks good on paper, but doesn't translate well in practice.

Address the Personalities First

EVERY ADVISER I KNOW who is in a partnership used the same words when discussing the relationship: It's like marriage. As a person who is married to her partner, I can reinforce that. In fact, it can be better or worse than marriage. For me, both relationships rely on successful teamwork. If we can just know how to construct the perfect teams, we've got it made.

Identify Successful Teams

BELBIN FOUND THAT the most successful teams were those comprised of individuals who complemented each other's talents. When complementary personalities were paired within the team, they were unbeatable. He determined that defining the key personalities and their function is a good starting point when looking for a partner.

Begin by identifying the attributes of a personality that will complement you. In order to identify your potential partner's characteristics, you'll need to have a clear sense of your own personality and style. Belbin defines four broad personality types that may be used in classifying yourself. These types are identified, as follows, on Belbin's extrovert-introvert vs. stability-anxiety scale:

◆ **Stable extroverts** are individuals who work best in cooperative or liaison relationships. They tend to be easy-going and well received by other personality types and may make great sales people.

◆ **Anxious extroverts** like to work at a fast pace and enjoy positions that allow them to motivate and influence others. They are good at seizing opportunities and respond well to rapidly changing situations. Anxious extroverts make great sales managers.

◆ **Stable introverts** work well with smaller groups, maintaining relationships for extended periods of time. They are strong in details, organization skills and planning. They make good administrators.

◆ **Anxious introverts** are self-directed and persistent. They work best on their own and are not particularly team-oriented.

If it is difficult for you to identify yourself with these brief descriptions, list the activities in your business that you enjoy most. Is it the rainmaking, the client meetings, or the number crunching? Which do you avoid or tackle last? Do many of your ideas fall away because you just don't have the time, opportunity or personnel to carry them out?

Belbin also identified eight distinct team roles that can be useful in identifying personality characteristics for possible partnerships.

Partnership design is analogous to portfolio design. The focus should be on the portfolio (i.e., the partnership) and not the security (i.e., the partner). Partnership is about balance. What is needed is not well-balanced individuals, but individuals who possess characteristics that complement and balance one another.

Assess Yourself as a Team Member

BELBIN'S THEORIES MAY HELP YOU identify personality types. However, you'll also want to explore work style preferences when considering partners or teams. Dr. William Taggart of Santa Cruz, California, has developed a Personal Style Inventory (PSI). Dr. Taggart's

Team Roles

TYPE	TYPICAL FEATURES	POSITIVE QUALITIES	WEAKNESSES
Chairman	Self-confident, controlled	Strong sense of objectives	Ordinary creative abilities
Worker	Conservative, predictable	Organizing abilities, self-discipline	Lacks flexibility
Shaper	Outgoing, dynamic	Drive, challenging nature	Impatient, easily provoked
Plant	Individualistic, unorthodox	Drive, challenging nature	Impatient, easily provoked
Investigator	Extroverted, enthusiastic	Explores the new	Loses interest easily
Evaluator	Unemotional, prudent	Judgment, discretion	Lacks inspiration, non-motivator
Team Player	Socially oriented, sensitive	Promotes team spirit	Indecisive
Finisher	Orderly, conscientious	Perfectionism, follows through	Worries about details

research suggests that there are six personal style modes that identify an individual's preferred behavior. The style modes—planning, vision, analysis, insight, control, and sharing—dictate how you will react in approaching your work, solving problems, and preparing for the future.

Dr. Taggart has been studying personality and the way in which we process information. In addition to the style modes, his research suggests that there are two possible dominant preferences (rational and intuitive) that can be measured by six style dimensions. Based on these conclusions, he has designed a Personal Style Inventory (PSI) to assist individuals in developing a picture of their rational/intuitive preference. In his terminology, an individual with a *rational* preference will prepare for the future by planning, solving problems with analysis, and approach work with procedures and control. An individual with *intuitive* preference, will prepare for the future with vision, solve problems with insight, and use a sharing (people-oriented) approach to work. Although Dr. Taggart's survey is much more comprehensive (PAR Psychological Assessment Resources, Inc. A "Dimensional Booklet" summarizing the Personal Inventory Approach to rational/intuitive flexibility can be obtained by calling 800-331-8378), the following "quick and dirty" questionnaire he devised as a teaser will give you an idea of its application.

Each of the four statements describes a behavior, a belief, or a preference that relates to a common work or life experience. Respond to each statement by rating it according to the answers that best describe you.

Response	Score
Never	1
Once in a while	2
Sometimes	3
Quite often	4
Frequently, but not always	5
Always	6

1 When I have a special job to do, I like to organize it carefully from the start.

2 I feel that a prescribed, step-by-step method is best for solving problems.

3 I prefer people who are imaginative to those who are not.

4 I look at a problem as a whole, approaching it from all sides.

First, add up the score for the first two questions. For example, if your response to the first two questions was a 5 and 3, your total score for the first two questions is 8. Then calculate the score for the last two questions. For example, if the responses are 6 and 6, your total is 12. Finally, subtract the score for the second calculation (i.e., 12) from the first one (8). In this example, the answer is –4. Look at the following scale:

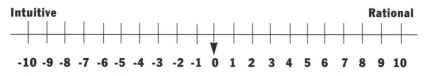

Intuitive   **Rational**

-10 -9 -8 -7 -6 -5 -4 -3 -2 -1   0   1   2   3   4   5   6   7   8   9   10

If your answer is a positive number, you have a dominant rational preference and will use rational rules to make a decision. If your score is negative, as above, your dominant preference is intuition. If you are in the middle, you have a nice balance between the rational and the intuitive, and can draw from both as necessary in your working environment.

Carl Jung, the first to identify intuition as part of the personality, suggests that some individuals have an innate sense of perception and process information in the unconscious. Rational individuals take a more analytical approach, emphasizing process and planning. In application, it is appropriate to be cognizant of your dominant preferences, but it is not necessary to search for a partner who is your complete opposite. Taggart and his associate, Dr. Anisya Thomas of Florida International University, conclude that "to succeed, most organizations must balance creativity and efficiency to nurture intuition in some parts while simultaneously promoting rationality in others. Our experience suggests that heterogeneous management teams that reflect a balance of reason and intuition are best suited to the task (of succeeding)." [*Integrating Intuition in Organizations*, (forthcoming).] Partnerships can work only if you recognize, respect, and utilize these differences.

Successful Teams in Practice

I ASKED DR. TAGGART to participate in one of our company retreats. It was magnificent. Through his survey of our partners and staff, we were able to identify those of us who could work well together. More importantly, we knew why we could accomplish more if we adjusted work responsibilities and teams. One of my staff members told me after the retreat that she had always had problems working closely with another member of the staff. "This was so revealing. I realize now that we have completely different work styles. I was relying on her to accomplish her tasks the same way I always do. Now that I know her personal style, my expectations for her will be different and I will be less frustrated."

Probably the most dramatic demonstration of how an understanding of differences in work styles can help an existing team was the work Dr. Taggart did for our Alpha Group. The Alpha Group is a study group of thirteen members from nine firms around the country. We began as an informal study group in 1990. We also had a cause to champion. Portfolio managers of mutual funds were not providing much information. We felt that it was important for us to know much more about their style, process, and thinking than could ever possibly be shared through a prospectus. As a group, we could approach various fund managers, ask for information, and even request phone calls with them. Collectively, we represented over a billion dollars in assets, so we were worth their time.

We developed our monthly manager calls. Each month we invited a different manager to conduct a phone conference with us. Soon, this idea caught on and managers began conducting their own calls, inviting any advisers to participate. There was no need for us to request our own calls any longer. Within two years, it was clear that on any one day, you could participate in any of at least five different calls with various managers. We thought we needed another cause.

As time went on, at our periodic meetings, we would devise wonderful projects and white papers. We would leave our meetings energized and excited. By the next meeting, none of us had carried out the things we intended to do. We simply could not figure out why we were not more productive. That's when we asked Dr. Taggart to give us the work style assessment. "It's amazing," he told me, "you all have an intuitive work style in the extreme. There isn't a planner in the bunch." This was a pretty big surprise to us, since we all considered ourselves top-notch financial planners. Taggart went on to explain that we would probably make a better industry think tank, arranging to hand off projects we design to those planners who enjoy carrying out the tasks. This was an amazing, liberating realization. Since that time we have pulled together ideas, then shared them with others in the industry who have acted on them.

The Myers Briggs Type Indicator (Consulting Psychologists Press, Inc. 3808 E. Bayshore, Palo Alto, California 94303, 800-624-1765, www.mbti.com.) is possibly the most well-known personality indicator. It is based on Carl Jung's theory of psychological types. The instrument divides personalities into sixteen types, each possessing certain distinct personality characteristics. Answers to ninety-three questions place the personality on four different scales:

1 Introvert or Extrovert
2 Sensing or Intuition
3 Thinking or Feeling
4 Perceiving or Judging

Because this is a fairly popular personality exercise, I won't go into detail. I have however referenced its availability, as we've utilized the Myers Briggs during our retreats and found it most useful. You may find it an effective method for identifying complementary personality traits in potential partners.

Collective Vision

ONCE YOU HAVE IDENTIFIED personality types, you must ensure that you and your potential partner share the same vision for the future of the business and the same ethical standards. There must be mutual respect and a comfortable working relationship before you establish a partnership, which cannot be formed overnight. Most married couples have had some kind of courtship before the wedding. Prior to formalizing a transfer of ownership, establish a formal courting relationship.

You can do this by keeping the relationship temporary or on a trial basis for a period of time, or you may structure a buy-in over a longer period of time. Whatever strategy you use, be sure that each participant has an equitable way out of the partnership if it does not appear to be working. Schedule frequent evaluations during the trial period and keep the communication flowing.

Threatening the Marriage

MORE AND MORE ESTABLISHED ADVISERS are considering bringing in younger partners to absorb the work overflow and/or participate in the succession plan. Unfortunately, it may disturb relationships that exist between the older partners. Peggy Ruhlin refers to this as "threatening the marriage."

A friend confided to me that he and his partner in an established fee-only practice had been approached by another planner in their town who suggested that they combine their businesses. This planner was a broker with a substantial commission-based clientele. He was willing to share his revenues for a percentage of the combined practice and a substantial, dependable salary. He was a good marketer and felt he could attract substantial business to the firm. They settled on a 15 percent share of the practice and $75,000 base salary for the new partner.

There were several unpleasant surprises not anticipated by any of the partners. Much of the business the broker expected to bring did not come with him. His existing clients, comfortable with paying commissions, were not happy with the fee-only philosophy of the new firm. The idea of paying an annual fee was not attractive. The minority partner was indeed a good marketer, but even the new clients he attracted did not match the new firm's client base, and as a result, they did not remain clients very long. Unfortunately, in all their planning, none of the three had considered an exit strategy. After four years, my friend and his original partner are exploring ways to buy out the minority partner. In hindsight, it would have been better to form an affiliation and cement or sever it at a later date.

Find Common Ground

ONCE YOU HAVE AGREED to take on a new partner, re-craft your positioning and vision statements to ensure that you are both (all) in agreement with your business plans and purpose. Eleanor Blayney suggests that the hardest thing to overcome in any business relationship is each partner's different sense of priorities. The more partners, the more varied the range and intensity of these perspectives. Clearly defined core values and a common investment philosophy help.

As you ponder the commonalties of your business styles, consider whether you and your partner share the same vision of growth for the firm. Ross Levin says that after having increased his client base many fold, he and his partner agreed that taking on more clients did not match their vision of growth. They would prefer to spend more time with fewer people than progressively less time with more people. As a result they mutually agreed to "grow down."

Then consider the practical issues. What will your work products look like? What investments will you use? For example, do you both agree on the efficacy of active money management? Are you both committed to the exclusive use of mutual funds, or will you also use separate accounts, or individual stocks and bonds? A successful partnership requires members who are flexible, adaptable, and possess an ability to communicate and compromise.

Finding the right partner is as important as deciding you want one. It is imperative that you both have a clear vision of how that relationship should work and what you expect from it. By carefully listing and analyzing the reasons for having a partner, you may decide that all you really need is a good administrator to run the practice, while you concentrate on gathering new business. Perhaps a good salesperson will free up your time so it can be devoted to existing clients. Partnerships still risk failure, even if you have thoughtfully analyzed your requirements, determined that you need a partner, and have selected someone to complement your personality. So plan carefully and consider an engagement first.

Who's in Charge?

ONCE YOU HAVE CONSTRUCTED your partnership arrangement, you and your potential partner must choose a managing partner. It is unrealistic to believe that more than one person can stand at the helm and steer the boat. The managing partner should be the person with the best management and organizational skills. All staff management and day-to-day business decisions should be the responsibility of the managing partner. Be honest and realistic. If managing people is not your forte, admit it and be prepared to let your partner take the helm. Then stay out of his way. Each of you has different responsibilities within the organization and respects the other for contributions to the company as a whole.

Periodic Evaluation and Review

AS A PRACTITIONER, you use benchmarks to gauge your client's progress. Similarly, you and your partners need to establish benchmarks and periodically review your progress. Set both short-term (e.g., three- to twelve-month goals) and long-term (e.g., three years) benchmarks. Include business goals, such as the number of new clients per quarter; and organizational goals, such as additional staff or the purchase of software. Finally, list personal goals. Quite often business and personal goals are inextricably linked, and it is wise to share these goals with your partners as well. Evaluate your process and your results. The following is our partner evaluation form:

Partner Self-Assessment

1 Did you accomplish your personal goals from last year? Describe your successes and failures.

2 What would you like to accomplish personally during the next three months? Six months? Nine months?

3 Are you satisfied with your performance as a partner? If not, where would you like to make some improvements?

4 What are your expectations for this company in the next year? Two to five years?

5 Where do you want to be next year at this time?
  a. Personally
  b. Professionally
  c. With regard to family
  d. With regard to friends
  e. Financially

6 Where would you like the business to be at this time next year?
  a. Number of clients
  b. Assets under management
  c. Number of employees
  d. Your salary and company profit

Regular Partner Retreats

FIVE YEARS AGO, my partners and I began having formal, scheduled partner retreats. These are separate from our company retreats, which everyone attends. We always meet away from the office, either at my home or a hotel. We believe it is important to meet outside the office. There are no distractions or interruptions, and often the new venue stimulates new thoughts and visions.

We begin the day with my "State of the Business" report, which includes detailed financial reports, staff evaluations, and growth projections. We continue with our benchmark and personal evaluations, and end the day with our strategic planning. We always review our mission and vision statements, making sure that our new objectives for the upcoming year are in keeping with them.

Partner Compensation

SINCE YOU AND YOUR PARTNER(S) presumably have different work responsibilities, you will need to address the partnership compensation structures. It should seem fair to everyone involved, and all partners should be satisfied with their share. In my experience, it is not wise to keep revisiting this issue unless something substantive in the relationship changes.

Of the firms I have interviewed, all have a partner compensation structure that considers the individual's contribution to the company. Every partner receives the same base salary, but bonuses are based on the income generated by each person.

A firm I've been advising recently discussed their compensation structure for a new partner who would function purely as a back-office person. It was not expected he would be directly responsible for new business. The other two partners had been together for seven years. They proposed a base compensation, plus a percentage of new business for the new partner. I challenged this rationale since only the original two partners would be bringing in new business. There seemed to be an eventual opportunity for resentment since the third partner's bonus would be based upon new business that he did not bring into the firm. I pointed out that their new partner influences client retention and suggested a compensation structure for him that was based upon client retention rather than client acquisition. Compensation should be linked to some measure of the partner's value to the company.

Granting Ownership to Associates

THERE IS A GREAT DEAL of controversy about granting minority partnership interests for career path personnel. Many CPA and law firms use this structure to encourage excellent professionals to remain with the practice. I have some objections to this, as do some other advisers I've interviewed. Many of the objections center on the lack of well-formed succession plans. Most of us have not yet decided how we will transfer our businesses and are reluctant to grant ownership until the succession issues are clear. On the other hand, granting ownership seems to be working well for some others, and is, in fact, an integral part of their succession plans.

Jerry Neill of Neill and Associates in Kansas City, Missouri, started as a sole practitioner. As his business grew, he added young planners. These new members proved so productive that Jerry felt he would not be able to keep them unless he provided some incentives. He believes that good salary, bonuses, and benefits are not enough to retain good people. He arranged for his key employees to purchase minority interests in his company. "It made a world of difference," he confided. "They have a stake in this company and they treat their responsibilities differently." Jerry is thinking about an Employee Stock Option Program (ESOP) for future incentives. "Frankly, these people are my exit strategy."

Conversely, Peggy Ruhlin does not want to dilute her company with minority interests. "When we took on our new partner, it was for the full one-third. We would much rather consider a phantom stock arrangement for incentives for employees." Phantom stock arrangements do in fact avoid the time-consuming administrative detail that accompanies actual stock transfer, since actual shares of stock are not issued. The company pays additional compensation to the employees, which is translated into shares, based on the number that could be purchased with that amount of compensation. Naturally, some fair valuation of the company is made periodically. Shares are valued at some date in the future, that is, date of separation, death, or disability, and compensation is made. They provide incentive by having employees participate in the growth of the company, but the cash required for these incentives is deferred.

Plan Your Future Before You Plan Your Clients'

AS AN ADVISER, you spend your career guiding individuals in attaining their financial objectives. It is virtually impossible for you to continue giving good advice when you've spent relatively little time developing your own future. Whether you choose a solo practice, an affiliation, or a partnership, planning your practice deserves as much thought as you'd give to planning your clients' investments. After all, their future depends upon how well you've planned for yours.

CHAPTER 5

PEOPLE MAKE IT HAPPEN

We desperately need meaning in our lives and will sacrifice
a great deal to institutions that will provide meaning
for us. We simultaneously need independence, to feel as
though we are in charge of our destinies, and to have
the ability to stick out.

—TOM PETERS, *In Search of Excellence*

IT IS VIRTUALLY IMPOSSIBLE for you to meet all of your

clients' needs without the help of good support staff. As

your practice grows, delegating to key people is crucial to

your growth and success. Yet, nearly every adviser I

know has experienced difficulty finding the right people, hiring them and keeping them. The larger the practice, the more difficult that job gets.

There are many proven ways to attract good personnel, but the only way to keep them is through quality training, good compensation and benefits, and a nurturing, stimulating, challenging work environment. The success of your practice depends on the people who interact with your clients every day. In fact, long-term clients are comfortable and secure with long-term employees.

You've probably spent significant time figuring out how to manage your clients' expectations. It's worth the effort to figure out how to manage your staff's expectations as well. Just remember, where clients are concerned, there is no way to compensate for lousy support staff.

Hiring, Mentoring, and Internships

WE'VE DEVOTED A GREAT DEAL of time in our practice to finding the most effective approach to hiring and retaining good people. We prefer the mentor-apprenticeship method of staffing. We search for people with good education and good personalities who demonstrate the most flexibility in terms of their work style. When someone meets these requirements, we can generally integrate him into our workplace by training him in our philosophy and methods. One of our favorite sources for new staff is through internships. However, this requires a two- to three-year training period, and a considerable corporate investment of time and money.

We nearly always promote from within and seldom hire someone who will "hit the ground running." This gives us ample familiarity of an employee's work style and capabilities, as well as how he or she will integrate with other staff members.

Currently, there are over 100 educational programs at colleges and universities nationwide who offer financial planning programs registered with the CFP Board of Standards. Their graduates may sit for the comprehensive CFP exam. The University of Miami offers the CFP program as part of its master's in accounting and personal finance. We approached the director of the program and expressed an interest in working with the school to provide business experience for interns. As a result, we've had some great intern relationships that have blossomed into permanent employment.

Texas Tech in Lubbock, Texas, has a very impressive internship program, designed by Dr. Jerry Mason, who heads their financial planning curriculum. His students are bright, capable, and well trained. The students volunteer as support staff for the IAFP Success Forum each year. This is a good opportunity to connect with possible candidates for your office.

Virginia Tech in Blacksburg, Virginia, has a new financial planning internship program as well, run by Dr. Bruce Brunson. Dr. Brunson's program is similar to Texas Tech's, and his students often attend the IAFP Success Forum to meet planners. I have provided contact information in the Resource chapter.

Cindy Conger of Arkansas Financial Group feels that technology has replaced lower-level positions in their practice. Nowadays, even assembling their files requires some financial knowledge. They use interns to help in all aspects of the business, particularly in assisting the planners. "It's a matter of attitude," says Cindy. "I can ask a file clerk to prepare our client files in a certain way, but that file clerk sees that job as menial. When our intern prepares those files, he knows it is vital to the operation of the practice. His attitude toward the job is different, so his end work product is different." Interns are young, eager to learn, enthusiastic, grateful for the work, and they can always teach you something.

In the early years of our practice, we called our professional support staff para-planners, then associate advisers. We discovered that clients tend to identify the term "associate adviser" with junior people. Since we are attempting to encourage closer relationships between our clients and these professionals, we need to make sure that they are professionally elevated and presented as seasoned staff. Therefore, these days, we use the term "adviser" to describe the professional staff who work directly with clients. All our advisers are Certified Financial Planner licensees or are working toward that designation. To differentiate, we now refer to the firm's principals as the "partners," rather than the "advisers."

Currently, we have three partners, four advisers, four executive assistants, a comptroller/office manager, a director of operations,

The Following Is an Agreement
between Joe Adviser and Planning Firm

1 In recognition of the costs incurred by the Firm for training and education, Joe Adviser agrees that if Planning Firm severs the relationship with him for cause, he will not form or join a competing investment advisory firm in Our Town for a period of twelve (12) months after leaving the Firm.

2 Joe Adviser acknowledges that all clients are clients of the Firm and he agrees, should he leave the Firm, not to contact any clients or prospects he has served or which were being served by the Firm during his relationship with the Firm. He acknowledges that the files and records of client accounts are records of the Firm and shall not be copied or used for any purpose other than that approved, in writing, by the Firm. Joe Adviser acknowledges that he recognizes that the Firm considers its material and process proprietary and that he will keep this confidential. Should Joe Adviser leave the Firm he will neither remove any material nor use the material for his own use.

3 Joe Adviser agrees to follow the policies of the Firm. Joe Adviser without the prior approval, in writing, of the partners will provide no correspondence or other printed material, other than strictly operational, to the public (including media). Examples would include market commentary, "interim reports," plans, and policies.

4 This agreement supersedes all previous agreements.

Signed_____   Signed_____
            (Joe Adviser)   (President (For the Firm))

Date_____   Date_____

a director of concierge services and an intern. I will discuss their job descriptions in detail later in this chapter.

Naturally, as soon as you bring other advisers into your practice, you will want to have a formalized agreement about whether clients are considered to be company or personal contacts and how situations will be handled if you agree to part company with the advisers. We request that our advisers sign non-compete agreements. I've included a simple sample on the previous page.

This document states that clients are clients of the firm. In essence, this precludes advisers from soliciting clients for business if they leave the firm. As your practice becomes less dependent upon you and more dependent upon others on your team, a non-compete document is vital. Additionally, if you are planning for the transfer of your practice sometime in the future, you will want these agreements to ensure that key personnel will remain with the firm, even if you don't.

Rick Adkins of Arkansas Financial Advisory told me that his decision to require a non-compete was a difficult hurdle. "Our biggest concern was letting ambitious junior staff interact with our clients, yet this was essential if we were going to grow into a viable business." Rick and his partner Cindy Conger explained that in exchange for signing the non-compete agreement, staff would have full access to clients and become instrumental in a shift in client control. "Once everyone signed," confided Rick, "we all felt a certain relief and freedom."

Taking Care of Your Most Valuable Asset: Your Staff

YOUR STAFF MEMBERS are the people who make the very first impression on your prospects and can enhance or destroy relationships with existing clients. If you want to attract great clients, hire great staff, train them, and then empower them. You must give them a sense of self-worth beyond their value as an employee, and then compensate them accordingly. Just as you would with your best clients, find out what they expect from this relationship and manage their expectations. We want our staff to know how important they are to our business, so we spend significant time demonstrating how much we value them.

Money Plus

IN 1998, PRINCETON RESEARCH found that workers aged eighteen to twenty-nine felt that advancement, opportunity, and benefits (health coverage, vacations, flex-time) were more important than money or number of working hours. Seventy percent of our employees are under age thirty. It is very clear that our staff wants flexibility, benefit choices, respect, personal and professional challenge, plus money. Money is essential, yet money by itself is not enough.

Jerry Neill of Neill & Associates in Kansas City told me that not long ago several of his employees abruptly quit. He conducted exit interviews to ask what some of the problems were. Among other things, they all said it wasn't "a fun place to work." "I just didn't understand that," Jerry told me. "This is not the kind of business I grew up in. Work is work." So Jerry hired a business consultant who made some simple suggestions to keep the troops happy. "These people would have killed for a casual-dress Friday. How did I know?" Jerry's consultant suggested they have more family-centered activities such as a company picnic and holiday party. Of course, now casual Fridays in his office are a must. Jerry and his partners hired an office manager who, along with other key personnel, has completely rewritten the employee manual. The office manager is closer in age to their under-thirty employees, and the change in the office has been remarkable.

Not everyone can afford to hire a business consultant like Jerry did, so you might want to check out Jane Applegate's *201 Great Ideas for Your Small Business* (Princeton, New Jersey: Bloomberg Press, 1998) for some great tips on taking care of employees and creating a better workplace.

Ross Levin explains that he and his staff go out together about once a quarter, usually to celebrate something, like tax day or some bogus event that requires a celebration. "Everyone loves this. We have a good time and enjoy each other's company." Karen Spero, of Spero, Smith Investment Advisers, Inc. in Cleveland, Ohio, also arranges company luncheons and outside-office activities. There is a trend among established advisers toward creating office-family activities with opportunities for employee bonding. We've seen our staff develop such strong relationships over the years that they create and plan activities on their own now.

Eleanor Blayney and I have had numerous discussions about managing and compensating staff. I suspect this is a hot topic among planners who started their careers as sole practitioners and wound up growing into larger firms with numerous personnel. Eleanor considers her staff members not only valuable assets, she has compared them to capitalizing a business. "If you wanted to capitalize a new business," she says, "you would probably have some bondholders and some stockholders. In staffing, the bondholders are the steady, loyal employees who are not particularly looking for advancement, but enjoy what they do and fully intend to do it as long as they work. They would like to be well paid for their efforts but are not generally motivated by entrepreneurial career path incentives. Bondholder staff wants security and income. Conversely, the stockholders, on a career path, want incentives, challenges, and opportunity." Eleanor believes that these two "asset classes" should be treated differently and offered different remuneration and benefit packages.

Compensation

WE HAVE DESIGNED our staff compensation based upon the career path the individual has chosen. Once a year, my partners and I take each employee to a private lunch and we review his or her personal goals. We want to ensure that they remain successful, satisfied members of the staff. Career paths are not written in stone. One of our advisers began working in back-office operations. Each year for several years we met and discussed his plans for the future. Each year, he told us he was happy in operations and had no plans to do anything else. Then one year, because of personnel changes, we asked him to sit in on some client meetings until we hired someone new. Within the month he declared an intention to take CFP courses and accept the responsibilities of an adviser. He has made it quite clear that his future plans involve entrepreneurial risks. He wants to become a rainmaker, developing his own client base, and eventually working independently. Because of his new career path, our requirements for him changed. He tells me that now he averages a sixty-hour workweek.

Bonuses

I NEVER REALLY BELIEVED in giving bonuses. Bonuses always felt so unpredictable. I also believed they were not necessarily the best incentives for everyone. I preferred ensuring a reasonably good salary. Then I discussed the issue with Dick Thaler, who is a behavioral finance professor at the University of Chicago. He reminded me that classical finance theory maintains that the rational investor makes decisions based on rational thought. Behavioral finance theory maintains that investors are not rational, but are predictable, basing their decisions on mental shortcuts or rules of thumb to solve complex problems. These mental shortcuts are known as heuristics. One of these heuristics Thaler refers to as "mental accounting." This is the human, non-rational approach to tracking and evaluating transactions. Thaler related the issue of bonuses to the mental accounting heuristic he calls "separate pockets." Applying this heuristic to your employees' behavior may elicit some interesting insights.

In his book, *The Winners Curse* (Princeton, New Jersey: Princeton University Press, 1992, pp. 112–16), Thaler discusses bonuses and windfalls. If you pay your employee $50,000 per year, he will live a $50,000 lifestyle. If, alternatively, you pay him $40,000 with a predictable $10,000 bonus annually, he will live a $40,000 lifestyle, using the extra $10,000 for something special, possibly even investing it. In other words, bonuses encourage savings. Thaler was persuasive. This, for me was a powerful argument for paying a bonus, and more compelling to me than just a calculation of how to get the most out of a worker. I consider it one of my responsibilities as an employer to encourage my staff to save and invest.

Peggy Ruhlin of Budros & Ruhlin explains that they have a "growth sharing" arrangement for providing bonuses for their advisers. Each year a percentage of the firm's gross is deposited into an account to be shared by the employees based on a point system. Peggy said they elected to base these bonuses on the gross, rather than the net profits so that the advisers will be assured of some extra compensation even if the company has no profit for the year. The staff is given points for longevity, client retention, support for new business, achieving a new professional designation, or completing continuing education courses. They are bonused annually based on the number of points acquired during the year.

Because of my discussions with Dick Thaler, we have two bonus programs. One is designed for the benefit of all employees and is calculated purely upon the number of years of service. It is not based on profits—gross or net. The bonus is paid on the first of December so I refer to it as the Christmas Club. The second one, the merit bonus, is much more subjective. My partners and I set aside a bonus amount, based upon our profits for the year. We assign one point for every $250, and each partner is allocated one-third of the points. We then cast our points for the employees we think have done the best job overall during the past year. For example, if we have $9,000 for bonuses, each partner would have twelve points to give away.

Bonuses do not necessarily have to be in the form of cash. One year Bugen Stuart Korn & Cordaro gave their staff gift certificates for a cruise. David Bugen made arrangements with the local travel agent so that each employee had a budget to design his or her own cruise. The company picked up the tab.

Empowerment

I'VE REQUIRED OUR ADVISER employees to investigate benefit options to help us structure them for the benefit of all of us. I have discussed the dollars we have available for benefits and I let them decide how to put this package together. They present their findings to all of us at a weekly staff meeting. A staff committee also designed our investment policy and manages our profit sharing plan.

We have devised a staffing philosophy, much the same as we designed a business and investment policy. There are several components that are key to this philosophy: worker empowerment, warm working environment, non-accusatory attitudes toward errors, and continuing education. We use cross training and team building to help facilitate our philosophy. Last year, for example, our employees divided themselves into teams, addressing our prospect and client delivery systems, such as brochures, data gathering questionnaires, and review documents. At a company staff meeting, each team presented recommendations for improving or redesigning our systems. We are still in the process of implementing their recommendations.

Our employees are given titles, commensurate with their responsibilities. Further, they are empowered with the authority to make a situation right for the client. Staff is trained to accept responsibility for errors, even if they are not ours. We never argue with a client or make him feel uncomfortable about a situation. We call this empowerment Nordstrom Authority.

If you've ever been to San Francisco, you may have been to Nordstrom's department store. They are nationally known for their superior service. During my first visit, I bought a suit that needed a minor alteration. When I went to pick it up later that day, it was not ready. I reminded the clerk that I was going home early the following day. After a profuse apology, the saleswoman reassured me, "Don't worry, the suit will be ready at 7:00 this evening. I will have it delivered to your hotel by 7:30 P.M." It was. She did not have to obtain permission from anyone else.

The first time one of our advisers used his Nordstrom Authority, a new client had just complained that during a transfer of funds, one security was liquidated when it should have been transferred in kind. The result was a loss of about $650 to the client. Although the transferring firm caused the error, our advisers told the client, "You are absolutely right. I will immediately call to have it rectified. Don't worry," he went on to say, "I will make your position whole as though the transfer had been made correctly." Later that afternoon the new client called once again, this time concerned that the adviser would be "eating the mistake himself." The adviser told the client he appreciated his calling but that he need not be concerned. It is the policy of the firm to stand behind the client and the adviser.

Aside from the usual benefits, we have also instituted a Personal and Professional Development Fund in our firm. Employees may spend up to $1,000 per year for courses or seminars to further their professional or personal development. In past years, staff has taken courses from Dale Carnegie Institute, Evelyn Wood speed-reading classes, advanced computer courses, neurolinguistic programming classes, and seminars for executive assistants and middle managers.

Naturally, we subsidize anyone who wants to pursue the Certified Financial Planner designation, and it is a requirement for those who will work directly with clients. Interested employees are required to pay for the first course. If they decide to continue, we pay for the remaining courses and examinations, and reimburse them for the first one upon successful completion of the program.

Because of Karen Spero we have formalized a program for staff to attend professional conferences and conventions. Karen and I were preparing for a practice management conference presentation two years ago and she told me, "This would really be great for my associates to hear. One of these days we're going to have to start sending our junior staff to these meetings. They would really benefit from the experiences." So one year, as an experiment, we sent six of our staff members to a Schwab conference in Orlando. Our comptroller and my partner Harold's assistant also chose to go. They expressed some trepidation, figuring that the sessions might be over their heads. They were wrong. They came away from the sessions, and the networking, with new acquaintances and great ideas. More importantly, they developed a different perspective about their knowledge and level of expertise.

Titles and Business Cards

WHEN I WAS FOURTEEN, I took a job working for an interior designer after school. She had a two-year-old daughter. Although my primary responsibility was looking after her daughter, I was also required to dust the store displays several times a week while Suzie took a nap. I figured this was busy work because my new boss did not want to pay me just for sitting around while Suzie napped, but I wanted the job, so I dusted well. After several weeks my boss presented me with a box of business cards with "Deena Lynn Boone, Assistant" printed on them under her store name. "You've done a great job," she said, "and you deserve a promotion." There was no actual change in salary or job responsibilities, but I was invited to place some of my precious cards in a small silver tray near the door. I didn't just have a job, I had a career. Now I not only dusted the displays, I re-arranged them with care and creativity. Especially in smaller organizations, titles ignite pride, contribute greatly to self-esteem, and, of course, impress mothers. In our office, everyone has a title; everyone has a card. Everyone has a career.

Realizing Potential

KAREN SPERO FEELS that it is her responsibility to help her staff realize their own potential. To that end, she has devised a self-assessment form that all staff members are required to complete at the beginning of each year. Karen says that she and her partner, Robert Smith, gain much insight into their staff and the growth potential of each one. They use the self-assessments to help guide the upcoming year's activities. From an analysis of these responses, you may discover that your people have interests in areas of which you were unaware.

For example, Karen's first two questions focus on goal setting and reviewing accomplishments in light of those goals.

1 What do you regard as your most significant accomplishment last year and why?

2 What do you most want to accomplish this year? Describe at least three goals and how you plan to achieve them. Please be as specific as possible.

Karen confided to me that from responses to these two questions she learned that one of her employees had a strong interest in spending more time with clients rather than in the back office. "Frankly," said Karen, "she was hired for her analytic expertise. I never really thought she was interested in client communications. Naturally, we were delighted to shift responsibilities to give her new opportunities."

The next three questions invite employees to offer perspectives on their current positions, the resources and support they want, and how Karen and her partner should evaluate the employees' work.

Thanks to Karen, I've used these questions not only in our practice, but as part of consulting for other firms. One response I received from a particular employee surprised me. The respondent prefaced his remarks by thanking me for asking. It seems that he had been given a work responsibility because the last employee to handle it left the practice. He was told that he would have this responsibility until a new employee was hired. New employees were hired, but no one ever revisited this work responsibility, and by default, after two years, he still had it. "I was not trained to do this and I really feel I am not doing the best job. I am certain that someone else would handle it better." When I asked him why he did not bring this up with his boss, he said, "He's not interested in how the work gets done, he just wants us to 'Make It So.'" By not encouraging his employee to provide feedback, the employer guaranteed that his staff would "Make It So-So" inefficiently.

It is vitally important to ask staff what resources or support systems they need to work more effectively. You might be surprised at some of the answers you receive to the next two questions.

3 What resources/support would make you more efficient in your job?

4 How much and what type of supervisory input do you feel you require to accomplish your job?

My comptroller presented me with a list of answers to the resources question. "Our director of concierge services needs her own credit card to purchase gifts and make arrangements for special events for clients. She should need authorization only for purchases in excess of $500. You should get our intern permission to use the law library at the University of Miami so he can have more flexibility in his research. He should be allowed to set his own schedule. He can just check in to see that we don't have anything more pressing for him here at the office. And," she added, with authority, "put a waterfall in the conference room. It will be very soothing to clients and will be a good retreat for us when we feel overwhelmed." She does, he does, I did, and we do.

The next four questions were helpful in creating our work teams. We were able to encourage people who complemented each other to work together on projects.

5 What three skills/abilities do you see as your strengths? What three skills/abilities do you see as weaknesses?

6 How would you further develop your strengths?

7 What aspects of your job are most appealing?

8 What aspects are least appealing?
Several of Karen Spero's employees answered number 5 stating that they felt they lacked skills necessary to communicate well with clients. As a result, Karen arranged for her staff to attend seminars on improving communication abilities.

The last three questions will help get a sense of the vision and goals each person has in the workplace.

9 Please write a description of your job as it now exists. (Be as brief as possible; bullet points are okay.)

10 Please write a job description of what you would like your job to be. (Be as brief as possible; bullet points are okay.)

11 Now describe your job in five years.
I particularly like this last question. On a consulting job, one employee told me that she pictured herself retired in two to three years. From this, I fully understood her demonstrable lack of energy and enthusiasm for her job. She was coasting until retirement. With an understanding of her personal goal, I was able to arrange for her early retirement over the next year, during which time she enthusiastically trained her replacement.

My sister owned her own business for twenty years. On the wall in her office hung a poster with the following line: "If you aim at nothing, you're sure to hit it." Karen's self-assessment survey encourages everyone to set goals and measure progress.

Food, Comfort, and Other Care

MY PARTNER PETER BROWN remarked that we have one of the few cafeteria benefits programs in this country that actually involve food. Our office kitchen, fondly known as the "great room," has become the center of our office activities and our home hearth, so to speak. I hadn't thought much about the impact this lunchroom has had on everyone until I sauntered in one day for my own coffee and found a couple of clients sitting at our lunch table, sharing sodas and jokes with two of our advisers. Everyone feels at home. It's what we had in mind.

Our food fetish started with an Alpha Group visit to Advent Software in San Francisco. As we were shown around the programmer floors, I noticed trays of fresh fruit and baked goods at various locations around the work areas. Advent's president, Stephanie DeMarco, told me that the trays are delivered each morning for staff to nosh on all day. She also has fresh flowers delivered once a week. The programmers told me it makes a comfortable environment, facilitating thought and creativity.

We grabbed the idea and expanded it. Rather than the same fruit and pastry plate every day, staff decides what they will order on a weekly basis. Mornings we all meet around the big table for morning coffee, breakfast treats, and vitamins. Yes, vitamins. A few years ago our office manager, Mena Bielow, decided that we were passing around colds and flu too frequently. She brought in a bottle of vitamin C and insisted that everyone take one 1000 mg tablet each morning. After a few weeks, we all felt better and had fewer illnesses among us. Now, the company provides a selection of multivitamins, and Mena monitors our intake. Mena also ensures that everyone has a company-paid annual physical and flu shot.

Often our morning coffee moments turn into brief, informal coordinating sessions with everyone discussing his or her planned activities for the day. Lunches are usually enjoyed together at the big table in our great room. At any time during the day there are pastries, fruit, cookies, and hot and cold drinks. For the staff meetings each week, the company provides a full breakfast, and Fridays are generally company-catered pizza lunches. This environment facilitates personal as well as business discussions.

Birthdays and anniversaries with the company are excuses to get together for conversation and cake. Our comptroller always assigns someone to choose a small gift and card that everyone personally signs. Often if clients are visiting, they join in the festivities. Everyone loves the special attention.

Owning Up to Mistakes

BACK IN THE 1970S I read a book on transactional analysis, *I'm OK, You're OK,* by Thomas A. Harris. One silly vignette stayed with me. Since then, I've used the concept numerous times in working with staff. Your spouse is fixing breakfast and inadvertently burns the toast. You know it's inadvertent because nobody gets up one morning and says, "I think I will burn the toast this morning so it's inedible."

You come down to breakfast and see the burnt toast. You could say, "How could you be so stupid to burn this toast?" or, "This toast is burnt; I won't eat it." Now, you know that your spouse already knows the toast is burnt, and that mentioning something he or she already knows is unproductive. Your spouse probably already feels bad about the toast. A transactionally aware person says, "You must be having a bad morning. What can I do to help?"

When staff makes a mistake, it is rarely intentional. It is usually for one of three reasons: our system isn't working, someone made a bad judgment call, or someone inadvertently did something stupid. Since staff is empowered to make judgment calls, there will be times when they will be wrong. If the mistake recurs, it's probably the system. If it's just plain stupidity, even the best of us does something stupid from time to time that's forgivable. If it's terminal stupidity, that's probably an indication that it's time to free up someone's future.

I believe in fixing the problem, not the blame. To encourage people to admit mistakes, I devised the Turkey Award. The Turkey is a goofy-looking stuffed animal suspended from a gold cord. At each Friday meeting, we discuss our mistakes for the week. The person who made the stupidest, craziest, most unbelievable mistake gets the turkey for the week. He or she is saluted with the Turkey "gobble" and the stuffed turkey sits on his or her desk for the week. We have given the Turkey for cutting off a tie in the shredder, trying to send a fax to our own fax number, confusing two clients with similar last names, and preparing a rebalancing proposal using the wrong portfolio policy. Despite the array of available scenarios, these days we are hard pressed to give the Turkey away. For all mistakes, I always ask, "Did this happen because the system is bad?" If that's the case, we revise the system.

I've noted earlier, each staff member has the power to do what must be done to make it right for the client. That means eating trans-action charges when we've made a trading error, sending an apology gift to a client for a mistake, or accepting the blame for a situation even though we know we weren't responsible for it. I support my staff and any of their decisions to make a situation right for the client. I only ask to be informed as soon as the problem arises. Most of the time, staff tells me the problem and their solution simultaneously.

Ross Levin tells the story of a huge trading mistake made in his office last year. One of his staff members thought he was buying one fund, when he actually purchased another. By the time the trader discovered the error two months later, the fund they actually bought was down $13,000. "We believe in owning up to mistakes immediately. This is a client who would probably have never known we'd made this mistake. Of course, we brought it to his attention and we made it right, which means we ate the $13,000. We were honest, no matter how painful. Now, we have a client for life."

Appreciation

I HAVE BEEN TALKING about appreciation that we as employers have for our staff and the ways we demonstrate it. We also provide opportunities for staff to show their appreciation for each other. The companion to our Turkey is the Star, a stuffed gold star with multi-colored streamers hanging from a long ribbon. The Star of the Week is nominated at our weekly staff meetings, right after we declare the Turkey. We have awarded a star for chasing down the mail carrier when we inadvertently mailed 100 letters without postage. We've given stars for fixing the stapler, volunteering to stay late and help an associate get out an important mailing, and for discovering an error on a client's death certificate that saved us and his attorney a great deal of aggravation. The Platypus Award is given to a deserving employee who has received both a star and a turkey during the same week. It is rare, but it has happened.

I particularly like Greg Sullivan's (Sullivan, Bruyette, Speros & Blayney) appreciation strategy. He buys a batch of lunch coupons at the local deli in his building. He gives everyone ten $5 coupons to give away to thank a co-worker for appreciation for something special. The only requirement is that if you give one away, you must inform a principal and report why.

Employee Reviews

JEFFREY PFEFFER, the Thomas D. Dee professor of organizational behavior at the Stanford Graduate School of Administration, said that many business people compare annual employee reviews with "filling out your income tax form. It's not a process that anybody likes, but you've got to do it." (Michael Barrier, "Reviewing the Annual Review," *Nations Business*, September 1998, pp. 32–34.) It does have to be done, but it doesn't have to be painful. Before my reviews, I talk with my partners and my office manager. Together we compare notes about each staff member. Using these discussions and my own observations, I formulate a list of strengths and weaknesses for each person. That list becomes the basis for my reviews. I used to use Employee Appraiser software (Austin-Hoyne), which I thought was fairly good. But I found the framework only made my discussions stilted since they were not formulated by me or directed by the self-assessments.

I also use this review time to elicit their recommendations; in essence, they are judging me as a leader. This has been helpful to me personally and I welcome their thoughts. From time to time when I have fallen behind in giving out my reviews, staff has asked me for them.

I usually conduct my reviews based on the self-assessment document that staff members complete. There are a few items to keep in mind when you conduct a review.

◆ Keep the review private.

◆ Focus on the employee. Do not make comparisons to others.

◆ Ask them how they think they are doing. You'll be surprised at how candid people can be about their own work.

◆ If you have tough criticisms, cover that first. Always end with something positive, encouraging, and upbeat.

◆ Give them an opportunity to make open and honest observations about anything, with no recriminations. Be sure to tell them that the comments will not leave the room, and mean it.

◆ Ask them how they think you can be a better leader.

◆ Take notes on what you have discussed and file them in a permanent employee file.

Little Things

THE BOTTOM LINE IS that we treat our staff the way we would like them to treat our clients: Intensive Customer Care. We surprise them from time to time with an impromptu party after a particularly grueling week. When we travel, we always bring them small mementos of the places we've visited, so they know we're thinking about them, and they return the favor. We have arranged to have the local dry cleaners pick up their laundry at the office each week. We have an annual company picnic to which families and friends are invited. We have even sent interested staff to a local nutritionist for counseling and menus. (With our food fetishes, is it any wonder?)

Our holiday party includes spouses and significant others. We choose a fine restaurant for dinner then retreat to my house for "The Rookie Show." For the past five years, we were hiring new people so fast that each time we got together for the annual holiday party, there were so many new faces, we practically had to wear nametags. My partner Peter decided we needed some sort of ice breaker and initiation rite, so he created the Rookie Show. At each holiday party, anyone who is new to the firm in the past year must perform for the rest of us. They can sing, dance, tell a joke—whatever they want to do. It's a great deal of fun and a wonderful bonding mechanism.

All of these little things demonstrate our support and interest in them as individuals, not just our employees. They show their support and interest in us by taking very good care of our clients.

If It Ain't Fixable, Break It Off, ASAP

I HAVE SPENT the better part of this chapter discussing getting and keeping good staff and promoting good teamwork. However, it would not be complete without a discussion of terminating staff. This is not an easy task. Most of us have never been trained as human resource professionals. Advisers don't like confrontation, we want everyone to like us. If the salesman's curse is to close the sale, then the planner's curse is the need for everyone to like us.

During the ten years that Murphy Brown was on television, she fired no fewer than ninety-two secretaries. They ran the gamut from bizarre, unskilled, or bossy, to timid, overqualified, or certifiably insane. This was great comedy, but it's not so funny when it sits outside your office. My partner Peter loves to tell the story of the time he had to fire Harold's secretary because Harold stopped coming to work in order to avoid her. He couldn't work well with her, but he just couldn't let her go. Peter didn't want to fire her either, but it was that, or let Harold work from home for the rest of his life.

Over the past twenty-three years in business, I have formed several hard and fast rules about hiring and firing employees.

◆ **Have a written job description and a salary range with an absolute maximum in mind before you start interviewing.** Always ask what their salary requirements are. If your offer and their requirements are too far apart, one of you has unrealistic expectations.

◆ **Don't hire on impulse.** Take time to evaluate the candidates thoroughly. Check references and ask them to visit more than once. Let staff interview them too. Good people are going to evaluate their job opportunities carefully. Be sure they are a good fit.

◆ **If it's not working out, fire sooner rather than later.** Don't wait for things to get better. They won't. "We had a very toxic person in our office once," Ross Levin told me. "It really affected morale. We should have terminated that relationship six months before we did. Today, we're happier and more efficient."

◆ **Keep copious notes on employees,** including personal discussions and your observations, as well as observations from others. You never know if you may need them later.

◆ **If someone quits, then later asks you to rehire, don't.** Office environments are dynamic. Although he may have been the right person for the job before he left, it does not necessarily follow that he will be the right person now.

◆ **Allow a limited time for two employees to solve their own conflicts.** Allow a limited time for you to mediate. When all else fails, terminate one or both of them. Forcing warring employees to work together can threaten the success of your company.

People Management Is the Key

HAPPY, EFFICIENT, HARD-WORKING staff is critical to your business. Learn how to manage them or immediately pass the responsibility to a partner who can. If you don't have a partner, or neither of you have the skills to successfully manage people, hire someone to do it for you.

You may be able to solve your management problems by hiring an office manager, someone who is capable of directing the daily activities of the practice. Your office manager can hire and fire, supervise personnel, and manage daily work responsibilities. Decisions of marketing, budgeting, and long-range planning still fall to you.

If you feel you need a higher level of expertise, it is unlikely that you will be able to hire someone with the skills necessary to take over the management of the entire business. Most people with chief operating officer level skills will be working for a large company, commanding a hefty salary, or they will be running their own smaller business. Consider taking on a partner who has administrative skills who will complement your own skill set.

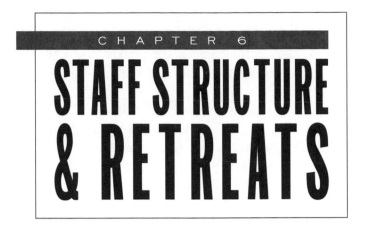

CHAPTER 6

STAFF STRUCTURE & RETREATS

An ounce of action is worth a ton of theory

— FRIEDRICH ENGELS

WHILE HAVING GOOD people is a critical element in the success of a business, those people must have a structure that will provide the best environment for personal and professional growth. One of my first jobs in the real estate business was for a man in his mid-fifties who possessed no management skills whatsoever. My first day at work he told me, "I own you from 9:00 A.M. to 5:00 P.M.

Whatever I ask you to do, you will do it with a smile and a positive affirmation such as 'Yes, Sir.' If at any time you don't want to do what I say, you can buy the paper and go job hunting." Fortunately, over time, more effective methods of managing people have come to the forefront.

In the early 1980s, I participated in a Quality Circle exercise for the first time. Quality Circle Team concepts were brought to the United States by the Japanese in the 1970s as a problem-solving technique. In our exercise, we sat in a circle while the facilitator put a problem on the chalkboard. Each person would have one minute to offer an insight or a solution to that problem. We then discussed the best suggestions, weighed the possible consequences and reached a consensus. It was the first time I'd witnessed the power of individuals working as a team to solve problems that individuals could not solve on their own. It was the first time I'd heard the word "synergy" to describe success-ful team activities.

Since the early 1990s, businesses have fully embraced the use of teams in the workplace. It has been proven that individuals who are fully coordinated and working cooperatively can accomplish more than individuals who are performing related but not coordinated tasks. I firmly believe that the development and use of effective teams is what has made our business a success.

Team Building

THE DEVELOPMENT of great teams does not happen instantly. Once the structure is designed (see the box on the following page), you must provide ample opportunity for your staff to recognize their identity within the team structure, learn to trust each other, and function together for common goals. We refer to this as team building.

Our organizational chart is designed to facilitate team interaction. You will notice the overlapping circles indicating that individuals from one service team may be a member of another team as well. We have improved our intra-office communications by making one team member active on another team. The overlapping circles also indicate that at least one person from one team is cross-trained to perform the activities of another team when necessary.

The client is at the center of the chart, indicating that all of our activities are for and about the client. Everyone in our office is very aware that it is the client who pays our salaries. We have divided the work responsibilities into three areas: Administrative, Advisory, and Concierge.

EVENSKY, BROWN & KATZ ORGANIZATIONAL CHART

Administrative Team

Managing Partner
Comptroller/Office Manager
Administrative Assistants

CLIENT

Partners
Advisers
Operations Staff

Director of Concierge Services
Administrative Assistants
Partners
Advisers

Advisory Team

Concierge Team

ADMINISTRATIVE TEAM

COMPRISED OF THE MANAGING PARTNER, comptroller, and the managing partner's administrative assistants, the administrative team is responsible for all activities relating to the operation of the company.

◆ **Managing partner.** This is my role. I oversee all the teams to ensure that we are delivering our services consistently, with quality, and in keeping with our mission statement.

◆ **Comptroller/office manager.** Prepares the company books, does the payroll, manages the benefits, and does client billing. She also manages the office, supervises staff, and runs the Friday morning staff meetings, and in her spare time she serves as our Compliance Officer.

◆ **Administrative assistants.** Each partner has his or her own assistant who coordinates their activities with the clients and the advisers. In addition, there is one administrative assistant who supports the advisers.

ADVISORY TEAM

COMPRISED OF PARTNERS, advisers, and operations staff, this team has the primary responsibility for clients, relating to the planning and management of their investments.

◆ **Partners.** Although a lead partner is assigned, the client is informed that only the adviser remains constant. The client will see the other partners during the course of the relationship. Clients usually like this arrangement because each partner has a different perspective in working with the client, demonstrating the depth of knowledge in our organization.

◆ **Advisers.** An adviser is assigned when a prospect makes an appointment. Advisers are responsible for the initial data gathering and the preparation of the client's plan. Partners and advisers design the investment policy together. Company policy is that at least two partners review all the plans. This is partly to ensure quality and partly to familiarize a second partner with the client from the beginning of the engagement.

◆ **Operations staff.** The director of operations and operations administrative assistant support the advisers and partners by opening accounts, transferring assets, preparing reviews and trading. Although the director does all the trading, the decision to trade rests with the advisers and partners.

CONCIERGE TEAM

WHILE OSTENSIBLY everyone at EBK is part of the concierge team, in reality, it is the partners, the administrative staff, and the advisers who are primarily responsible for the work that is done in this area.

◆ **Director of concierge services.** The director of concierge services provides the finesse to our relationships with the client. She also coordinates the activities of the administrative assistants as they relate to clients. Among her responsibilities are coordinating our advisory boards, preparing client surveys, and designing our intensive care program. Chapter 14 describes our concierge services in detail.

◆ **Administrative assistants.** All company administrative assistants function as part of this team, assisting the director of concierge services in sending notes, gifts, and tracking data for each client.

◆ **Partners.** Partners are provided "Care Call" lists on a monthly basis to make phone calls and social appointments with various clients.

◆ **Advisers.** Advisers are also provided with "Care Call" lists for their monthly contacts.

Our many personal and family activities, our annual retreat, and the structure of the daily workload all facilitate our team building. Personal time with each other fosters friendships and mutual respect outside of the work arena. Often staff members from different teams spend time together after work or on weekends. My partners and I think that we now have the best teams we've ever had. We attribute this to the pseudo-family environment in our office.

One year at our annual retreat, I asked our three teams what makes them a success. They supplied me with the following list:

◆ **Common goals.** We want personal success, client success, and business success.

◆ **Trust and support.** We trust and support each other, our employers, and our clients.

◆ **Common values.** Ethical, honest people who work with ethical, honest people.

◆ **Perspective.** We don't take our work too seriously. We can laugh at our dumb mistakes and apologize for and learn from the grave ones.

◆ **Balance.** There is life beyond the office walls.

Although our annual retreat is built around a different theme each year, at least one team-building activity is included in our agenda. The end of this chapter is devoted to a discussion of retreats.

Cross-Training

FOR STAFF TO BE so empowered, knowledgeable, and flexible, it is necessary for them to be cross trained. Each person has developed and written his own job description, and has compiled a checklist for time-sensitive or important activities that must be accomplished whether he is there or not. These are guidelines and checklists, not detailed directions. As a private pilot, I have a pre-flight checklist in the cockpit. Even though I know the pre-flight routine, I use the list each time I fly to ensure that I have not missed an important activity. Our checklists serve the same function. We keep copies of our checklists in a notebook we call HELP (Having Everything Like Perfect). In addition to the written material, each employee is required to identify and train at least one other person he/she feels can accomplish his or her job in an emergency. When someone is out for the day or on vacation, we use the opportunity to conduct practice drills where everyone changes jobs for the day.

Open-Book Management

AN ALTERNATIVE OFFICE structure, Open-Book Management, is popping up in American businesses, thanks to a book written by John Case, *Open-Book Management: The Coming Revolution* (New York: HarperBusiness, 1995). John is a nationally known expert in business management and editor-at-large of *Inc.* magazine.

There are three basic essentials in this management style. First, every employee sees and learns to understand the financial statements of the company. You show your books to every employee and have training courses to ensure that they have a good working knowledge of cash flow and net worth—yep, this means information on everybody's salary, including yours. You hang these numbers on the wall, make sure they are in the computer, and you and your staff revisit them constantly to see how you're doing.

Second, every employee understands how his or her production relates directly to the bottom line and learns that bad decisions mean lower profits. You'll need to explain to everyone from your para-planner to your file clerk how valuable his or her contribution is to the company. They need to know this as a real dollar figure, too. How much is their time worth? How much money does it cost to produce a review? What if they can produce it faster? They know whether the company is making money, and more importantly, why. Their job now includes the responsibility of moving the financial numbers in the right direction. In essence, everyone focuses on helping the business make money.

Third, all decisions, such as whether to upgrade your computer system, purchase new office equipment or hire a new employee, are put up for discussion and voted upon. Employees are empowered, with regard not only to their own performance, but also with making important business decisions. Finally, everyone shares in the profits, including making the decisions of where and how they will be distributed.

I have never quite warmed up to the idea of total open-book management. I believe we have a considerable amount of open communication with our staff, but there are certain aspects I don't buy. For example, it's my partners and I who personally sign for the credit line to cover business lulls or expansion costs, not our employees. If bad decisions are made, we take the salary cuts, not our employees. When open-book employees make bad decisions, do they take salary cuts? I don't think so. Still, some other planners find open-book management a most effective model.

Lou Stanasolovich, of Legend Financial Advisors in Pittsburgh, Pennsylvania, has been using it since he opened his own office in 1995. Lou reports that his staff is fully committed to open-book management. "I let them (his staff) have considerable influence on the decisions made in this office. They expect to receive benefits, such as becoming shareholders, receiving bonuses from the bonus pool, pension and profit sharing plans, and competitive salaries. Because they feel like owners, work the same hours as the owners do, they expect the rewards and losses."

Charlie Haines, of Haines Financial Advisors in Birmingham, Alabama, has been using open-book management for a few years as well. "Because of open-book management, I feel I have twelve partners. My staff feels they have more control over what happens here. When we have a troublesome relationship with a client, they evaluate the relationship compared to the income and decide whether it is worth keeping. When it's their decision to keep that client, they will be sure to make it work." Charlie explains that the only possible downside is that so many meetings are necessary to make a decision. "But," he adds, "we're getting better at those too."

John Case has a Web site, **www.openbookmanagement.com**, and a newsletter if you are interested in learning more about this management style. I believe in nearly every aspect of open-book management except opening my books and sharing the decisions that should be the responsibility of those whose names are on the line. We have found innovative ways to empower our staff and encourage them to take "psychic ownership," without giving them complete control of everything we do. If you too are somewhat uncomfortable with total open-book, you may want to explore a modified version, involving your staff in discussions such as the allocation of the bonus pool, investing the company pension plan, or purchasing new office equipment.

Employee Manual

WRITING AN EMPLOYEE MANUAL will give you insight into the current operation of your business, and will help you formulate new structures and procedures to lead your company to the next level of achievement. For instance, while we were writing our manual, we decided to make arrangements for flexible working hours to accommodate working parents or employees who must drive long distances. This decision helped us attract a working mother who has been essential in the growth of our practice. Without our flextime policy, she probably would not have been able to accept the position.

There are a few software packages that may help provide a framework, but much of their content is unnecessary boilerplate. A close friend gave me a copy of his software-generated employee manual to review. There was an extensive section establishing a rather strict dress code. It discussed the appropriate length of skirt a woman can wear, and it required jackets and ties for men. I was surprised because his office is informal, and South Florida businesses tend to be rather relaxed because of the heat. I questioned it. "Oh, we never enforce that," he said, "we left it in there, just in case." The dress code should state exactly what you want your staff to wear and when. Anything else invites confusion and misunderstanding. One day, someone is going to show up in an off-the-shoulder, sequined ensemble or a well-worn college sweat suit with patched knees.

Reading further, I found a lengthy discussion prohibiting the use of perfumes or colognes, "except Old Spice." When questioned about this one, he said, "Well, we had an employee here who used to drench herself in cologne and no one could breathe. But," he added, "I wear Old Spice and I'm not stopping." It is important to be consistent and non-discriminatory in your manual. I followed Jerry Neill's suggestion that key personnel devise the manual together with the principal(s).

Your employee manual does not have to be complicated. You'll want to outline your policies regarding benefits, vacation and sick days, holidays, and working hours. For example, our workday is officially 7½ hours. Each employee may choose his starting time, from 8:30 A.M to 10:00 A.M. There is a 45-minute paid lunchtime. In this way, our office is covered from 8:30 A.M to 6:00 P.M. As I said before, this flextime allows staff with young children to get home earlier or people who live further away to avoid rush hour traffic congestion. Budros & Ruhlin have workdays from 8:00 A.M. until 5:00 P.M. four days per week, with Friday afternoons off.

Our employees receive nine paid holidays per year. This appears to be standard with many advisers around the country. Our vacation policy allows one week after six months service or two weeks after one year. Then, from one to eight years, an employee is entitled to two weeks paid vacation, and over eight years, three weeks. We have seven paid sick or personal days per year.

Budros & Ruhlin always give the week between Christmas and New Year's as a paid vacation week for their staff, in addition to their accrued vacation time. I've always liked this idea, but I guess we haven't trained our clients as well as Budros & Ruhlin. During that week, our clients have more questions and requests for tax information and open more qualified accounts than at any other time.

Company Retreats

ABOUT FIVE YEARS AGO, while Eleanor Blayney and I were discussing our practices, she mentioned that her firm had just returned from a company retreat. She felt it was a great experience and her staff thought so, too. I asked Eleanor for the agenda. It had great activities like an icebreaker, team building, and role-playing. The main thrust of the weekend was centered on "learning-by-doing" activities, but the lagniappe was the cementing of personal relationships. We took Eleanor's agenda, and with some modifications, planned our own. Our comptroller is still talking about the success of our first retreat.

One of the best reasons to have a retreat is to ensure that you, your partners, and your staff are focused on the same goals. It is an excellent time to devise or revise your mission statement, core values, and employee manual, or to take on any number of activities that will help your organization become more systematized and efficient.

The dynamics of a retreat are unique. It is important that from the outset there be no normal employer/employee distinction. Each person brings his individualism, as well as his ability to meld into the team. Everyone's opinion is important. Activities should be developed around encouraging rather than forcing change. Each retreat has a different theme, but certain activities are repeated each year to create continuity to the experience.

Icebreakers

WE USUALLY START with an activity that gets the group talking about themselves and loosened up for the day's events. Our first year we used one of Eleanor's ideas. Everyone takes paper and pencil and completes this sentence, "One thing no one knows about me is...." Answers are folded up, dropped into a container and drawn out randomly and read. Everyone tries to guess who wrote what. Mena, our controller, told me that she was amazed at how little she knew about some of the people she had been working with for years.

My partner Peter is usually responsible for the icebreakers. One year, he set the question in the early days of Rome. We all needed to fill out a job application for one of three locations: the Coliseum, the Pantheon, or the Aqueducts. Whatever we selected, we had to explain why we felt we would be suited for that job. Then, we each had to guess who chose what job. Peter wanted to be Nero. Nobody guessed that. Everyone's answers helped us understand our job responsibilities and why we liked or didn't like certain aspects of our daily work responsibilities.

Encounter Group

ANOTHER ACTIVITY we got from Eleanor that we always use, I call the Post-It Note Pique. Everyone has a Post-It Note pad and five minutes to complete the phrase, "The thing that drives me crazy is...." Everyone can write as many Post-It Notes as they want, sticking them to the wall when we've finished. During a break, I reorganize them according to topic. Later, we read them aloud, and determine if there is a pattern of dissatisfaction. We then offer solutions and attempt a consensus. It is important to remind everyone from the outset that consensus is not the same as unanimity; it is simply a general agreement. All notes are anonymous so everyone feels comfortable in airing their frustrations. One year, because of a constellation of comments, we added voice-mail to our phone system, although admittedly, it does not get much use.

Team Builders

ONE YEAR FOR OUR RETREAT, Dr. Bill Taggart facilitated his Personal Style Inventory (PSI) program, a system he devised to determine our personal preferences. Weeks in advance we provided Dr. Taggart with a completed personal assessment inventory, the survey that Dr. Taggart developed to determine work styles, discussed in Chapter 4. At the retreat, Dr. Taggart assembled us according to our work styles, from rational to intuitive.

According to Taggart, intuitives are creative and spontaneous, while rationals are planners and calculators. In our company, the partners were all, to varying degrees, intuitive, while our assistants leaned somewhat to the rational side. This, Taggart pointed out, was a good team balance, because we could be creative, then hand our ideas to our assistants who would make our ideas concrete.

Once we understood our own personal work style preferences, we were able to function better as teams. We understood who must see the big picture, making plans more globally, and who was goal and task oriented, not requiring a big picture perspective. In assigning new job responsibilities, my partners and I consider these employee work styles. This exercise also helps all of us to understand our different perspectives on issues, as well as our different senses of urgency to complete work.

Last year, Andy Vladimir, a professor at Florida International University and a well-known consultant and author of hospitality textbooks, facilitated our retreat. Andy presented a classic Harvard

Business School case, Shouldice Hospital. (Harvard Business School, Sholdice Hospital, 1983.) As part of its MBA program, Harvard Business School pioneered the case study method, which allows students to learn by doing instead of by theory. These are actual cases highlighting organizations in some situation that requires a decision. Students must analyze the alternatives and provide advice to the organization.

Shouldice is a hospital in Canada that specialized in only one surgical procedure: hernias. It took only people who needed a hernia operation but were otherwise healthy. The hospital enjoyed 100 percent success and 100 percent patient satisfaction, but now they were considering growth possibilities. One alternative involved providing other types of surgery, but this would mean they would risk their patient satisfaction record. They could take less healthy people who needed hernia operations, but this might also risk their success ratio.

Our job was to work in teams to provide Shouldice with a strategic plan for growth. Everyone in our office was able to participate in this case, and everyone offered ideas. Andy used the Shouldice dilemma to give us a clearer picture of how and why we need to manage our growth. We used his morning presentation to segue into the next day's discussions of our own company growth and how we could give superior, intensive customer care.

Because our focus in recent years has been on team development, a close friend, Karla Curtis, vice president of PIE Technologies in Midlothian, Virginia, administered the Myers-Briggs personality instrument at one of our retreats. Myers-Briggs is an assessment survey designed to identify personality characteristics. (You can hire a Myers-Briggs facilitator to administer this test for approximately $1,000–$1,500.) Responses to questions on the survey are used to group individuals into four basic categories of personalities (described briefly in Chapter 3). This process not only helped us to understand ourselves, but also to understand the makeup of our work teams. A further benefit was that our staff learned to identify certain traits in our clients that would enable us to work better with them. For example, they discovered that our extrovert clients would probably ask for our opinions much more often than our introverted clients.

Role Playing

ROLE-PLAYING CAN ADD significantly to the understanding of the value of different people within the company. One year I wrote a case about a retiring couple. We followed this hypothetical couple from the prospect stage through an ongoing client relationship. Everyone participated, but not in his or her traditional role. Peter and our comptroller, Mena, became the couple, while one of our advisers and our operations director became the adviser team, designing the plan and making the recommendations. Some of our administrative staff functioned as the operations team, opening accounts, trading, and preparing reviews. We then came together as one group, making suggestions about how we could be more efficient or service oriented. Each of us left that experience with a new appreciation for how important our responsibilities are to the company and a renewed sense of self-worth.

Shared Vision

"SHARED VISION" is another activity we used one year at our retreat (see the box on the following page). This encourages staff to consider long-range planning. Without revealing authorship, we discussed future plans for the company and tried to pinpoint weaknesses and strengths from the employees' point of view.

Facilitators

FACILITATORS ADD PERSPECTIVE, creativity, framework, and depth to retreats. We usually divide the session into facilitated and non-facilitated, so that we also have some time to digest and consider the results of the work done with the facilitator.

Charlie Haines hired an industrial psychologist to facilitate his company's first retreat. "We were suffering from rapid growth and needed help fast." Charlie credits the retreat with "completely turning around one employee." The psychologist took them through a series of activities to help identify their strengths and weaknesses. Their first exercise was survival. They were all told that they were on an airplane that crashed in the Amazon and they needed to devise a plan to get to safety. First, they attacked the problem individually,

Shared Vision Questionnaire

INSTRUCTIONS: Be honest. There will be no retribution. If anonymity makes you more comfortable, don't include your name. This exercise is to help us see your working world clearer. Please bring this completed questionnaire to the morning session at the retreat.

1 What does this company do?

2 What is your responsibility within the organization?

3 Do you think this is an important responsibility? What would happen if your job was eliminated?

4 If this company grows 10% next year, what changes would need to be made (either in personnel, physical plant, or systems)? By 25%? By 50%?

5 If this were your company, what change would you immediately implement?

6 Finish this sentence. "If I had _____, I think my work would be infinitely better.

7 If I had to pinpoint one problem within this company and put it in ONE WORD, that word would be _____.

8 If I had to describe, in ONE WORD, the best thing about being a part of this company, that word would be _____.

then as a group. They began to see how much they could accomplish working together, as well as observing the roles that their colleagues performed within this group.

Free Association

OFTEN WE ENGAGE in an activity I refer to as free association. Someone poses a question. We then go around the room, saying the first thing that comes into our heads in response to that question. Quite often, we have gained some wonderful insights. For instance, last year, my question was, "You are my client. What are you paying me for?" One of our people said, "I am paying you to

---

Portable Initiatives Form

Objective: **Improve Services and Client Relations**

Why: The volatile market

Actions:
1. More frequent care calls
2. Custom designed birthday cards
3. Timely, accurate reviews
4. Immediate follow up
5. Survey—Are we doing things right, not are we doing the right things
6. Family involvement
7. Prepare detailed client profile
8. Client advisory board
9. Client picture wall
10. Refreshment preference

How: Design new database to accept customized information about clients. Include a tasking program so we can set up regular contact calls, e-mails, and faxes, and can send correspondence faster and easier.

---

worry for me." We've used this statement many times with our clients over the past year. It has worked well.

Another question was "What is a client?" Among the answers we got, "A client is family." Our free association activities help us all to change our perspectives with regard to our work and relationships with each other and our clients. We form new initiatives so that when we return to work, it is with a renewed enthusiasm.

The Game Plan

AT THE END OF THE RETREAT, we develop a game plan, or portable initiatives for the following year. We write down our objectives, why and how we want to accomplish them, and what specific actions we will take to meet our goals. Our game plan for one of our goals for 1997 is shown above, Portable Initiatives Form.

Designing Your First Retreat

IF YOU'VE NEVER taken part in a retreat, and many of the planners I spoke with have not, you may want to engineer it yourself the first time. Eleanor Blayney's agenda was a great start for us, so I have included it here. Additionally, there are numerous books with team building and retreat activities that you can use to customize your own program. I have listed what I consider to be some of the more useful ones in the Resource chapter.

If you feel uncomfortable running your own, you might also contact the business department of your local college or university who can provide you with ideas or facilitators, or ask other businesses in your area if they have retreats. I've included a few agendas from some of our retreats to give you an idea of activities you might incorporate into your own plans. The first one is a modification of the format that Eleanor Blayney shared with us years ago.

Organize and Strategize

DEVELOPING AN ORGANIZATIONAL chart can help everyone in your office understand the responsibilities, contributions and value of each person in the firm. It can also help you visualize work flow and outline team functions. A retreat environment is a good opportunity to consistently refine your organizational chart, inviting input from each member of your staff.

I spoke with many advisers who indicated that they had not yet had a retreat. Some reasoned that they were just too small a company to consider it. Don't confuse a retreat with the formality of the agendas I've presented. If there is someone else besides you working in your organization, you'd be wise to take an afternoon, find a quiet place to talk, and strategize the future of your business. No matter how big or how small your office is, you and your business will benefit from taking time for strategic planning.

Business Goals

1. What is the direction of the business?

◆ Growth of business

◆ Changes in format of presentations for more attractive appearance and faster preparation time

◆ More high touch

How should work flow be handled? Review Associate Adviser duties

◆ Marketing—newsletter and client communications

◆ Heavy reliance on data base to get things out for clients—new database

◆ More local activity

◆ What do you enjoy doing? Dropping our outdated paradigms

◆ Job operations manual

◆ Where do you want to be in one year?

2. Identify performance problems and come up with solutions which, when implemented, will turn the situation around.

◆ Tell what is happening in observable, measurable terms.

◆ Tell what you would like to be happening, in behavioral terms.

A problem exists only if there is a difference between what is actually happening and what you DESIRE to be happening.

3. Identify problems in the physical plant which require restructuring to produce the desired results in performance.

◆ Tell what is happening in observable, measurable terms.

◆ Tell what you would like to be happening, in behavioral terms.

◆ Tell how the change in the physical plant will produce desired results.

A SAMPLE RETREAT AGENDA

EBK FIRST COMPANY RETREAT

8:30–8:45 AM   INTRODUCTION (Deena)

Taking it to the next level. A brief discussion of why we're here and what we want to accomplish.

8:45–9:15 AM   ICEBREAKER (Peter)

Getting to Know You, Getting to Know All About You.

Answer the following questions:

In my next life, I will be_____.

My favorite_____is_____.

The place I would most like to spend the day is _____.

Something you probably do not know about me is _____.

We will fold up the sheet, put them in a bag and take turns drawing the sheets out, reading answers and then trying to guess the identity of the responder.

9:15–9:30 AM   BREAK

9:30–11:30 AM   CASE STUDIES

Getting the staff to think like clients and senior planners.

What's important from the Client/Planner point of view.

Services to be rendered and who does what, when. Each member of the organization will assume a different role for the purposes of exploring our interactions with clients. Three different scenarios will be attempted: the initial and data gathering meeting; the plan delivery; and finally, a review session.

Mr. & Mrs. Jerry Atrick   Initial Meeting and Data Gathering

Mr & Mrs. Jerry Atrick   Plan Delivery

Mr. & Mrs. Jerry Atrick   Review meeting

11:30–12:00 PM   PORTABLE INITIATIVES

Case critiques. What can we take back to the office to improve our interaction with our clients?

12:00–1:00 PM   LUNCH

1:00–1:30 PM   POST-IT NOTE PIQUE (Encounter Group)

"The thing that drives me crazy is…" Everyone has five minutes to write their day-to-day pet peeves on Post-It notes and stick them on the wall. We will then walk around the room reading (and agreeing) with the "things that drove us crazy." We hope to discover that all irritants are solvable and that everyone is mature enough not to direct their frustrations personally to other people. Everyone has different gripes.

1:00–3:00 PM   TEAM BUILDING

What activities can we refine for better internal communication?

3:00–3:15 PM   BREAK

3:15–4:30 PM   BRAINSTORMING

Standardization vs. Customization. How can we become more efficient, yet not lose our "high touch"?

4:30–5:00 PM   BUSINESS/PERSONAL GOALS FOR FOLLOWING YEAR

What would YOU like to accomplish both personally and in business next year?

SECTION

THREE

THE
ENVIRONMENT

NO MATTER HOW GOOD your partners and staff are, inefficient back office systems and bleeding-edge technology can stunt your business growth. A company overcommitted to technology will find staff constantly struggling to scale the learning curve. This section explores the effective use of hardware and software for an expanding practice and discusses the necessity of systematizing operations to ensure success.

CHAPTER 7

HARDWARE MAKES IT HAPPEN QUICKLY

Fatal error. Contact systems manager to rebuild.

Have a nice day.

—EBK ERROR ROUTINE

GOOD TECHNOLOGICAL SUPPORT can improve prof-

itability, and it can help you provide seamless service. In

our office, we have worked diligently over the years to

use low-tech and high-tech hardware and software effi-

ciently, and to appear high touch to our clients.

I have divided this discussion of technology into two

chapters. The first, which follows, discusses physical

infrastructure. It is in turn divided into two categories: low tech, covering such things as physical space, filing, and phone systems; and high tech, covering computer hardware, peripherals, gadgets, and electronic storage. The second, Chapter 8, discusses software.

Physical Plant

FIVE YEARS AGO, we had a conventional layout, with small offices distributed around a small core. This core area served as the filing room as well as copy room, mailroom, and binding room. Each adviser handled a defined number of clients, performing all operational activities for them, including plan preparation, trading, and review preparation. The trouble with this method was that if an adviser was absent when a client called for help, no one else was prepared to deal with the problem. Furthermore, if a key adviser left the firm, getting existing clients comfortable with a new person while trying to bring the replacement up to speed was a nightmare.

We also had no checks and balances. If an adviser made a trading error, it might not be discovered until the client's next quarterly review, and maybe not even then.

As we grew, it became clear that we needed to divide work responsibilities differently. We also had to rely much more on teamwork. We developed a formal team system in order to encourage interaction, but due to the physical layout, staff found themselves rushing from office to office, trying to find files, picking up reviews, talking with each other about client calls, and wasting time.

One day, my three advisers marched into my office and asked me to break down the office walls. "You could open up the whole inside of this space, build in desks and work areas. We can save time, energy, and keep each other apprised about client activities." That afternoon we drew up the plans for the Great Room, a huge area with built-in desks, plenty of file storage and work surfaces, and small and large conference tables. My partners were sure that one huge room with workstations would be too noisy and distracting. In fact, it has worked so well, we broke down the wall to the kitchen area and incorporated that into the Great Room as well.

Around the room are several tables for impromptu meetings, daily lunches, and birthday parties. Initially, the copier, fax machine, postage machine, and other time savers lined the walls too. They proved to be too distracting, so they were relegated to an unused office nearby.

The open-area concept is not for everyone, so it is important to talk about structural plans with staff as well as partners. When designing your office space, discuss your ideas with the people who will be working there. Ask for further input to create a work area that is both comfortable and functional.

Filing

FILING SYSTEMS SEEM to be everyone's nemesis. Archiving documents is especially difficult in this business where some records must be held for several years. We have solved this problem by outsourcing the operation to a company that stores and destroys the files for us at our direction. This was infinitely better than our old system of using a rented storage space and moving files ourselves. That was inconvenient, hot, and dirty. Staff hated it and my partners hated it. Only the rental storage company was happy. Now, periodically, we pack up archive boxes, label them with dates for destruction, and the storage company picks them up and stores them off-site until the destruction date. The company provides us with a notarized letter verifying the confidential destruction. You are charged per cubic foot of storage space you need. We currently pay approximately $40 monthly. Costs will vary depending upon geographic area.

Phone System Enhancements

VOICE MAIL SYSTEMS have popped up everywhere, and they are admittedly efficient. Many of our friends have complex systems that allow a caller to spend a minute or more wandering through the system, punching in last names, leaving messages, and flagging levels of importance for those messages.

I am not a big fan of this aspect of technology. Our clients rarely leave voice mail messages; they prefer a live person. So do we. Our voice mail system, therefore, gets about as much use as a Maytag repairman, and is relegated to collecting after-hours messages and posting after-hours notification of our business hours, holidays, and absences.

On the other hand, Sullivan, Bruyette, Speros and Blayney find their voice mail system indispensable. "I think it's just the nature of our clients. They are comfortable with electronic messaging and prefer to get directly to us or leave a message directly for us. They find the voice mail system more efficient in their busy world," says Greg Sullivan.

Should you elect to incorporate a working hours voice mail system in your practice, be sure that you frequently call in to see how it feels to be a client or prospect. Then ask some of your best clients how they like it. Barry Freedman, of Freedman Financial Associates, Inc., in Peabody, Massachusetts, reports that he received a standing ovation from his client advisory board when he announced that his firm would "never have a voice mail system in our office."

Caller ID was another one of my bright ideas that hasn't worked as well as I expected. We installed it on the receptionist phone, but the first time she picked up the call and said, "Good morning, Mr. Shultz," Mr. Shultz got paranoid. For that matter, it was impossible to tell whether it was Mr. or Mrs. Shultz on the other end. At least it was good for verifying phone numbers. Randi Grant of Morrison, Brown, Argiz, says her caller ID saves her plenty of time. "I am really able to screen my own calls. I can then return them at my convenience, not the caller's." A state-of-the art phone system may have caller ID on every phone.

One of the best purchases we made were telephone headsets. I personally hate them, but our advisers find them invaluable. Headsets allow staff to talk while they grab files, enter data into the computer, and fill out documents. They're really an efficient addition to the office.

Low-Tech Equipment

WE USE SPIRAL BINDERS and heat sealing binding machines for assembling plans and presentations. Our reviews are three-hole punched for the clients to insert in the leather binder we provide at the beginning of our relationship. These binders are embossed in gold leaf with our firm name and the client's name. Prior to last year, we sent out the binders to be embossed. This year we bought our own embossing machine to avoid the turn-around time required for outside imprinting. Because this has worked so well, we have been experimenting embossing different items. We have even embossed cocktail napkins with clients' names before their appointments. When we serve beverages, they really are impressed with this detail.

Hardware Consultants

WE HAVE ENOUGH computer hardware to run several nuclear power plants. This should not necessarily be the standard of the industry; rather, it arises from a combination of the interests of our three partners and the wild enthusiasm of our computer consultant, Rick Medina of Netrus. Rick and his company have designed, built, and maintained our system for over ten years. If you haven't done so already, get a good computer consultant who is not only familiar but comfortable with many different kinds of applications. It is worth the money.

Norm Boone, of Boone & Associates in San Francisco, considers himself a sophisticated user, yet he uses a professional computer support person. "Every day you are telling people that they need a professional when it comes to their financial planning. Take your own advice," he says. "We tell our clients not to listen to a half dozen advisers but to find one they trust (i.e., us). It's the same principle when it comes to your computer system. Hire a good consultant, not multiple consultants." In other words, it's not a good idea to try to diversify your source of technical help. As Rick Medina says, "Good luck in getting us guys to talk with each other and agree on anything. We spend all our time arguing, trying to convince each other that we have the right approach and the best solutions." My advice is similar to what you might tell your clients. Find someone good you can trust and don't let the cost be your guiding factor. Your business is too dependent on a good working system to skimp here.

The Service You Pay For

ONE OF MY CHICAGO CLIENTS told me of his visit to a Cadillac dealership years ago. He went into the showroom and walked the sales manager over to a gorgeous brand-new Cadillac. He pointed to the sticker on the side window and said, "See that sticker price? I'm going to pay that price, no negotiating. In return, you are going to give me the best service you've ever given. When my car needs repair, you are going to send someone for it with a loaner car for me. When you tell me the car will be ready at 5:00 P.M., it will be ready. Even if you are overbooked for repairs, you will take mine. Now, if that's acceptable to you, let's draw up the paperwork and let me take this baby home." He always paid top dollar, but boasted about the extraordinary service he always received. We used this same concept for our computer maintenance service. We have a blanket service contract with our computer consultants, and it guarantees one-hour response time. We pay for it, but it is exceptional, dependable service that we've decided is necessary.

Rick and his partner Ernie built our IBM clones. This is an optimum method, because they can find less expensive parts and build upgradable systems. Even if you don't go this route, consider carefully before purchasing your system by mail. Your success depends on being in business *all* of the time. Some mail order companies will offer service within twenty-four hours, but this usually entails swapping out your system for a new one. You will get all the pre-installed software, not your carefully customized software. You may have to retrieve any proprietary software from your old system and restore it yourself, assuming you have proper backup copies and you can recover it. Like anything else, if you have a relationship with someone, the commitment is different.

It's frightening to realize how computer-dependent we all are, particularly in this business. Rick Adkins and Cindy Conger of the Arkansas Financial Group in Little Rock maintain that their biggest expenditures by far are for their technology. "When we started in business," said Cindy, "we made a conscious decision to stay on the cutting edge of technology. It is a huge financial commitment, but it does assure our abilities to provide our clients with the best possible service." Your computer systems should be fast, efficient, and dependable. If you are not a computer junkie, and perhaps even more so if you are, hire a consultant—fast.

When you do buy systems, get the maintenance contracts. You'll need them, guaranteed. Only naive amateurs think they can fix any problem themselves. If computer maintenance is not your primary business, buy the contracts, and hire experts.

If you're in the market for a good computer systems person, ask other professionals whom they're using. You'll get much more useful advice if your computer people know their business and yours. Interview several people, ask for references, and solicit a proposal for current work as well as for a contracted, ongoing relationship. There are plenty of people getting into the computer business these days, but it doesn't mean they are qualified and capable.

Because our record keeping, analysis, and client maintenance are heavily reliant upon technology, there are some things I don't think we can be without. In this section, I have divided the hardware into two categories, required and optional. I'll start with the required—printers, redundant drives, online uninterruptible power supplies, power surge protection strips, and data backup.

Required Hardware

PRINTERS

WE HAVE SIX Hewlett Packard DeskJet 1600 color printers. You may not need six but you need at least one color printer. We elected to use good quality lower end printers, rather than buy one really expensive one. We have these scattered about the office. Three of them are on the network, available to anyone. The rest are resident in partners' and assistants' private offices for their personal use. These DeskJets may be slower than lasers but they provide consistent output and are dependable. The prices of color lasers have dropped substantially in the last few years.

You also need at least one good laser black and white printer. Get at least one good workhorse printer that is dependable and fast. A fast printer is a necessity, but when it comes to deciding how fast is "fast," you really need to weigh the costs against the time savings.

REDUNDANT DRIVES

THERE ARE AT LEAST half a dozen ways to structure redundant drives on your system. Only a good technician can tell which is best for you, your company needs, and your hardware system. When I asked Rick what we had, he informed me it was a RAID (redundant array of independent drives) level five with three drives for data striping storage, although shortly we'll convert to clustering. If you're like me, you'll want a translation of that, which is simply, if one of our hard drives is destroyed, our recovery time will be minimal because we are simultaneously writing to more than one drive. I cannot imagine living without that security, even if I don't understand the techy language. Redundant drives are not a luxury; they are a necessity.

ONLINE UNINTERRUPTIBLE POWER SUPPLY (UPS)

A UPS WILL PROVIDE electricity to run your system for a time in the event of a power failure. Our office is in Florida and we're subject to a combination of heavy storms and an unpredictable electrical system; power failures are a daily event. An online UPS maintains a battery charge that takes over if electrical service fails.

Online power supplies can run your computer for several hours and will, if you want, notify you with an alarm or page if the system goes down. If you do use a UPS, be sure that your network has power-down software as well, so your system will close down in an orderly fashion and not just stop when it runs out of power. Unexpected stops can destroy files. Sadly, I speak from experience.

POWER SURGE PROTECTION STRIPS

IF YOU ARE NOT using a permanent connection to the Internet, don't forget to protect your modem phone lines from power disruptions as well. Use surge protector strips and plug the phone lines into the strip so that the phone line is protected as well.

DATA BACKUP

EVERYONE HAS A BACKUP horror story, so I won't bore you with mine. If you've never experienced the sheer helplessness of finding you have no way to retrieve essential data except to recreate it, you're just lucky. You can lessen your chances of experiencing this loss by instituting excellent backup systems immediately. We use tape backups because they have the capability of high capacity, while they are relatively inexpensive to use. If your company has a large hardware budget, consider installing removable hard disk drives, which generally back up faster than tape. Depending upon the capacity of your backup facilities, you will want to devise a system of copying and archiving.

You can back up your system to many kinds of devices: hard drives, floppy drives, CD-ROMs, tape drives, and magneto optical drives, which is a combination of magnetic and optical technology that compresses data onto CD-type disks. The question is, would you want to? Would you want to back up an entire system onto 3-inch floppies? It would take you forever. Realistically, you want to have a backup system that is reasonably priced, fast, reliable, and has good storage capacity. Presently, tape drives have good capacity and are the most economical. Although it may be faster to back up to removable hard drives, it may be more costly.

We back up all our network drives onto tape automatically each night. You may want to consider a schedule that includes automatic and manual backups. For example, Kathy Day's office automatically backs up their entire system each night, then once a month they prepare a manual backup of just the clients' data and company files.

You will want to design a calendar system for scheduling backups, and a backup storage plan. Our archive system saves each backup for the week. Then, the following week we overwrite the prior week's tapes, with the exception of the Friday tape. It is set aside for storage. On the last day of the month we back up and set aside that tape for storage. When the new month begins, we reuse the earlier saved Friday tapes. At the beginning of a new year we save the last business day and begin reusing the monthly tapes. On Friday, our weekly, monthly and yearly tapes are stored off-site. As a result, at any given time we have backup for the prior five business days, the prior four weeks, the last day of every month for the year and the last business day of every prior year.

Recheck your backups periodically. Even the most powerful backup system has the potential for failure. Don't ever assume you have complete data. Prior to long-term archiving, take a few minutes to attempt a restore to ensure that you will be able to retrieve data if necessary.

Optional Hardware

JUKEBOX CDS

WE INSTALLED A JUKEBOX CD (that's a unit that allows us to mount and read multiple CDs), anticipating the eventual custodian and mutual fund company delivery of statements via CDs. We have also been able to install huge CD-based programs on the jukebox, giving everyone access to the program CD when the disk itself is required for every user. Caveat: if you do an installation this way, be sure that you have a license agreement for multiple users.

SCANNERS

SCANNERS MAKE IT EASY to bring pictures and data to your system without manually reentering it. Have at least one multi-page high-end scanner for bulk scanning projects, particularly if you are migrating to an electronic filing system. If you produce your own company newsletter, a scanner makes is easy to integrate pictures and articles for communications with clients.

NETWORK HARDWARE

ALTHOUGH NETWORKS ARE really software-driven solutions for multiple system communication, network implementation is so integral to the design of your hardware system that I've elected to include their discussion in this chapter. If you have just one or two users, you probably don't have to worry about a network. If you need to share information, you can probably just copy a floppy and run it over to the next machine. If you have more than two computers, I consider a network mandatory (assuming you plan on growing your practice).

LANtastic, Novell, and Microsoft Windows NT are the most popular network software. We use both Novell and Microsoft NT networks on separate servers. We have worked with Novell for ten years. We selected it because it was the biggest company for network software at the time, and running it required relatively few computer resources. There are advantages to using NT, primarily because as a Microsoft product it is compatible with our key applications. We put up two NT servers, one for our Access database, HOMER, which is a resource hog, and one for the Windows version of Centerpiece, the portfolio management software we use, because it, too, is somewhat piggy. Currently, the NT network is a much better application server than Novell, but it requires a lot of computer memory. My computer consultant assures me that in the not too distant future, there will be plenty of alternatives that will need much less processing power and will be even more flexible in handling different applications.

I believe that even smaller companies can benefit from a network system, but don't try to learn all of this stuff yourself. Find a competent expert to build it for you. Before you meet with him, prepare a list of the technology you'll need:

◆ How many devices (CD-ROM, printers, tape backups, fax/data modem, etc.) will you want to hook up to the network?

◆ Will you need a dedicated server or do you have a lesser-used PC that can serve double duty?

◆ What type of communications connectors will you need? How many people will be connected to the Internet?

◆ What are your plans for growth? Remember my buddy with the boat, and plan for the day after tomorrow. Some network systems expand better than others.

Although we use NT for very specialized programs, I'd still recommend Novell for its flexibility in network handling. Once you decide on a network, you must decide on its configuration. Two years ago, if someone inadvertently disconnected a computer from our network, the entire system failed and everyone's computer went down. If one of the cleaning crew tripped on a wire, loosening the connection, the network crashed and nobody's computer worked. I remember running around the office at least once a week, crawling under each desk, looking for the loose wire so we could work again. Back then we used coaxial connections that were run in a single loop. A break anywhere in the circle shut everything down. Today we are connected directly into a hub that allows each system to run independently. If one is disconnected, there is no disruption. Given a choice, opt for a hub.

PALM PILOT

KATHY DAY SAID she cannot remember life without her Palm Pilot. When she's out of the office, every piece of information is readily available on the Palm Pilot in her purse. It also synchronizes data with many different client contact and scheduling programs, so information can always be current. My partner Harold practically sleeps with his. Try visiting **www.palmpilot.com** on the Net to get a list of hundreds of trial Palm Pilot programs to download, which just might improve your data manipulation and storage efficiency. If you are often away from your office, but don't need a laptop, consider a Palm Pilot.

The Internet

IF YOU HAVEN'T YET put up a Web site, I encourage you to consider it. Mark Ralphs, of The Financial Planning Corporation in the UK, described Web sites as "virtual brochures." That's exactly what they should be. They should tell who you are, what you do, and why, but should never replace human communication with prospects or clients. We have found it useful to familiarize people with our company, as an alternative to investing in slick brochures.

One of the first things you should do is lock in your domain name. Many speculators are purchasing rights to company and product names on the Net, then selling them at astronomical prices to those people wanting the name. One of the other unscrupulous Net gimmicks is to figure out a common typo in a domain name, then sell that variant to a competitor. In any case, you can work with your Internet provider to see how to lock in the names you want, or visit InterNIC, the group responsible for registering all domain names **www.internic.com**, who will complete it for you online. The costs to host your domain name start at about $70 per year.

Next, I recommend that you find a Web site designer to help you get started. Did you ever notice how much time it takes to pull up some sites rather than others? Every little spinning ball on a site takes time to load. People surfing the net may not have the powerful equipment that you have. They can grow impatient and click off before they ever see how pretty your site is. Professional web designers know what will work and what won't. Creating a site is time consuming—time you probably should be spending on your company and clients. If you really must keep your hand in, professionals can get you to a certain point, then show you how to maintain some of the information yourself.

Jim Lamb, senior staff writer at Lightport, Inc., our Web site provider **(www.lightport.com)** offers these hints for designing a Web site:

◆ Make it simple

◆ Be direct

◆ Be conversational

◆ Be personal

◆ Be interactive

You may want to consider giving your clients access to their portfolios on your site. Lightport can set this up if you use Centerpiece or Advent as your portfolio management software. Some planners are already marketing this as an added value for their clients. Basically, you can enable clients to download any report that you can produce through Advent or Centerpiece. Lightport reports that over 100,000 portfolios were on line in the Fall of 1998.

Just remember, if you do put performance reports on your site, you may be encouraging your clients to look at their portfolios more often than they should. Professor Dick Thaler maintains that portfolios should be rebalanced every thirteen months and that's how often the investor should look at them. Anything more often risks the danger of micro-managing.

Lightport was the first to design Web sites specifically for Registered Investment Advisors and the first to offer access to portfolios for clients. We selected them because they provide the consulting and design work and the results are very professional. They are not inexpensive, but they produce quality. If you want more hands-on, check out Advisor Square **(www.advisorsquare.com)**. It is similar to Lightport, but does not include the design and consulting work, so is less expensive. You build your own site using pre-designed templates. The company also supplies interesting features including analytical tools that you can make available to your clients. Similarly, Web Dynamics **(www.myfrontdoor.com)** provides templates that you can modify to design your own site. There are many more Web designers available; just check out the Internet. A search under "web designers" will yield enough Web sites to keep you busy for days. Here are some things to keep in mind when you select one:

◆ How long have they been in business? There are plenty of start-up companies related to the Net. You want to select one with some staying power.

◆ Do they have an office, or are they just two guys and a dog in a garage? Having an office is not a necessity, but you really should know who is providing the support and how they work.

◆ Do they have any experience in the financial field? Someone who understands your business and your client base will provide an additional level of advice.

◆ What are all the charges, from start-up to ongoing maintenance fees? Fees for Internet services, consulting services, and Web site support can add up to big dollars.

CONNECTIONS TO THE INTERNET

THERE ARE SEVERAL WAYS you can make the connection to the Superhighway. The best method for you will be dependent upon your usage, the cost, and what is available in your area. You will also want to consider whether you will be downloading client data from your custodian(s). You may want to check with them to get recommendations if you have not yet made a connection for this purpose. Probably the most commonly used is the POTS (plain old telephone system). You connect through the telephone lines with a modem (modulator/demodulator) device that converts the signals from a computer to code that can be transmitted over the phone lines. At present, you can buy modems with different transmission speeds (baud rates), but for now the fastest modem speed is 56 kilobits per second.

Many advisers I've talked with have put ISDN (Integrated Services Digital Network) lines in their offices. We have one. These are actually multiple phone lines that function together to give you a constant connection to the Internet and higher transmission speeds. Some ISDN services are charging tariffs on these lines, so check to see how charges are generated. It may surprise you. For example, the base charge for our ISDN line is $135 per month. We then may have additional charges depending upon the number of hours of usage.

Satellite connections use wireless microwaves to transmit data from Internet servers to a satellite dish at your location, sometimes via a tower located elsewhere. This type of connection has downloading capabilities in excess of 200 kilobits per second and may cost in excess of $200 a month to start, but the upload is only as fast as your modem.

Now some TV-cable companies are offering connections to the Internet also. Conventional connections are likewise set for fast downloading through them, from 400 to 600 kilobits per second, and slower uploading. There are some two-way transmitters that send and receive on the same line; this is not at the present time a standard feature.

Hardware Blues

IT IS IMPOSSIBLE for anyone to keep up with the technological advances in today's world. In fact, when you purchase a new computer, it is virtually obsolete when you walk out the door. Although I recommend purchasing state-of-the-art hardware and upgrading often, don't travel too far into cyberland. It can be far more expensive than it should be. If you purchase the newest Pentium processor as soon as it becomes available, it can cost three times as much than if you wait six months for the price (and the demand) to come down. Temper your desire to have the latest and greatest, knowing that it's a race you can't win. The goal is not to own the latest hardware, it's to have the most efficient office.

CHAPTER 8

SOFTWARE MAKES IT HAPPEN PROFITABLY

Isn't it great when things work together?

— Z A C H E R Y   W E L L S , 9 Years Old

TECHNOLOGY IS RESHAPING our businesses drastically.

However, the same technology that can leverage time

can also absorb it, along with personnel and money.

Every adviser I've talked to around the world expressed

the same concern: There is no integrated system to help

us do business efficiently.

Ed McCarthy is the editor for *CFP BIZ*, an online mag-

azine at the ICFP Web site. In an article for the *Journal*

of *Financial Planning* in June 1998, Ed summed up the financial planners' quandary. "In a perfect world, the software programs that resided on your PC would work as one seamless productivity tool. You would manually enter or electronically retrieve new data just once." (The Data Dilemma," *Journal of Financial Planning*, Vol. II, Issue 3, June 1998.)

Right now, the only option for total software integration is to design some yourself. Our firm hired a programmer to build a bridge between Centerpiece, our portfolio management software, Excel, and PowerPoint. We can now use the data from our portfolio management software to produce custom reports and graphics. Unfortunately, the process can be costly and time consuming. The biggest drawback to attempting your own software integration is that you are at the mercy of a programmer. Unless you employ an in-house programmer/systems manager, you will need to develop an ongoing relationship with someone for maintenance and upgrades. Having done it, I have to tell you that it sometimes reminded me of the old joke about owning a boat—a hole in the water into which you pour money.

Appropriate software can make an entire office function more efficiently and allow for more time to be spent with clients. If the software crashes, or doesn't handle the data effectively, you can waste hours that add up to days and weeks. You can consume days just adapting to new software; we've made whopping big mistakes underestimating that learning curve. The more complicated the program and the more people needing to learn it, the harder it is to climb that curve.

More than once we purchased big, powerful proprietary software and did not introduce it to our staff until they were required to use it. One year we bought a massive, complex, integrated financial planning and portfolio management program. It was not particularly user-friendly, but having seen it at one of the IAFP conventions, we believed it was the answer to our prayers. Instead of including our staff in the evaluation, we bought it, brought it home, and essentially said, "use it." Staff looked it over, decided that it added little besides complexity to what we were already doing, and threw it out.

Nearly every adviser I've interviewed admitted to the same experience. "Frankly," says Ross Levin of Accredited Investors, "we stay with some of our older software relationships, even though we know we'd be more 'efficient' going elsewhere. We just don't relish facing conversions and steep learning curves that are required when implementing new software."

I would like to offer some recommendations for software support that can improve profitability and help provide seamless service, as well as some ideas that may bring you closer to that perfect technological world we'd all love to live in.

Electronic Data Storage

THE PREVIOUS CHAPTER discussed our solution to the problems we faced with low-tech filing. Now let me tell you what software-based solutions we see in the future and what some planners are doing today.

Last year, our comptroller, Mena, decided that our firm should become a paperless office. She researched scanners, document scanning companies, software, hardware, everything she thought we would need to accomplish this. When she presented this idea to the partners, we looked at her in horror! We were not yet ready to give up our paper client files. She reminded us we would have Boolean search capabilities; that is, we'd be able to search on any combination of words to find just what we needed. She showed us we would be able to use the present filing area for workspace. We are always desperate for workspace. She explained that if we did not do this, we would have to buy new, larger files and build new shelving to accommodate our growing business. She made a remarkable presentation for the paper-free office; still, we bought new filing cabinets and built new shelves for more documents. We know we'll have to do it soon; we're just not yet ready to give up that physical file.

David Strege, of Syverson, Strege, Sandager & Co., in West Des Moines, Iowa, spent a significant amount of time researching hardware and software to do document scanning and storing. He also spent time weighing the costs of making the move. "It's not the investment in hardware and software that is the real expense," he says, "it's the cost of the conversion time." Sharon Kayfetz of Personal

Financial Consultants in San Ramon, California, agrees. "We've spent over a year converting twenty years of data, and we're still doing it," she says. "On the other hand, once you have the system in place, it immediately saves retrieval time." Eventually, that really affects your bottom line. But not every office may benefit. David feels that offices with one to five people may not feel the benefits as much as offices with more than ten employees, but Sharon counters with the fact that she and her husband, Loren, have only one support staff person. They have been able to cut their space requirements by 40 percent. Sharon argues that electronic data storage can "lower overhead and upstream personnel." They have no use for minimally skilled personnel in their office anymore.

Two years ago, Kathleen Day, of Kathleen Day & Associates in Miami, successfully transformed her office into a practically paperless one. They bought a heavy-duty flatbed scanner that accommodates multiple pages; she also put a scanner on each employee's desk. When something lands on a desk, it is either scanned and filed, or thrown out. Kathy uses a software program called Worldox, which she found on the Internet at **www.worldox.com.** "It is mostly used by the legal community. It's inexpensive [at $295 per user], easy to learn, and easy to set up." Kathy explains that they handled the conversion problem easily. "We just made the commitment to start the system going forward and pick up the history if necessary. When a file was frequently used, we would set it up for conversion. Files we didn't touch remained stored away until we could legally destroy them." Doing the conversion piecemeal may mean your system is less reliable for a time, but it may also lift the burden of making your conversion a showstopping event.

All three advisers I spoke with about a paperless office agreed that the most critical decision is how you define your filing system. Some electronic filing system companies will provide design support. Naturally, they are more expensive. David Strege recommends you use a company that will give you this support. "They know just how to make the most of their systems. It's worth the money." Kathy Day chose her system because it was easy to design the

Kathy Day's Story

WALK INTO KATHY DAY'S OFFICE and she'll proudly show you the one and only filing cabinet in her work space: a four-drawer lateral that's hardly filled. "We've got only original-signature documents in here," she proudly proclaims. "Anything that we can copy is stored electronically on our system."

Kathy investigated many software systems before choosing Worldox. "I sat literally for hours on the Internet, researching electronic storage systems that I felt we could put into place easily, yet would be powerful enough to store everything that we're required to keep for years." Once she decided on Worldox, she and her son began the job of installing it on the system and designing their electronic file cabinets.

They looked at their hard copy files and determined that their current system was logical. Everything pertaining to a client was stored under the client's name, then subdivided by applications, plans, trading confirmations, and personal documents, such as copies of wills and trusts. They used this same logic to design the electronic storage system. "Click on Jacobs and you'll find all of Jacobs' files."

Kathy created separate filing cabinets for company, compliance, and resource files. "When I need information about a mutual fund I'm using, I click on the resource drawer and call up the fund." It all sounds so easy, yet Kathy warns, "Be sure your staff has plenty of time to learn the program and get comfortable with it. It works well only because everyone was well-prepared for it."

filing systems herself. "If you currently have a good filing system, it will translate well to an electronic one. No one knows better than you how to organize your files."

If you are considering a paperless office, consider and weigh the costs as well as the time commitment and ultimate savings:

◆ **Assess the physical space.** How much room will the new equipment require? How much can you save by giving up your filing cabinets?

◆ **Estimate how much labor you can save,** but don't think you can eliminate your file clerk completely. You can't; in our business, bulk scanning is an ongoing task.

◆ **Interview four or five different companies,** and take your time deciding. You are facing a huge commitment in costs and conversion time. No matter how exciting the new company's story may be, don't be a guinea pig; choose experienced professionals.

◆ **Be sure your employees embrace the process enthusiastically.** It's wasted money if staff are still emotionally tied to the files and feel the need to keep paper.

◆ **Don't short-cut file design.** You want to ensure success by thinking through this process carefully. Once you've committed to a structure, it is difficult to change.

◆ **Choose your hardware carefully.** What additional hardware will you require? Computer storage is getting cheaper, but keep in mind that you will still need to plan for expansion, so choose a system that will grow with you. You will need to consider snap drives, CD jukeboxes, or similar systems for easy retrieval.

◆ **Select software for ease in operation and flexibility.** You should be able to search by keywords and customize the reports you can generate.

◆ **Will you use OCR (optical character recognition)?** OCR capabilities allow you to manipulate the data using any word processing program. This feature makes the system more expensive, but will allow you to search by any word in the document. Alternatively, you could just have keywording capabilities, meaning that each file will have a number of keywords assigned in order to retrieve the document easily.

The future of the financial planning offices is definitely in the paperless office world. Sharon Kayfetz is certain that one day, through enhanced technology, she will eliminate office space and personnel altogether. "With so few necessary hard copy files, and our data on disks, with laptops, mobile telephone, and fax, we'll just be an office-in-a-box."

Anti-Virus Software

PROGRAMMING TO PROTECT your files is another one of those required pieces of software, especially if you or anyone in your office spends any amount of time on the Internet. The three most popular programs are from MacAfee, Norton, and Dr. Solomon. We use MacAfee, for no particular reason other than our consultant likes it. It runs resident on the system and is set to scan automatically at certain times of the day. There are hundreds of new viruses each week, thus, it's imperative to keep your virus-scan software current to avoid being crippled, particularly if you retrieve data or files from the Internet. We download every week, directly from MacAfee on the Internet. In fact, we get most of our updates of any software directly over the Internet. I haven't been to a computer software store to purchase software in ages.

Backup Software

MANUAL BACKUP PROCEDURES are such a nuisance. They can also be unreliable because of human involvement. It is far easier to set automatic backups and let them run sometime during the night. We use Cheyenne Backup Software, the largest provider in the industry. Is it not particularly user-friendly, but it is, in my opinion, the most powerful and flexible one for us at the moment. Seagate and Norton both have good backup programs as well.

It is imperative that you have a good backup program and good backup procedures in place. However, no matter how good your hardware and software for backups are, if you store on site and fire, flood, or natural disaster destroys your offices, you're exposed. Be sure that you have a system for storing backup tapes off-site, not just in your office.

Word Processing, Spreadsheets, and Graphics

I ADMIT IT, WE'RE WIMPS. It is pointless to fight the trend. Long ago, we commited to use Microsoft so that all our programs would be integrated. Many of the planners I interviewed made this same decision. This makes it incredibly easy to design and build your own financial plans, reviews, and other documents. I didn't mind giving up WordPerfect for Word and Lotus 1-2-3 for Excel, but I held on to my Harvard Graphics for a long time before embracing PowerPoint. Now I can't imagine using anything else. We've designed a PowerPoint presentation for client meetings, complete with animation. It's fun to create spinning allocation pies and walking Ibbotson "mountain" charts.

Financial Planning Software

WHEN IT COMES TO business application software, I opt for the largest and oldest companies. No one can afford to commit to some great software application that may become obsolete or unsupported. I learned this lesson the hard way by purchasing Softbridge financial planning software in its early years. This company built one huge comprehensive program, made no plans to modify it for the future, and within a short period of time sold it to someone else who didn't really support it. Look for a company that has been in the business for some time and ask what their modification and upgrade plans are.

Financial planning software should be flexible enough so that you can address the issues important to you and customize your work product so it will not look like everyone else's. But pretty presentations are not enough; you must be able to have confidence in the underlying calculations as well. Look for detailed audit trails. Unfortunately, the programs that do the best analysis are not necessarily user friendly, and the programs that produce pretty plans are not necessarily analytically sound or flexible.

We have reviewed many financial planning programs and have found that most problems occur in the retirement planning modules. Focus on the detail allowed in the input process. The capital needs analysis calculations should be entirely flexible so that you can change the input for expected returns by asset class. A program that just allows one input for all the investments, with one expected rate of return, for example, is a poor program. The capability of varying the expenses for time periods, including terminating items such as mortgages that mature prior to the end of the projected goal, is also essential. Additionally, you will want to be able to override automatic calculations, such as estimated social security income, and vary the income for time periods as well, to account for part-time work, inheritances, or other unusual inflows.

Very few advisers I interviewed actually use comprehensive financial planning software. They have, over time, devised their own systems, as we have, using a combination of a word processing program, a graphics program such as PowerPoint or Harvard Graphics, and a spreadsheet such as Excel or Lotus. Many claim to have some planning software, such as Leonard or ExecPlan, but few admit to using it on a regular basis. "I just couldn't get comfortable with any packaged software," said Rick Adkins, "so I wrote my own. I know how the calculations are done, and my plans don't look like anyone else's."

We don't use comprehensive financial planning software any longer, either. We prefer to design our own, along with modular programs, and put together a package that looks the way we want it to. I have listed some of the larger providers of software in the Resource chapter. Rather than tell you what experienced advisers are saying about the various products, I have compiled a list of questions that many advisers suggest you pose prior to selection.

◆ **Are you doing comprehensive planning?** If you have no need to prepare net worth, cash flow, and budgeting analysis for your clients, you may consider a stand-alone capital needs analysis program.

◆ **What requirements do you have for the output?** Will you be delivering a big plan with all the graphs and charts, or do you prefer to give summaries and provide education sessions to explain the backup documentation? Some programs have wonderful graphics but you wouldn't want to show the analytical tables to anyone.

◆ **How many people will be using the software?** Does the software work on a network? Do you need multiple licenses?

◆ **Who will be preparing the plans in your office?** Some of the software is big, cumbersome and not user-friendly, but good analytical software just the same. If you're relegating some of the input to assistants, they may not have the level of expertise to pick through the entry screen correctly.

◆ **Is the program flexible?** Can you customize the reports to your own needs and circumstances?

◆ **Will the program allow you to modify information easily** to create different client scenarios?

◆ **Are upgrades included in the basic costs?** How often is the program updated?

◆ **Can it integrate with any other software programs?**

Although we do not use a full comprehensive planning program, we do use retirement planning software to analyze capital needs, the basis for some of our asset allocation design. We have been using M-Preps for this purpose. It is a bit cumbersome but the mathematics are good, and since we don't give our clients the output anyway, it works well. Advisers Jack Firestone and Lynn Hopewell use Golden Years, as do many other planners. In fact, Lynn was instrumental in its design. See Chapter 15, the Resource chapter, for more information on these and other planning software packages.

Portfolio Management Software

ASSUMING YOU WILL be producing your own periodic reviews, you will want to select software providing dependability, mathematically sound analysis of time and dollar-weighted returns, customizable reports, and, at the very least, a Windows-based platform. We have been using Centerpiece since it was first developed. My partner Peter proudly announces that we are user number sixty-four. We have found the Centerpiece folks extraordinarily accommodating as we have grown and made more demands on their software. We have built macros exporting data from Centerpiece to Excel to produce some of the charts that we use in our reviews. Although Centerpiece has rebalancing capabilities, they are limited, so we have written macros to produce our own rebalancing page. A copy of this chart is contained in Chapter 14.

Advent is another one of the biggest players in portfolio management software for advisers. It is expensive, but state-of-the-art. They have customized reports available that you can purchase separately, or for a fee they will design special reports for you.

The other two major players in portfolio management software are DB Cams and Captools. DB Cams has the most comprehensive system, which includes client contact, but because it is so powerful, it can be complicated to learn.

Most planners agree that there are great features and drawbacks to each of the portfolio management software choices. Because software is so difficult to change once you have made the commitment, talk to many advisers before you make your selection. There may be conversion capabilities from one software system to another, but rarely can historical data (such as tax lot basis) be converted effectively. I have included a list of software firms and contact information in the Resource chapter.

Scheduling, Contact Software, and Relationship Management

THE CORE OF YOUR BUSINESS requires good technical and analytical skills. Your expertise will assist you in attracting good clients and gathering assets. Consistently good advice and superior service will help you keep those clients. At the heart of superior service is the ability to know your clients and to manage their expectations. To do that best, you need a good information manager.

In the summer of 1998, Bill Gates gave a speech about technology and business at the Microsoft Summit. "A customer is at the center of your business. That's pretty basic, but how many companies really find it easy to browse and bring up all the information about a customer? Not just the billing information, but also who at that customer company makes the decisions, how do they make use of your product, what is your history with them? Is all that information available in one place so that different parts of your organization that touch the customer can work with each other, know who the others are, and always make sure they are on the same page in terms of what's going on with the customer? I think there are very few companies that even meet that basic level of information availability."

With the advent of the Internet, most people have become information junkies. Those people who have become most successful have also learned that information is power. The hitch is organizing it and learning to store and retrieve it efficiently to your benefit. That is why a good database is essential to success.

There are three alternatives available to you in the selection of a database. You can buy generic contact-management software, buy a ready-built database that is set up for the financial advisory profession, or build your own using database programs such as Microsoft Access.

Pre-Packaged Software

THERE ARE TWO general types of pre-packaged software: contact managers and personal information managers (PIMs). Despite numerous contact software programs available on the market, the planning community primarily uses only two, ACT (www.symantec.com/act/) or Goldmine (www.goldminesw.com/). Both integrate with other Windows-based software and both have many enhancements such as caller ID, direct connection to the Internet, and ample space for client notes and details.

Programs such as the Day-Timer Organizer 200 (www.daytimer.com/technology/software/index.html) and Steven Covey's Franklin/Covey Ascend 97 (www.franklincovey.com/sitemap.html) are personal information managers. They track and manage your schedule, addresses, calls, and so on and share information with popular handheld electronic organizers like the Palm Pilot.

One of the benefits of using pre-packaged software packages is that they are constantly being upgraded, and since the development cost is spread over thousands of users, they are extremely cost efficient. The downside is that the software is generic and you must live within the constraints of the proprietary system. For example, if there are four lines allocated to an address and you need a fifth, there is nothing you can do about it.

Professional Proprietary Software

THE NEXT ALTERNATIVES are those programs written specifically for the industry. Unfortunately, there aren't many, but you can find a fairly comprehensive list along with a brief description at the ICFP BIZ Web site, www.icfpbiz.net/vendorguide/clientmngmtsoft.htm. A few that you should look at include: Financial Planning Consultants Text Library; ProTracker System; Captool Professional Investor; and DbCams+ V1.5.

Warren Mackensen, a financial adviser in New Hampshire, wrote ProTracker, a fairly comprehensive relationship manager. I call it that because it allows more information tracking than most other software offerings. For example, you can keep track of beneficiaries, health care powers, wills, and over-70½ mandatory distribution methods. Warren has spent a significant amount of time refining his program, taking advice and hints from his users to renovate and upgrade frequently. Contact information for all these companies is listed in Chapter 15.

Home Grown Database

THE MOST COMPREHENSIVE (and problematical) solution is to design your own. Our first client database software was Day-Timer. When the data we kept in Day-Timer became too voluminous for us to manage within that system, we recognized we had nowhere to go. About that time, Microsoft had refined Access, their relational database program, so that it was easy to build, flexible, totally integrated, and user-friendly. We made the commitment to hire an Access programmer to build the perfect contact system at $65 an hour, spending over $50,000 to get the exact system we wanted. Everyone in our office participated in the project. We started by making a "wish list." If we could have the perfect system, what information would we want to be readily available? Aside from the obvious information in contact software, we wanted vital items such as "permission to speak to," clients' unique asset allocation models and their history, mandatory distribution methods, and links to client notes and client rebalancing spreadsheets. We soon discovered that we didn't want or need a PIM or a contact manager, we needed a relationship manager.

Probably one of the best illustrations of how useful an in-depth relationship manager can be is my experience with the family and advisers of my client who died last summer. We record a note in our database, which we call HOMER (Helping Ourselves Make Everything Relate), saying whether we have permission to speak with family members or other professionals. We also list beneficiaries and other important data about clients' wills, trusts, and accounts. Shortly after the funeral, my client's attorney called to request that I help him get information to probate the estate. He asked if we knew who the beneficiaries were on all the accounts.

First, I found the client's file in HOMER to ensure that I had permission to speak with the attorney without prior authorization from my client's wife. Since the beneficiary designation and relative percent of interest for each beneficiary is already stored in our database, once I verified my authority to share the information, I simply printed a copy and faxed it to the attorney. He was so impressed with our efficiency, he has subsequently given us several excellent referrals.

Many advisers have taken a similar route and developed their own systems based in Microsoft Access. These solutions are specific to each practice, but all capture the usual data. Karen Speros, of Spero, Smith Investment Advisors, Columbus, Ohio, added an action section to her database, which tracks the progress of a prospect call, through the final disposition. All their correspondence, including letters in response to IAFP, NAPFA, and ICFP referrals, are generated automatically from their database. Karen's office staff is also able to generate engagement letters and referral letters to other planners directly from their system.

Karen divides her client database into financial planning clients and asset management clients. She captures different information for each. For example, for asset management clients, the data include meeting frequency, first billing date, and a termination date (if any). For a financial planning client, Karen's system includes client-specific items such as estate planning details, retirement, and business planning information.

Ross Levin's database is designed around his wealth management index, which he describes in detail in his book, *The Wealth Management Index* (see Chapter 15). At the beginning of the year, Ross, his staff, and his clients decide what tasks need to be accomplished for the year. This may include drawing up new wills, reviewing insurance policies, and investigating long-term care. Whatever the projects, tasks are created in his Access database then e-mailed to the staff involved, as well as his client. Each task becomes a tickler item until it is completed. Access allows Ross complete control and flexibility.

The biggest drawback to developing a customized program is that the design and writing of the database is labor intensive,

Ross Levin's Story

"WE DEVISED OUR Wealth Management Index and built it in Excel spreadsheets. We soon found that although we liked the concept, this format wasn't very efficient." Ideally, Ross wanted to be able to create the action items and send them to those responsible for getting the items completed, including clients. They also needed to be able to report progress on those items, so that everyone involved was up-to-speed. After researching open-format databases, Ross and his group decided to hire a programmer to design their own database according to their specifications. "It's important," says Ross, "when you select your programmer that it is understood that you retain the rights to the end-product. Further, life will be much easier if you select someone who will still be available to you after the project is completed, because, realistically, the project is never completed. Our database is constantly evolving."

disruptive, and expensive. Ross Levin confided, "If I had known all the cost and complications of designing our own database, I would never have attempted it." After $50,000 and hundreds of hours to connect data, our office feels that way, too.

What to Look For

WHETHER YOU DECIDE to design your own or buy proprietary software, you should begin the process by determining what results you're ultimately looking for. The following are items you might want to consider:

GLOBAL
◆ Data integrity: one-time-only entry of all data items
◆ The ability to link directly to your primary word processing, spreadsheet, and portfolio management software
◆ The ability to access the database from outside your office

◆ The ability to synchronize with your portable computers
◆ The ability to sort and mail merge
◆ The ability to link with your existing e-mail, or independently handle e-mail

CLIENT RELATED

◆ Classification(s): prospect, VIP client, asset management client, planning client
◆ Account Information: account location and account number, date opened, type (trust, joint, IRA, etc.), investment policy history, review schedule, billing schedule and source (to account or to client), related account(s), owner(s), trustee(s), beneficiary(s) (and their interest)
◆ Relationships: family, dependent, birthdays, to other client accounts (e.g., trustee, beneficiary)
◆ Advisers: profession, name, phone, address, permission to share information (verbally, copies of reports, statements)
◆ Financial planning issues such as estate planning: wills, trusts, health care powers, date last reviewed, recommendation made, implemented, on file in office
◆ Miscellaneous: 70+ distribution method, gift level, client picture

Whatever you decide, it's imperative that you have a solid system. The average gestation period from inquiry to clienthood approximates that of an elephant's pregnancy. One of the reasons we transfer our prospect information to HOMER is so that we can impress prospects with information they gave us the last time they called. When a prospect calls and says, "You probably don't remember me, but I called two years ago...," I simply pull up my HOMER screen and say "Of course Mr. Winthrop, how is your grandchild Andrew? He must be almost two by now." This is very impressive.

Bells and Whistles

MY PARTNERS ARE gadget and gimmick freaks. I am by nature somewhat lazy, so I am always looking for a faster, better, more efficient way to do anything. They are always looking for something that's fun. Other "techy" advisers I know admit to falling for the latest gimmicks, too. Whatever our inclination, many of us have stumbled across some good stuff that added greatly to our office procedures. We've also stumbled across some that add nothing whatsoever, but could be fun. Here are some of the better discoveries.

Fax Serve Software

ONE OF THE BEST timesaving programs we installed was Cheyenne Fax Serve. Our Novell server functions as a fax, and with this software we can fax materials directly to and from our computers. We still have our fax machine, but it doesn't get much use. If it is necessary to fax a copy of something that is not in our system, we can always scan it in, or send it the old-fashioned way from the central fax machine.

Dictating Software

IF YOU KEEP copious client notes, you may want to consider a nifty little software program that will allow you to dictate your thoughts right into a word processing program on the computer. Our advisers are given the option of using Dragon Dictate to chronicle their client notes. Some find it easier to dictate, then go back and clean up the misunderstood words and strange grammar, and some find it easier just to sit down and type it.

I like doing my dictation on Dragon. It does away with the two-step process of my dictation and my assistant typing it. She just corrects the copy and dispatches it. Dragon is one of two major programs available for this purpose. The other one is Via Voice by IBM. The drawback to any of these programs is that you have to train it by reading to it for an hour before you can even begin to use it. Each time you use it, you can train and correct as well, so that the program gets better and better as it learns your speech style and pronunciation. One of my clients dictated John Grisham's novel *The Firm* to train his system, and now claims 98 percent accuracy.

The Final Word on Technology

THE TECHNOLOGY you acquire is, next to your clients and your staff, the most important asset to the operation of your business, but it should not be the focal point of your business.

◆ Use a professional to help design and develop your technological support. Your consultant's job, ultimately, is to save you time and money.

◆ Don't sacrifice your identity to your software. If your output looks like everyone else's, it may be difficult for people to see your value.

◆ If you are a computer junkie, make a decision. Are you a financial adviser or a computer geek? Time spent with your computer is time you can't spend with clients. If you can't control your computer involvement, change careers.

◆ Customize everything you can.

◆ Involve your staff in major technological decisions; they will be using it, too.

◆ Take extraordinary precautions to protect and back up your data.

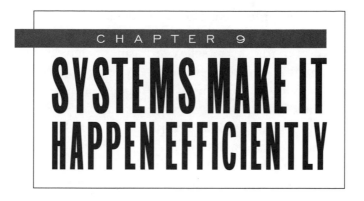

CHAPTER 9

SYSTEMS MAKE IT HAPPEN EFFICIENTLY

The mark of a good executive is to design his company
so that it runs efficiently without him.

— UNKNOWN

THE MORE YOU MOLD your practice into a business, the

more systematized it should become. Whether you are a

sole practitioner or a partner in a firm, systems not only

reduce errors and provide consistent service, but also help

stabilize the business in the event of a crisis, and position

it for eventual sale or transfer. Many advisers have

designed specific routines to ensure completion of tasks,

and to keep clients informed. The key is to keep the systems from interfering with the high-touch customized service you give clients.

If you expect to transfer or sell your business someday, you will want to ensure that you have appropriate systems in place. "Transferability is one of the most important aspects of business valuation," said Mark Tibergien, of Moss Adams LLP in Seattle, whose primary business is valuing financial industry practices. "Businesses that are easily transferable are usually highly systematized, but this does not mean they aren't personal."

I have divided this chapter into two sections: Company Staff Systems—methods that facilitate smooth running of the company, as well as those that keep the staff functioning efficiently; and Client Systems—standardized, systematic procedures for working with clients.

Company Systems

YOU MIGHT REMEMBER pads of paper from about twenty years ago that were used for inter-office memos. Printed at the top were the words, "Avoid Verbal Orders." Today, thanks to the wonders of computerization, almost all advisers I interviewed have an e-mail system, generally as part of their contact or scheduling software, and view it as an integral part of their communication system.

There is no question e-mail has improved intra-office communication drastically. Yet as valuable as we find e-mail to be, it was necessary for us to learn to use it properly. It is never a replacement for face-to-face communication. When we first got our e-mail system running, I would leave long directives to my new secretary each evening. She would answer these directives each morning. I would answer, then she would ask for clarification. This went on for three days until I realized I hadn't seen her during that time. I walked into her office and remarked that she hadn't been in to see me all week. "Oh," she replied, "I thought you felt more comfortable communicating from a distance, you know, the *Wizard of Oz* management style."

Even Bill Gates, at his Microsoft CEO Summit in Seattle in 1998, has acknowledged a problem with the emphasis we often place on e-mail today. "Sometimes people must meet face-to-face. If they are going back and forth more than three or four times on e-mail and are disagreeing, the wise thing is to get together and discuss the matter, because it's very hard to come to an agreement in an electronic mail exchange."

Clarity begins at home, inside the office, by promoting face-to-face conversation among staff. All our office systems are based on checks, balances, and cross training. No one person is totally responsible for the completion of any single project. For small companies or workgroups, this is important. If someone is absent, the work can still be completed.

COMPLIANCE

OUR COMPTROLLER IS also our compliance officer. She subscribes to the National Regulatory Service (NRS) online system, and receives compliance information from our custodian, to ensure we stay current with new regulations. Once a month we meet to discuss any substantive changes in our reporting. She has this information entered in the NRS software program so items are easily changed when necessary. NRS is certainly not the only program available, but most advisers told me this is the software they use. Compliance is one area in which having well-organized, current information is vital. Under present law, our firm has to file only Federally. However, because states do not want to give up the revenue, in reality we are also required to file in the different states in which we have clients. There is far more to compliance than I am able to cover within the scope of this book, but I have learned one important thing: you can never know too much about compliance. Because it is such an important issue, I recommend you get a copy of Katherine Vessenes's *Protecting Your Practice* (Princeton: Bloomberg Press, 1997). Be sure your compliance officer has it as well. It commands high priority on my Gotta Have list in the Resource chapter.

STAFF MEETINGS

ON FRIDAY MORNINGS the office buys breakfast and the staff holds its Up to Speed meetings. Our comptroller/office manager runs these weekly confabs, used to report new information about clients and the status of projects, including our reviews. Principals are not invited unless specifically requested by the staff. Company policies, workflow systems, and client relationships are scrutinized, tweaked, and refined. Only policies that affect core values or a major shift in work responsibilities need to be vetted by me. With this much flexibility, staff is constantly reviewing their processes in favor of more efficient, less time-consuming, or labor-saving programs. The important part of this activity is that staff is empowered to make changes for their benefit and for the benefit of the client. Each staff member views the responsibilities from a different perspective. Their discussions, negotiations, and consensus are the ultimate in teamwork.

Not long ago, our concierge reminded us that although we communicate well with our clients and prospects, we often forget that

---

Task Directive Form

EBK

Internal Directive Sheet

Today's Date: **Re:**

Need by: ❏ **VVIP!**

File In: **Create:**   **Copies:**   **Send:**   **Send by:**   **Other:**

❏ Client File	❏ File in Word	❏ Need ___ Copies
❏ Mutual Fund File	❏ File in Excel	❏ Stapled
❏ Morningstar	❏ EBK Client Blue Bndr	❏ Paper Clipped
❏ Value Line	❏ EBK Prospect File	❏ CC:_____
❏ Schwab Stmnts	❏ City Client Binder	
❏ SEI Statements	❏ Morrison Client Bndr	
❏ Other:_____		

❏ Telephone _____

❏ Schedule _____

❏ Draft _____

Additional Instructions _____

_____

FROM: _____

communication between us is equally, if not more, important. Because we support each other so regularly on various projects, our concierge designed an inter-office directive (see the box below), which gets attached to the material that needs attention. This directive includes everything from mailing instructions to entering information on our database and creating or copying files. This form also allows us to prioritize. VVIP is Very, Very Important, or "If I needed it tomorrow, I would have asked for it tomorrow." ASAP is As Soon As Possible, or "I can wait today, but it better be on your list for tomorrow." Finally, R2 is Round Tu-It, do it when you "get around to it, it's not priority." Additionally, the form facilitates follow-up and has

To:_____

❑ **ASAP**   ❑ **R 2**

❑ Return Envelope   ❑ Messenger   ❑ Enter in H.O.M.E.
❑ Puff PackageqFedex Priority   ❑ KEYWORD
❑ Questionnaire   ❑ Fedex Std
                         ❑ Fedex Box
                         ❑ UPS
                         ❑ Mail

❑ And say_____
❑ Arrange_____
❑ Edit _____

_____
_____

COMPLETED: _____

been designed as an Access template to be e-mailed. This seems like a simple idea, but it saves time. Many advisers have developed similar forms using their personal information or contact manager software.

KEY WORDING

WITH THE VOLUME of materials that pass through advisers' hands each month, some sort of key wording system is essential. We use Day-Timer because its Boolean search capabilities let us search on any logical combination of words that we want. Whenever we see information we think will be useful later, we keyword it, give it a unique number, and type the name of the document and its keywords into the Day-Timer notes section. When someone asks us about variable annuity expenses, for example, we call up the program and search under "variable and annuity and expenses." The program will then list each document containing all of those keywords.

BACK-OFFICE OPERATIONS

WE ARE CONSTANTLY challenged to systematize workflow to save time, be more efficient, and most importantly, to be error-free in our back-office operations. We have met this challenge, as have many advisers, with cross-training efforts. Consequently, our operations teams, as well as all of our advisers, are fully capable of opening accounts. We have selected Schwab as our custodian-partner, and they have provided us with Schwablink, their proprietary software to support advisers. Through this program, we can open accounts, trade electronically, and track client accounts. Jack White, Fidelity, and others have similar programs for their independent advisers. I have included a list of questions to ask custodians in Chapter 12, Transitioning Your Practice. I have also placed in the Resource chapter additional information about the most widely used custodians.

In addition to cross training, our operations director has developed a reference book listing all the different documents required to open any type of account. If he is unavailable, nearly anyone can figure out which form is needed and complete it. One of the other responsibilities of operations is to track the transfers. Our custodian makes that easy by producing a status file we can access at any time.

The status report contains an expected delivery date so we can keep our client informed of the progress.

One system that gets a big workout is the electronic trading facility. Since our own Excel sheet becomes our trading directive, our operations director simply transfers the information to Schwab's form and uploads it. Electronic trading makes it easier for both our office and Schwab's office to catch errors.

Schwab also makes it possible for us to send our billing requests electronically. What a time-saver! Our billing is automatically prepared from Centerpiece (our portfolio software). After spot-checking, our comptroller uploads the file to Schwab; we have a check in twenty-four hours. Of course, we send invoices to clients the week before, but for notification purposes only. Charging the account directly ensures that we can produce performance reports with net-of-fee numbers.

As you review or design your back-office systems, try to computerize routine activities as much as possible. If you are not currently trading online, I recommend that you spend time investigating it.

PROXIES

AS YOU PROBABLY KNOW, if your client gives you a proxy to vote, you have fiduciary responsibility to vote that proxy for them. Moreover, if you are a Registered Investment Advisor, you must have a proxy policy in place stating who makes the decisions and how they are implemented. Custodians such as Schwab and Fidelity provide forms for your clients, giving you permission to accumulate your proxy votes. Take advantage of their offer to provide proxy support.

Over the years, we have found that clients haven't a clue about how to vote these proxies and are more than willing to assign that task to you. We include these documents with our initial paperwork. There are three potential advantages in doing this:

1 You can block-vote all the proxies you hold

2 You vote with authority and knowledge, and the fund companies know it

3 You can work together with other advisers to affect the mutual fund company's proposals

PROTECTION: LOW AND HIGH TECH

IT IS NO EXAGGERATION that a good hacker can probably get into any computer in the world (and probably has). Your obligation to clients, it seems to me, is to do whatever you can to prevent sensitive material from becoming public information. For years we always ignored this issue; after all, we trust all the folks who work for us. This is a mistake, especially if you have outside cleaning people, many visitors, or connections to the Internet. It's important to protect your client files, data, and programs from invasion.

BE CAREFUL WHERE YOU SEND IT

SEVERAL YEARS AGO one of our clients asked us to send a position statement to his office. A helpful assistant decided to fax it, not thinking to alert the client that it was coming. Two hours later, our irate client called screaming that his assets had become public knowledge around his office, since we'd sent the statement to the fax machine in the secretarial pool. Confidential cover sheets rarely "cover" more than the sender's derriere and should at best be a backup security procedure. If you must send a sensitive fax, phone ahead so the receiver can be there to pick it up personally, or ask for a secure fax number.

SHRED IT

YOU DON'T REALIZE how important protecting clients' documents are until you walk outside your office one windy day and one of the papers swirling at your feet is a client's current position statement with his name and address glaring at you from the top of the page. It is sobering to run around, trying to find the trash bag it came from, wading waist high into the dumpster behind your building, ripping open bags with your teeth. I won't reveal who this was, but I will tell you we bought a high-volume shredder the very next day.

CONFIDENTIALITY AGREEMENT

ALTHOUGH OUR OFFICE operates on a need-to-know basis, every staff member must sign a confidentiality agreement. I have included our confidentiality agreement here. We customized it from one that Lou Stanasolovich of Legend Financial Advisors in Pittsburgh shared with us.

Confidentiality Policy

CLIENT CONFIDENTIALITY is of paramount importance in the financial services industry. All client information is considered confidential in accordance with the provisions of the "Code of Ethics and Professional Responsibility" for CFP licensees.

All information about EBK and its clients is considered to be confidential. Employees shall not disclose any confidential information at any time during, *or after*, employment with this firm.

Company files are available to employees in the course of their work on a need to know basis only. No employee shall permit any person whatsoever to examine or make copies of any reports or any other documents prepared by EBK for its clients, or documents that come into an employee's possession by reason of employment with this firm. In the event of confusion regarding the use of information, any person associated with EBK who has a question regarding the propriety of using client information in any manner other than for the benefit of the client, shall ask the Compliance Officer of EBK for a determination of propriety.

Unauthorized use of client lists, or client names, addresses and/or phone numbers, both during employment and after termination of employment, is a potential criminal violation of the laws of the State of Florida.

Upon termination of employment, an employee shall turn over to the Compliance Officer all documents, papers, memoranda, electronic files, and other matter in his or her possession or under his or her control, which may have, in any way, to do with the above-described confidential information.

My signature below indicates that I have read this policy and agree to comply with it.

_____   _____
Employee's signature   Date

Once a year, when we offer our clients a copy of our form ADV Part II, as required by the Securities and Exchange Commission, we remind our clients that our professionals are all bound by the CFP Board Code of Ethics. We also state that everyone in our office has signed our confidentiality agreement.

DATA PROTECTION

NEXT TO TAKING EXCELLENT CARE of your client, protecting their data is of utmost importance. Here are some tips to make your job easier:

◆ Protect entry to your data processing system using the password facility incorporated into the operating system.

◆ Change your password frequently and don't use obvious names or numbers.

◆ Put a screen saver on your system that requires a password to remove. This will guard against someone's copying data onto a floppy disk while you are away from your desk.

◆ Consider using programs such as FolderBolt by Citadel Technology to protect individual folders or programs.

◆ Never leave sensitive data on your monitor if you walk away from your desk, or if you have visitors or staff who do not need to have access to sensitive files.

◆ Password protect your backup files, so that if someone grabs one of your tapes, he or she would not be able to copy it onto another disk without proper authority.

◆ Eliminate guest accounts that have no passwords.

◆ Restrict access from external sources using a firewall or other password protected environments.

Client Systems

I BELIEVE IN INVESTING time to find ways to complete a job faster or more efficiently. Many of the systems I've been talking about were designed to save time.

Our client-related systems were designed specifically to ensure consistent and quality treatment for everyone. We feel good knowing that anyone who calls or visits will go through much the same experience as everyone else.

EBK Client Qualification Form

Person taking call: Date:

Partner assigned: Adviser assigned:

Name of caller:

Address: Telephone home:
Telephone work:
Fax #:
E-mail address:

Communication preference:

___regular mail   ___telephone   ___e-mail   ___fax

Result of 1st Communication:

a. Send puff package & Data Gathering Questionnaire (DGQ)

b. Who are we referring this prospect to: _____

c. Follow-up phone call. When: _____Who:_____

d. Not compatible/do not need to send information.

Receipt of Data Gathering Questionnaire

Date received in office:_____

Does the prospect meet our requirements: Yes____ No____

Date prospect called: _____   By Whom: _____

a. Set an appt. with: ___HRE ___DBK ___PB Time:____ Date:____

b. Other: _____

_____

Action:

a. Puff sent (including DGQ
    & Return Envelope)   _____   _____

b. Added to HOMER (including
    DGQ reference in notes section)   _____   _____

c. Marked as prospect/newsletter   _____   _____

d. Thank-you card sent to referrer
    for sending prospect   _____   _____

e. Notified outside referral source
    of pending prospect   _____   _____

f. Take off of prospect/newsletter list   _____   _____

g. Is any pertinent prospect information   _____   _____
    in the notes section of Homer:

ARE ALL THE BASES COVERED?

Because of our high media profile, we receive many inquiries from people who are not part of our target market. Our client qualification forms (see box on page 179) have been designed on an Access template so that the information we gather can be manipulated easily later. Usually, the responsibility for qualifying the client rests with one of the partners or advisers. However, each staff member is trained to handle an initial call.

Since all of our Access forms are manipulated through Outlook, we can check off material we want to send, record whether there is an appointment pending, and note any other actions that we might want to take. This form is then e-mailed to the advisers, partners, and assistants who may have responsibilities as a result of this call with the prospect.

The reverse side of the client qualification form asks the usual questions: Why are they calling? What do they think we can do for them? We also ask how they learned about our firm and whether they have seen a planner before. We feel it is vitally important to know if they have met with others and what that experience was like. Sometimes it is easy to see a pattern developing. A prospect who tells me that he is suing his last planner is someone I may want to avoid.

We call our informational brochures "Puff Packages." We have elected to forgo slick brochures, instead printing what we want with our color printers. This way, we can customize the package for the person who calls. We used to send many newspaper articles, along with a lengthy missive on who, what, why, and how we work. It is my contention that most people do not really read this stuff. This is one place where our Web site has been useful. My friend, Mark Ralphs, a planner in the United Kingdom, pointed out that a Web site is a better glossy brochure. Bingo. We now refer prospects to our Web site for more information.

Unlike most advisers, we have two puff packages. One is what I refer to as the "tire kicker." This is business-envelope size and tells, as concisely (and inexpensively) as possible, what we do and what it costs. We use these when we suspect that the people who called are not appropriate to our client base, or if they have not been willing to share any additional information with us over the phone.

The other puff package is much more detailed and describes who we are and how we conduct our meetings with clients. We attempt to put people at ease by familiarizing them with the people they will see and the types of issues we will discuss. Seeing a planner can be intimidating. After all, we want to know everything about them, including every stupid investment they've made in the past twenty years. The easier and more comfortable we make this first hurdle, the better. If people want glossy and impressive, we refer them to the Web site.

In preparation for this book, I reviewed dozens of puff packages from some of the most successful advisers around the world. Some were formal, some informal, some colorful and slick. Some just included copies of newspaper articles in which the adviser is quoted. Through this exercise, I discovered one important thing: it probably doesn't make a damn bit of difference how much you send, as long as it correctly reflects your firm and what you have to offer.

THE FIRST APPOINTMENT

PROBABLY THE BIGGEST MISTAKE we made early on was creating a mystique around the partners. When prospects came in for an appointment, they met with one of us. I felt then that our planning sessions were like counseling sessions and should be kept private. Staff was kept at a discreet distance. We finally realized that in order to grow, we needed to dispel the mystique and emphasize the team concept. Today, everyone in our office takes responsibility for some aspect of our clients' lives, and the clients appreciate seeing more brains working on their problems.

Our concierge is usually the official greeter. She gets the clients settled, sees that someone brings in refreshments, and alerts the partners and advisers. We meet in one of the partners' offices, which are more casual and comfortable than a formal conference room. I'd love to take credit for eliminating our conference rooms, but we just outgrew our space and needed them for offices. When I visited Gary Mockler at Kessel Feinstein, in Benmore, South Africa, some of his conference rooms were mini-living rooms, with couches and comfy chairs. There isn't a good reason for putting a desk or table between our clients and us.

Investment Strategy Form

STRATEGY ANALYSIS

RESERVE	OWNER	STYLE	DESCRIPTION	
			CURRENT MMA RESERVES	
			NEW MMA RESERVES	
			TOTAL RESERVES	
MMA	SP		MMA	SWMXX
US-FIXED INC	SP	Sn Govt/Co	D1-A 1	DHHX
	SP	Sn Intm G/O	P-Low Dur	PTDX
		Intm G/C	Black H	BT-MCX
		Sn Muni	Vang M	VWSTX
	SP	Snint Muni	Ihom	LIMIX
	SP	Intm Muni	MorgG	MGMBX
US LARGE	SP	Core	BT Eq	BTIIX
	SP	Value	DI-A Lg	DI-LVX
	SP	Growth	WilsG	WLCGX
US SMALL	SP	SmCap Val	DI-A6-10	DI-SVX
	SP	SmCap Gro	BlackH	PSGIX
INTL EQ	SP	Developed	SEI Intl	SEIIX
	SP	Emerg Mkt	Mong	MNEMX
REAL EST	SP	Reits	DI-A Heal	DFREX
ALTERN	SP	Com Index	Oppen	QRAAX
	SP	Mkt Neutral	Mkt Neu	BMNIX

CURRENT POLICY		RECOMMENDED POLICY		PROPOSED POLICY	
				$0	
				$0	
				$0	
1,000,000	100%	$20,000	2%	$20,000	2%
		$70,000	7%	$70,000	7%
		$40,000	4%	$40,000	4%
			0%		
			0%		
		$80,000	8%	$80,000	8%
		$180,000	18%	$180,000	18%
		$60,000	6%	$60,000	6%
		$100,000	10%	$100,000	10%
		$50,000	5%	$50,000	5%
		$60,000	6%	$60,000	6%
		$40,000	4%	$40,000	4%
		$140,000	14%	$140,000	14%
		$50,000	5%	$50,000	5%
		$30,000	3%	$30,000	3%
		$30,000	3%	$30,000	3%
		$50,000	5%	$50,000	5%

PLAN FORMS

WE PREPARE an investment policy for every new client. The policy document includes the client's goals and objectives, our expectations for returns, a target return, asset allocation policy, and financial planning observations. Because we have not found financial planning software that we like, we designed our own, using several pages of Word documents, some Excel spreadsheets, and Power-Point charts. Since my partner Harold describes the process in his book, *Wealth Management* (New York: McGraw-Hill, 1997). I will not go into that here. However, I will describe some of the forms that we find useful in putting this policy together.

The heart of the policy document is the Excel spreadsheet, we call "Investment Strategy," that lists all of the clients' assets by asset class, ownership of the assets, and current value. If necessary, we include two sheets, one that lists all of the clients' assets, and another listing only those assets they wish us to manage. This Excel spreadsheet is stored in the client's data file. This sheet (see box on pages 182–83) also lists the optimal investment policy to accomplish the clients' goals (marked "recommended policy"). We also include a column we call "proposed policy," which takes into consideration the constraints of the clients' existing portfolio. Hidden columns also include names of the new assets we want to recommend, as well as their CUSIP numbers. We expand these when we present our action plan. This form is also a trading ticket when we are ready to implement. The asset ownership column controls hidden columns on the side of the spreadsheet so we can easily tally the value of each account. This is especially useful when we are rebalancing accounts. We have built a macro to move data from our portfolio management software to Excel so that we can download existing prices for rebalancing purposes.

CLIENT FILES AND DIRECTORIES

WE KEEP OUR CLIENT FILES in large notebooks, with dividers for different aspects of their planning engagement, such as their financial plan, estate plans, and investment recommendations. Each adviser is assigned a number of client relationships and client files are kept in a central file area .

Mark Balasa's Story

"WE NEVER WANTED OUR reviews to look like anyone else's," says Mark Balasa of Balasa & Hoffman, Inc., Schaumburg, Illinois. "Unfortunately, most portfolio management software is not integrated. A few years ago, you couldn't even transfer performance numbers to Excel documents. We would print them, then enter them to Excel by hand so we could make them more attractive and add little pie charts. This made the preparation for our reviews cumbersome. Then we discovered the capability of using a macro to convert the data to a template. The macro would dump the data to Excel then drop the numbers into our predesigned template. No more hand entering. It saved us days every month in review preparation time."

Often some of the simplest and most obvious things are overlooked. One year we hosted an intern from Jerry Mason's financial planning courses at Texas Tech. Our intern, Dan Mauck, spent the summer with us, working on special projects and assisting in the preparation of plans. At the time, our printer was located in a narrow hallway and filing area that had doors at either end. In order to get material from the printer, it was necessary to close one of the doors or reach around it to the printer. This was a nuisance, but we had no other place to put the printer. At his exit interview, I asked Dan if he had any comments or observations about our practice that he wanted to share with me. He led with, "Why don't you take the door off the hinges so you can get to the printer?" When I stopped laughing, we called the building engineer immediately and had the door removed.

Similarly, for the first five years of our practice, we kept our electronic documents in separate files according to the programs that were needed to run them, Word files in a Client Word file, Excel files in a Client Excel file, and so on. One day it occurred to me that Word and Excel applications default to look only for the documents with their own extensions (.doc or .xls). Now we know how much easier it is to have all the client documents stored in one place, regardless of what file extensions they use. This is infinitely easier for archiving as well.

STANDARDIZING REVIEW APPOINTMENTS

WHEN I WAS in the real estate management business in Chicago, the renters all over the city moved in October and May because that's when rental leases expired. This meant that twice a year we worked long hours reviewing all the upcoming leases to ensure that we caught all the escalation clauses, assigning new rents or drawing up new documents. The load was lighter the rest of the time, but during those weeks before May and October, I seldom went home before midnight. After years of this, one day we figured out that if we staggered the lease expiration dates, we could monitor just a certain number each month, avoiding the mad rush twice a year. Since many of our renters were students, they appreciated the opportunity to have odd lease expirations, anyway.

People's lives are not divided neatly into four calendar quarters either. It is generally immaterial to most people when you sit down and review their portfolios, so we do not review everyone on a calendar quarter. Each person is assigned a review schedule according to the month he became a client. As a consequence, we review one-quarter of our client base each month.

One happy quirk of a staggered schedule is that since most indices are reported by calendar year, it is hard for clients to track their short-term returns when they have odd review quarters, which is great—we don't *want* them to think in the short term. We don't assume that clients will want a quarterly review appointment, so we call them early in the month, offering alternatives, such as a phone review instead of an office appointment.

In our effort to de-emphasize short-term investment performance and emphasize the greater importance of ongoing financial planning, we design our review meetings around one of four financial planning themes: estate planning, income tax, property and casualty insurance, and retirement planning. These themes alternate every second review. Thus each theme lasts for two quarters, all planning aspects are revisited every two years.

For example, prior to the estate planning quarterly we request updated copies of clients' estate planning documents. We have these reviewed by a qualified estate-planning attorney prior to our meeting and we discuss the issues with clients during our meeting. The next quarterly is a follow-up estate planning discussion to ensure that any required action has been taken. The subsequent quarterly might be focused on our clients' property and casualty issues. Prior to that meeting we will obtain updated copies of all appropriate insurance policies and have them reviewed by a P and C specialist. We will discuss the recommendations and follow up to confirm all is well at the next quarterly meeting.

Naturally, at all meetings we discuss the investment portfolio. However, we minimize the importance of performance. Our investment reviews are specifically designed to manage our clients' expectations. We purposely put the performance pages last. I will cover this in greater detail under managing client expectations in Chapter 14.

Many internal eyes see our reviews, starting with the operations assistant who runs the intervals and prints the positions and performance pages. Our reviews are customized, using charts from PowerPoint and Excel. We include a manager review list generated in Word. The reviews are collated, then sent to the adviser who analyzes them for rebalancing and adjustments. Finally, they are presented to the partners. A quality-control sheet is attached to each review set. The operations assistant, the adviser, and the partner must all sign this sheet before the review is bound and presented or delivered to the client.

Most advisers prepare calendar-quarter reviews for no particular reason other than that is how they started. They also tell me they like to get their reviews in clients' hands within two or three weeks after the close of the review month. We used to aim for that too. Then I realized that the review time is not about producing the paper. As Joe Kopczynski so aptly puts it, "we are not in the paper pushing or report business." We now take as much time as we need to review the notes, client goals, allocations, and reserve accounts. Clients want it right, not necessarily fast, especially if we have told them that is what they should expect.

"NON-MANAGED" ACCOUNTS

BECAUSE OF THE UNIQUE WAY we design portfolios, it is necessary that we divide our accounts into a number of master accounts. Most of our clients are near retirement or retired. They may require cash flow from their portfolios. However, we do not design conventional income portfolios—that is, those built around stocks, dividends, and bond interest. This would force us into using higher income-producing stocks, such as utilities, and higher allocations to fixed income. Those are less growth-oriented investments than the client may need to satisfy his goals.

Individuals do not need dividends and income from their portfolios; they need cash flow. Since our portfolios are designed for total return, we have elected to segregate cash equivalents of eighteen to twenty-four months of expenses in a liquidity reserve account, reinvesting dividends, interest, and capital gains in the investment account. When we rebalance, we review the liquidity fund balance and fund it when necessary. This avoids selling investments for a loss in a down market when the client needs money.

Clients draw their required cash flow from their liquidity account. It is our belief that most people spend their adult lives relying upon a periodic payment in one form or another. Generally this is a salary. When they retire, they instinctively want the assurance that the money they need next month will be available, which is one of the reasons that retirees like municipal bonds. We refer to this as the paycheck syndrome. When up to two years of expenses are socked away in a reserve account, clients are less likely to be irrational about short-term volatility, because they know that the next two years of needed cash flow has been provided for. We refer to these accounts as "non-managed, with discretion" accounts because we do not charge for the balances in these accounts. Let me repeat that—we do not charge for reserve accounts. We do have limited discretion, for the purpose of moving money between investment and reserve accounts. However, we do not download information from the client's brokerage account to our portfolio management software or report on them. Yes, I know that we are giving up a sizable revenue stream. We think this is what separates us from asset managers. To us, the liquidity account is part of our service.

Managed investment accounts are those for which we have discretionary authority. We download the data from Schwab to our portfolio management software, bill on these accounts and produce performance reviews on these accounts. These are maintained under an investment management account.

Because of an SEC ruling requiring us to keep employee-family related accounts separate, we also maintain a separate master account through Schwab. This is much easier for us to track in the event we are audited; we just bring up the electronic file.

We also maintain a master account for a few, non-managed/ non-discretionary tracking accounts. These are for clients who want to do some things on their own. We are happy to maintain the data on these investments; we even offer to provide performance reports. We call these Las Vegas portfolios, explain that we think they will churn themselves to death, but offer to report the performance for them, anyway. We know that after awhile the client will recognize how poorly they're doing. In the interim, we do ask the clients to sign a statement acknowledging that we have no responsibility for them.

CLIENT CONTACT FORMS

WHEN ROSS LEVIN WROTE the *Wealth Management Index* (Irwin New York: McGraw-Hill, 1997.), I gave a copy to our concierge. If you haven't read Ross's book, I recommend it highly. Ross's suggestions for client contacts inspired our own tasking forms. These forms are built on an Access template, and can be sent as e-mail through our personal information manager software, Outlook. Each month, our concierge gives us a list of clients who need care calls, meetings, notes, or other attention. The box on pages 190–91 is a sample of our form.

SYSTEMS MAKE THE DIFFERENCE

SYSTEMATIZING YOUR PRACTICE is essential for client retention, for saving money, for efficiency, consistency, and ultimately, for transfer or sale. I've given you some ideas about systematizing your own practice. As you review what you're doing now, keep the following hints in mind:

Task Manager 1999

Client Name: Level:

Personal interests/possible reason for call

_____

_____

_____

_____

_____

Client Contact	Jan	Feb
Care call from partner		
Care call from adviser		
Flash report		
Article of interest		
Review cycle—ptnr/adv		
Estate planning review		
Special event		
Birthdays		

Client Contact	Aug	Sep
Care call from partner		
Care call from adviser		
Flash report		
Article of interest		
Review cycle—ptnr/adv		
Estate planning review		
Special event		
Birthdays		

Goals: 1 _____

2 _____

3 _____

Mar	Apr	May	Jun	Jul

Oct	Nov	Dec	Jan-00	Feb-00

◆ Any activity that has multiple steps should have a checklist so that no steps are forgotten.

◆ To the extent possible, important tasks should employ a system of checks and balances, necessitating more than one pair of eyes to review.

◆ For critical tasks, have a designated backup person and complete documentation.

◆ Consider outsourcing activities that are time consuming and not productive. In the long run, buying these services may save you money.

SECTION

FOUR

THE
GROWING

ADVISERS MAY AGREE TO special services or a poor fee structure for difficult or needy clients, because they want the work. As a practice matures, these relationships are the most time-consuming, the least rewarding, and often the most unpleasant. A profitable client base with healthy rapport is threatened when time and money are wasted maintaining unsuitable relationships. This section is concerned with defining, profiling, and positioning the practice, including transitioning from one style to another, and making the most of public relations.

CHAPTER 10

KILLING THE SACRED COWS

Do it now. The business obituary pages are filled
with planners who waited.

— HARRY BECKWITH, *Selling the Invisible*

ENTREPRENEURS ARE VISIONARIES and dreamers,

but most of all, risk-takers. Considering that the

financial advisory profession has been largely entrepre-

neurial, it is interesting to discover areas where advisers

balk at taking risks. Sacred cows—"we do it this

way because we've always done it this way"—are

akin to Linus's security blanket. They provide a false sense of safety.

Reverence for sacred cows seems to be an endemic problem in planning firms. I find it most often when I talk to advisers about committing to minimums or limiting practices to a finite and narrow client base. Some of this risk avoidance may stem from many of us having started out in the product business. We learned sales techniques. We took courses in it. The goal was to make the sale, any sale. All sales were good sales.

Once I took a "closing" seminar. I walked out with no less than 112 one-liners to "close the client." "Don't let the prospect get out the door," they told us. Never ask, "Would you like to buy this one?" Ask, "Which one of these are you buying?" This emphasis on closings may account for our need to capture every prospect that walks in the door. I have a good friend, an adviser who tracks his monthly and annual closings. He keeps these statistics at hand, impressing everyone in our business with his 80 percent conversion ratio. Meanwhile, he complains that he is overworked and his staff is overwhelmed. I talked with his planning director about this. "We do comprehensive plans here, but many of the people we take don't fit our profile. We really don't get paid for all the work we do on the plans." It's not that his firm doesn't have specific client profile and minimum criteria. My friend simply ignores his own standards because a prospect turns up and he loves the challenge of "closing" him.

The Sacred Cows

IF YOU'RE BREATHING, YOU CAN BE MY CLIENT

I LOVED THE Julia Roberts and Richard Gere movie, *Pretty Woman*. The heart-of-gold-hooker, rags-to-riches theme is appealing to nearly everyone. In the film, these lovable street-walkers always leave each other with the salutation, "Take care 'a you." This is my advice to all you planners out there. I use it to mean, "don't take troublesome clients." (I cleaned that up.)

Stewart Welch told me that once he decided to grow his practice, he set a dollar amount goal for each month. Quite often he agreed to take inappropriate clients or difficult relationships because it added to the bottom line and helped him reach his monthly goal. In Stewart's office, he is the rainmaker. But once he establishes the relationship, his director of planning maintains the relationship. It finally dawned on Stewart that he was not committing himself to these difficult relationships; he was committing his staff. "It's kind of like the movie *Jeremiah Johnson*," Stewart says. "Two hunters have been stalking a huge bear for days. One day, one of the hunters is sitting in the cabin, cleaning his gun. The second man rushes through the door, the bear chasing close behind. 'I caught 'im,' the man yells breathlessly, 'now you skin 'im!'"

If you are the rainmaker for your firm, resist the temptation to close each prospect. Rather than tracking "closings," track the "openings;" those people who fit your criteria and with whom you'd enjoy an ongoing relationship.

I NEED LOW MINIMUMS TO ATTRACT CLIENTS

THERE IS SOME CONTROVERSY about creating minimum criteria for your practice. Note here that "minimum criteria" do not necessarily have to translate into a dollar figure. It is good business practice to restrict your advice to those clients with whom you have an affinity and whose problems you're interested in solving. You shouldn't try to be all things to all people. At the very least, you should like the people you take on as clients. Diana Kahn, at The Financial Pharmacist, Inc., in Miami, Florida, has the following minimum criteria for the clients with whom she will work. None of these criteria involves minimum investable assets.

◆ They want to do the planning themselves.
◆ They nevertheless recognize that they need help.
◆ And they're willing to be guided and educated.

When planning the future of your practice, it is necessary to address the use of minimums. For example, you may wish to increase your practice by increasing the number of clients and would consequently set a low minimum portfolio size. We elected to expand our practice by attracting fewer but higher-net-worth clients. We set our first minimum at $100,000 investable assets, but we still took anyone who walked in the door or in any way expressed interest in becoming a client. A year later, I proposed we move the minimum to $300,000. Both of my partners choked. Yet, each time we raised minimums, and actually stuck to them, more business came in the door. When we decided to join Schwab Institutional's AdvisorSource, they tried to discourage us from using a million-dollar minimum, but we did anyway. Schwab was sure that we'd get no referrals. On the contrary, we got quality referrals that we turned into great client relationships.

Last year at our annual retreat, our staff requested that our minimums be increased to $2 million. Let's think about this for a minute. This is not a leap of faith here. It just makes good sense. Who do you get your referrals from? Existing clients? Existing clients tend to refer friends who are in the same financial situation. It is rare that someone with a half million in investable assets will pal around with someone who has four times that much. Do you really think that the CEO of a major corporation will want to use the same financial planner that his secretary uses? The success of this philosophy has been proven to us time and again.

Two years ago a woman called us for an appointment. We agreed that she did not fit our client profile. It is our policy and commitment to prospects that we will help them find the appropriate planner, so we gave her the names of two advisers in our area. We think highly of them and they have lower minimums. The following year, the woman's father called us, at her suggestion, because he had substantial assets and was not happy with his adviser. Although she was still working with her adviser, she did not recommend him because his client base consisted of people with fewer dollars and she did not think that he would be appropriate for someone with her dad's significant net worth.

MAYBE THEY KNOW SOMEONE RICH

THE EXAMPLE ABOVE is a first cousin to what I call "opportunity" clients. You know they are not particularly desirable clients but they may lead to an opportunity. I fell for that sacred cow and played that game for years. None of these people proved to be a great referral source for my target market. They required time and attention and often had different needs than my regular client base. Often I felt I was short-changing my opportunity clients because they needed services that I didn't have or want to provide.

For example, for my target clients, planning their cash flow needs did not involve budgeting or entail preparing a cash flow statement to help them identify discretionary income to accomplish goals. It usually concerned planning techniques for retirement distributions, or maximizing their estate transfer. It is far easier, and more profitable, to offer to find a new and appropriate planning relationship for opportunity clients than to attempt to do something that you are not really prepared to do.

IF YOU ASK, I WILL STAND ON MY HEAD

THIS IS ANOTHER COMPROMISE we make early on in our practices when we don't have many clients and customized, irregular services don't cost us much. If you're new to this business, don't start it. If you've got a seasoned practice and you are still doing it, cut it out.

Jack Firestone of Firestone Capital Management in Miami, Florida, shared this story with me. He had been working with his client Mr. Reeves since 1991. Suddenly, during the great bull market beginning in 1996, Mr. Reeves asked him to change his reviews to the calendar quarter so that he could compare his returns to the S&P 500. Jack explained that this was an inappropriate benchmark, since less than 20 percent of the client's assets were in large company stocks. The client insisted. After all, he said, "that's what's in the news every day."

Jack began to review his relationship with this client. Over the prior five years, the client spent more time on the phone with Jack looking for more reassurance than any other client he had. In 1994 when the market ended relatively flat for the year, the client was unhappy that he did not get a better return. When 1995 began an amazing run in the domestic large company market, his client was upset because he wasn't getting those returns in his portfolio.

Jack could do one of two things. He could do what the client requested or he could do what he knew was right. I related my similar circumstance to Jack. I asked a client of mine, "Just what do you pay me for?" "I pay you for advice," he answered. "Then why don't you take it?" I responded. I explained that I did not feel it was in his best interest to compare his returns to the S&P 500. I then offered to recommend another adviser. The client asked to stay. He's still my client. Jack still has his, too.

Presumably clients come to you for your expertise and advice, not for the frequency of reporting, the format of the reports, or the additional material you have to include in each different report. If the suggestions you receive from clients are good and worth implementing, then offer them for everyone. If it's not appropriate, yet your client insists on extraordinary special requests, introduce your client to another planner. Life is too short. Furthermore, if you want a profitable, efficient, and marketable practice, you'll want to systemize as much as possible, without losing the uniqueness of your service relationship.

YOU MUST MEET WITH CLIENTS QUARTERLY

ROY DILIBERTO MAINTAINS that it took him "only several years" to realize that quarterly meetings were not essential to client retention. When a client asks, "How often will we meet?", Roy asks, "How often do you want to meet?" Every year he completes a questionnaire with the client to note if anything substantive has changed. Some clients talk with him two or three times per week; others two or three times a year, their choice.

Paul Brady of Brady & Associates of Sydney, Australia, says he does not have regular quarterly appointments. He does have what he terms "cluster meetings" for his clients, however. At least once a year he invites a select group of clients and a top-notch speaker from the financial services field to a private room in a luxury hotel in downtown Sydney. Clients are encouraged to bring friends. This becomes not only a client information meeting, but is also a good source for referrals.

I'LL BE RIGHT OVER

MY FIRST CLIENTS were little old ladies in the Chicagoland area. I didn't have many clients so we both had plenty of time. It seemed logical to go to their homes to discuss their financial plans over tea and cookies. After all, I was in the service business, wasn't I? They showed me pictures of their grandchildren and we planned their futures, too. Many of us in this industry started that way.

In the early days of planning, we were considered salespeople, not professionals. We traveled to make the sale. With my new partners, we agreed that we would not visit clients, except under extraordinary circumstances. Early on, this wasn't a hard and fast rule and many times we traveled, rationalizing that our high net worth clients wanted superior service, which included accommodating their schedules. Most of the time we found that the more accommodating we were, the more we were treated like salespeople, not professionals.

Today, it is very rare that someone will ask us to leave our offices for meetings. We generally refuse if they do. We consider ourselves professionals. Doctors and attorneys expect to conduct business in their offices. So do we. Clients come to see us from all over the country. (I'll admit that it doesn't hurt that we are in South Florida.) This is one choice that has never cost us a relationship. In fact, prospects and clients appreciate that we take the use of our time seriously.

IF YOU FEED THEM, THEY WILL COME

IN MIAMI YOU CAN hold a seminar every day in the high rise condominiums on the beach. You can usually get about fifty to sixty people to attend depending upon the weather and what you serve. If it's a sunny day and you serve only orange juice and doughnuts, you'll get a handful of attendees. Rain and brunch yields tons of warm bodies; most of whom won't fit your client base or already have more financial advisory relationships than they can handle. Unfortunately, rain or shine, none of these people is particularly interested in what you have to say but they are interested in what you have to serve. They're bored and you are the entertainment. Better yet, you're paying for lunch.

Small-scale, exclusive seminars have worked well for many advisers. When Robert Levitt, of Levitt Novacoff & Co., wanted to generate new business in his firm's location of Boca Raton, Florida, he put an ad in the paper, advertising a seminar on selecting mutual funds. The ad specified that space was limited. When ten people signed up for the seminar, he told the rest of the callers that the seminar was filled, offering to sign them up for the following week. It worked. People liked the exclusivity and took the seminars seriously. He gave these seminars every week for a month.

This isn't really a book dedicated to marketing, so I won't go into detail about what will work and what won't work for you. Just remember, whatever you select as a marketing strategy, don't pander.

IF I DON'T TAKE THEM, THE SHARKS WILL EAT THEM ALIVE

YOU CAN ARGUE with me all you want but it is my personal belief that most financial planners are closet social workers. We love getting into a case, coaching, counseling, and giving substantive advice that really affects lives. We go home each evening feeling renewed, energized, and full of self-worth.

Things go along pretty well, then one day a little old lady steps into our office, has limited investable assets, a ton of personal problems beginning with the facts that her husband just died, her daughter is on drugs, and she knows absolutely nothing about finances. You know that if you don't take this one, she will get lousy advice from someone else, lose all the money her hard-working husband left her, and wind up living on the streets within five years. She doesn't fit your profile, probably can't even afford your fees but, if you help her, by the time you're finished, you could probably get her daughter into drug rehab and double her money, while improving her quality of life. It won't take much time, either. Get real!

Truthfully, I still do so much pro bono work in my professional career, I often think I work for a nonprofit organization. It is perfectly okay for you to get paid for the work that you do. But remember, it is perfectly okay for you to take clients that you want to take. Just be sure you know why you are taking them.

Dorothy Bossung, a financial planner at Ernst & Young, told me that she would suggest that all planners work for a big accounting firm, logging in hours and billing hourly for their time before they try to work on their own. "Billing for time really helps you put time management, and the selection of the clients you will work with, in perspective."

PERFORMANCE IS PARAMOUNT

WE ALWAYS PROVIDED quarterly and year-to-date performance returns in our reviews. Everyone does. One day we asked ourselves what message we were sending our clients by listing short-term performance, when we are constantly preaching the need for a portfolio with a long-term time horizon. It really made no sense, but of course peer pressure is mighty. We argued over this point for months until we took Nike's advice to "Just Do It." We did. We waited for the barrage of calls, questioning us about the absence of short-term performance numbers. We received three calls, all of them just asking if we had forgotten a line in the review. When we explained, they agreed it wasn't necessary.

We took the same tack when we omitted the page of index returns in our quarterly reviews. One day we just agreed that comparing managers to their benchmarks was a function of our job, not the clients'. Although we were perfectly willing and prepared to discuss it with any clients who asked, no one called.

CLIENTS NEED A FULL UNDERSTANDING OF MPT

ROY DILIBERTO ADMITS that at his firm they used to beat clients over the head with education on Modern Portfolio Theory. They'd explain Sharpe Ratios, Alphas, Betas. They would, in fact, have a lengthy discussion of whether Beta was dead. Most people didn't know what Beta was, let alone whether it was dead or not. Furthermore, they didn't care. "We finally shot this cow," said Roy. "Clients only want to know two things: 1) Are you competent? and 2) Do you put their interests first?"

SHE'S TOO OLD TO SURF THE NET

MY AUNT RUTH, who is eighty-six, sent me her e-mail address last year. She told me she knew how to do only one thing on the Internet—send and receive mail. However, weekends her son was training her to "surf the Net." This year on a weekly basis, Aunt

Ruth sends me electronic, musical, animated Care Bear cards with cute, "Thinking of you," notes that she's composed herself.

Last week my partner's eighty-three-year-old cousin e-mailed him to get his parents' (also in their eighties) e-mail address. They were developing an e-mail list of all their friends and family.

I assumed we could not communicate by e-mail to our over-seventy-five age group. We sent flash-faxes and e-mail notes to many clients, but just assumed that at a certain age, technology would be beyond them. How wrong I was. Our over-age-seventy-five clients is the group that is the most active online with me. Go figure. They find something that piques their interest and write me to ask what I think about it. They suggest Web sites for me to visit; they download their positions into files they keep current themselves.

I DON'T HAVE ANY SACRED COWS

I WAS AMAZED at the number of planners I interviewed who emphatically stated that they did not have any sacred cows. I have been in business over twenty years and from my experience and perspective, these people are in denial. It is virtually impossible to resist complacency, especially when you are preoccupied with other issues like increasing your practice. Keep in mind, just because something works doesn't mean it is working well.

I use the "T" account principle to locate hidden sacred cows and review any changes I may contemplate within the practice. To do this, draw a "T." As you review your procedures, systems, philosophies, put the positive attributes on the left, the negative ones on the right. This will allow you to visualize the impact these various decisions can have on your business. Consider:

◆ Why do we do it this way?

◆ If we change it, will it have a substantive effect (positively or negatively) on our clients, our office, or our company?

◆ What could be the "worst case" outcome?

◆ What could be the "best case" outcome?

Challenging your current practices and exploring new solutions and systems will make your business dynamic, successful, and profitable.

Finally, One Sacred Cow to Keep...

REMEMBER YOUR ROOTS. Just what brought you to this business, anyway? For most of the advisers I know, it was not the money. I'm not downplaying the money, but I think we all appreciate that we have a unique opportunity to affect lives. I like Charlie Haines's mission statement, "...to improve the quality of our client's lives." Notice he doesn't say, "improve the quality of their *financial* lives." If you think you've moved away from managing the client to managing the portfolio, I suggest a return to your roots.

CHAPTER 11

POSITIONING & PUBLIC RELATIONS

So you were misquoted, but did they spell your
name right?

— HAROLD EVENSKY

DR. MARTHA ROGERS, partner of 1:1, Inc., of Stamford,

Connecticut, has written an exceptionally insightful book

called *Enterprise One to One.* Her premise is that your mar-

keting should not consist of blitzing a huge audience offer-

ing the same thing to many. Instead, her model is to provide

an array of services to one customer at a time. Think about

your practice. It is built on relationships with individuals.

You get to know them, educate them, watch over their money, and help them meet their goals. We've spent years convincing people that they are unique. Their goals are different from anyone else's. In fact, twenty years ago, one of the standard lines I used was, "You wouldn't take your neighbor's prescription medicine. Why would you take his investment advice? What's good for him isn't necessarily good for you." Yet, as soon as the prospect became my client, I began to treat him the way I treated my other clients. I made a financial plan for him, which essentially looked the same as every other plan I wrote. I put him in the same investments as every other client, and my reports to him were exactly the same as everyone else received. I justified this by explaining that standardization was necessary to ensure that each client received the best service. Furthermore, I could help more people, using mass production. Horse puckey! I was institutionalizing and standardizing a very personal, unique relationship. My service was a system and my clients were being processed through the system. Henry Ford's first customers could have any color car they wanted as long as it was black. My clients could have any service as long as it was the one I offered.

Mark Ralphs, of Financial Advisory Consultants in the United Kingdom, told me that he can work with, at most, fifty clients. When the number of clients gets perilously close to that, he reviews his client base to determine if anyone should be graduated, or he stops entering into new relationships. "I realized early on that I can only be effective in the lives of so many people. But while they are clients, I am the adviser of the whole person, not just their financial affairs."

Judy Shine, of Shine Investment Advisory Services in Englewood, Colorado, explains that her company remains small by choice. Her client base is limited to people whose needs and circumstances are similar, but her relationship with each one is dictated by the services and support they believe they require. "In a way," explains Judy, "my client base has defined me."

Believe It!

I AM NOT A MARKETING EXPERT. Neither are any of the advisers I know. But, we've got two things going for us. We believe in the service we have to offer our clients, and because we are able to communicate that, our clients trust us. We are constantly positioning ourselves—with prospects, with our clients, and with the media.

When I was a kid, my sister Sharon had a Tupperware distributorship. Tupperware was sold on a home party system. My sister's sales force would go into a home, set up a display, and demonstrate the use of various plastic storage containers to the attendees while serving them coffee and cookies. One day, Sharon took me along while she trained a new sales person. Sharon and her trainee set up the display and sat down with cups of coffee. The party attendees wandered to the table, picked up the brightly colored containers. Soon they were telling each other how they used this piece and how they loved that one. Many sat down and filled out an order form on the spot. Sharon and her trainee drank coffee and kibitzed with the other women. Later I asked her why she didn't get up and demonstrate the pieces like the other salespeople I'd seen. "Deena," she said, "when you believe in your product, it doesn't have to be sold. It's bought."

I apply this concept to our services. Our clients come to us for our expertise and advice. I used to have difficulty giving an answer to the question, "What is your performance?" This question is plain enough to the money manager who needs to maximize returns and, in fact, stakes his reputation on making the list of the top ten mutual funds of the last ten minutes. But, I meandered through my answers, giving performance numbers for different asset classes, explaining that overall performance is based on the percentage of exposure to each class. It was a miserable response. My clients wanted a number. I was giving theory.

Today, the very first statement I make goes something like this, "If we work together, we will teach that performance is not the primary criterion for a successful portfolio. We will teach you the value of a consistent return over time and how that return can help you reach your goals. After all, isn't achieving your goals your primary concern? Wouldn't that make your portfolio a success?" I firmly believe my services consist of helping clients sleep well at night while they achieve their goals. I don't promise performance. I don't promise to beat any market. In fact, when one asset class is booming, I can promise that their portfolios will not do as well as that one asset class. Asset allocation does not maximize the client's total return; it helps them reach their goals. From the very first meeting, my main responsibility is to get that message across. I believe it will improve their lives, and I tell them so.

Joe Kopczynski believes that his honesty helps manage the client's expectations as well. "When someone knows what you know, it really changes things. I sit down with a prospect and tell them every screw-up I've ever made. I want people to know that they are dealing with human beings." My partner Harold tells new clients with large accounts that need to be transferred, "I guarantee you that along the line, someone will mess up one or more of the transfers. I also guarantee you that we'll monitor the process, assume the responsibility and see that, in the end, everything comes over properly." David Diesslin goes right to the heart of their expectations and asks them, "If we look ahead five years, what will have made this relationship a success?"

Promote the Whole, Not the "Core" Business

I AM ORIGINALLY from Chicago, home to McDonald's corporate headquarters. Some of my clients worked for McDonald's. In fact, I had the pleasure of visiting Hamburger University one year. Imagine my shock to learn that McDonald's is not in the hamburger business. They will tell you that they are in the thirty-minute-eating-experience business that happens to include hamburgers. One of their most famous tag lines is, "You deserve a break today." It does not say, "You deserve a hamburger today." Although their core business is food, they provide toys, playgrounds, consistency, and an atmosphere for taking a break from a busy day.

Successful advisers have figured out that they are not just in the investment advisory business. Just look at Ross Levin's philosophy statement in Chapter 1. "...we define wealth as integrating all of your resources—financial, emotional, physical and spiritual." Ross is not confining his practice to one aspect of his clients' lives.

Paul Brady of Brady & Associates in Australia says he's a lifestyle consultant. David Diesslin is a self-described client coach. Judy Lau and Judy Shine position themselves as counselors. Smart advisers know that they cannot segregate a client's financial life from the rest of his life. Successful advisers have found ways to incorporate that concept into their practices.

The box below can help determine how you can position yourself in the marketplace. The picture represents the core and supplementary service elements for Federal Express. As you can see, Federal Express does not merely position itself as an overnight transportation and delivery service company. It is in the corporate support business.

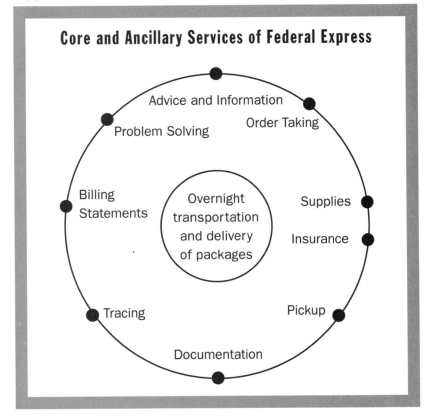

Core and Ancillary Services of Federal Express

Advice and Information

Order Taking

Problem Solving

Billing Statements

Overnight transportation and delivery of packages

Supplies

Insurance

Tracing

Pickup

Documentation

On a blank piece of paper, draw your own circles and write your core business in the center. Then list around the outer circle all the supplemental services you provide. Review all the supplementary services you provide a client and, ignoring for a moment what is written in the core circle, try to devise a statement that focuses on those supplemental services. This exercise may help you position your practice in an entirely different way—the way a client perceives it.

A few months ago my partner Harold was to deliver two speeches, back-to-back, on two coasts. Upon arriving in San Francisco, he discovered that he had not brought his overheads for his second talk, which was in New Jersey. It was a Saturday, and I had the responsibility of getting the overheads to him in New Jersey on a Sunday so that they would be available for his talk at 8:00 A.M. Monday. I called Federal Express and explained my dilemma. The support I received from their representative was amazing. "I think we can make this work," he told me. "It happens that we have Sunday delivery at the Newark airport. Is he going to Newark?" I was relieved to say that he was. "Great. Now," he said, "is he a member of any airline club?" Yes, he was a member of the American Airlines Admiral's Club. "Wonderful," he told me, "they have one at the Newark airport. Here is the address of the local Federal Express office in your town. You deliver your package by 7:00 P.M., addressed in care of the Admiral's Club at Newark. Then call the Admiral's Club in Newark and tell them to expect your package and hold it until your partner arrives. He can pick it up when his flight arrives from San Francisco." Federal Express is definitely not just in the overnight package delivery business. And their employee understood that.

If this sounds as though I am dismissing financial knowledge, expertise and skill in favor of counseling and handholding, rest assured I am not. Obviously, financial advice is the core of your business and you must do it all very well. McDonald's makes good hamburgers. Federal Express delivers packages fast and efficiently. Otherwise neither would survive. You just don't have to promote your core service as if it were the only thing you do.

Who Is Your Competition?

IN THE MID-1980s, I joined Rotary in Chicago. At one of my first meetings, I met the regional director of Delta Airlines. In an attempt to make small talk, I asked him who he considered to be his competition. Since Chicago is the home of United Airlines, I naturally assumed he would name United. He looked me straight in the eye and said, "AT&T. In the future, teleconferencing will probably eliminate the need for much of the business travel." I was shocked at his insight, and began wondering what it meant for my business.

A few years ago, David Pottruck, chairman of Schwab, was asked who his competition was. To our surprise he did not name Fidelity or Jack White. "Merrill Lynch," he told us, "because if they ever want to get in this business, they're so big, they could own it overnight."

Your competition probably does not come from the obvious quarters. Step out of the box and figure out who it is. Then you can prepare to meet it head on. At our firm, we have determined that our competition is not from other advisers, but from a local trust company. They have a 100-year-old tradition of service and fine china in their private dining room. Their fees are high and their returns are mediocre, but their service is impressive. That's where we've attacked. We can't compete with our own private dining room, but we do have superior, attentive service, intensive customer care, and a classy gourmet restaurant nearby, where my nephew is the chef.

Position and Promote Subtly

LAST YEAR I GOT a little booklet in the mail. It was twenty pages on how to create a good business plan. Initially, I didn't pay any attention to who sent it, nor did I much care. Still, it contained some good information, so I stuck it away for future reference. Then another one arrived, this time about hiring and recruiting. Then I received another about designing office space, then one more about business succession. I began to look them over carefully. They were damn good. They were from Chase Vista Funds. Chase didn't write the books, they hired experts to pen them. The last page in each one explained that as a financial company, they understood my needs and wanted to be a partner in my success. There was not one statement in any of those books that touts the excellence of their funds, or their performance. I'm sure they have that material, but that's not what they sent to me. Through these books, this company was subtly telling me that they did not see me as just a distribution channel for their funds.

They saw me as a partner in our mutual future success. The positioning was powerful. I had never looked at these funds before, but I made it a point to visit them at the next industry show. Imagine the impact on your prospects when you position your services differently.

Use Public Relations Wisely

MY PARTNER HAROLD is probably the most widely quoted financial adviser in the nation. He got there because he worked hard at establishing relationships with the media. He stays popular because he learned the value of the "fifteen-second quotable." Harold says he realized years ago that in order to compete with far larger companies, he needed visibility and credibility. While advertising can certainly develop visibility, it is costly and in our industry does not address issues of reputation or status. Good public relations can. He figured that the best way to reach the media was to write to them. So, he began to address letters to specific journalists, commenting on some of their columns. If he found an item of interest, he'd write to compliment them on the effort, then add an additional tidbit to suggest related areas for stories that they may want to pursue in the future, while at the same time demonstrating a knowledge of the subject. The journalists he wrote would file his letters for future reference.

After he started getting calls from the media, he realized that he wouldn't get more unless his remarks were thoughtful, pointed, and memorable. One day while watching a morning news show, it struck him that the best interviewees speak in fifteen-second sound bytes. They must sound intelligent, and they must have something to offer that makes the experience richer for the listener. These attributes are no less important when working with the print media, since reporters are usually on deadline, have limited space to make their point, and must consistently be informative.

It also occurred to Harold that he could not be an expert on every subject, but he could be a good resource. He spent the time and energy to compile a list of other financial service professionals and their expertise. When he received a call that he did not feel comfortable fielding, he would offer another name. Soon, journalists on deadline would call him asking for sources.

You Need a Plan

NOT EVERYONE SEES the value of good public relations. I think it's essential for growth, but it does take time. If you decide to cultivate the media, you will need to develop a public relations plan. It should include the following information:

◆ **Your organization.** Who are you and what sets you apart?

◆ **Public relations objective.** How do you want to influence public opinion?

◆ **Current public exposure.** How much and what type of exposure do you have now?

◆ **Expected public exposure.** What exposure do you want to have, specifically?

◆ **Define the target audience.** Who are you trying to reach?

◆ **Develop a strategy.** What steps will you take to accomplish this plan?

Once you have a plan in place, you will need to have specific action items before you can get started.

◆ Evaluate your publicity strengths: What are your oral and writing skills?

◆ Design a media package: It should include your biographical sketch, brochure, and reprints on your firm and its principals.

◆ Compile a media list: These are the people you want to get to. Don't just use the books in the library. Construct your own by reading the publications and watching and listening to the programs that the audience you wish to reach will be reading, hearing, and seeing. Notice who's writing the stories and producing the programs.

◆ Join a local community or service organization like Rotary or Kiwanis to raise your visibility.

◆ Contribute your time and talent to professional organizations at both the local and national levels. This will raise your visibility within your profession and attract industry media.

◆ Develop your speaking abilities by giving lectures or conducting seminars.

Hone Your Skills

AFTER YOU'VE MADE all these preparations, you still must decide how you will act and react when that first call arrives. Many of the advisers I interviewed for this book have enjoyed good relationships with the media. I have compiled a list of their best suggestions.

◆ **Be aware.** Read everything your clients are likely to read. You should be familiar with what the public is reading and thinking. Your value to the media will be your ability to integrate the issues of concern to the general reader with your own professional expertise.

◆ **Be available and prompt.** If for no other reason than media availability, keep a pager so your office can alert you to a media call. Reporters generally need answers "now." If you are not available they will move on to the next source.

◆ **Be professional.** Don't make negative comments about others in the profession.

◆ **Be prepared.** Always ask if they have a deadline. If you are not comfortable speaking spontaneously, ask to make an appointment to discuss it later.

◆ **Be honest.** If you don't know, don't answer. However, ask the reporter if he or she would like you to find someone who does know. If they say yes, do so *immediately*. If you are unsuccessful, let the reporter know posthaste.

◆ **Be clear and concise.** Journalists rarely have time for long stories or ramblings. They will let you know if they do.

◆ **Be controversial.** Stick your neck out. Say something worth hearing. If you're really a professional you presumably have opinions on professional issues. Be prepared to defend them after they appear in print.

◆ **Be interesting.** Pithy comments will likely wind up in print. News today is as much entertainment as it is information. Recommending that investors buy low and sell high is a good way to send a reporter on to a new source.

◆ **Be confidential.** Don't offer details about specific clients or their circumstances without first discussing it with the clients.

◆ **Be circumspect.** Don't say anything that you would not want to be made public. If you have to preface your statements with, "This is off the record," you probably should not say it in the first place.

◆ **Be respectful.** Good reporters are also professionals. Credit them with knowing more about their profession than you do. Don't try to persuade them to refocus a story. They know why they're asking the questions they do; you don't.

◆ **Be realistic.** You won't always be quoted in a story even if you have been interviewed. Life's not fair, but if you're patient you'll get your fair share.

◆ **Be responsive.** If you're misquoted, determine whether the mistake is serious enough to do something about. You then have two choices: you can ignore it, while vowing never to speak to that reporter again, or you can write a non-confrontational letter, stating "I appreciate your interest in my thoughts. However, it seems that I did not express myself clearly because the quote you used in your article did not reflect my point. What I was trying to say was..."

Why Bother?

I ATTENDED A SESSION on public relations for financial service professionals not long ago. One of the planners explained that he had all the business he wanted and couldn't figure out why he would want to spend time courting the media. We all agreed that this might not be the most effective use of his time now. This is for you to decide. If you believe that your client base is stable, and you can attract new clients without establishing even a local media presence, then by all means, forget it.

Bear in mind that the financial advisory profession is changing rapidly. Conventional marketing techniques may not be enough to ensure growth, and can even be counterproductive if you're selling the wrong features. Subtle positioning of your practice, as well as effective use of public relations, can poise your business for dynamic growth.

CHAPTER 12

TRANSITIONING YOUR PRACTICE

Companies are a lot like people. They go through different stages throughout their lives. Businesses, however do not automatically move forward toward the next level just because they celebrate another birthday.

—JIM WOOD,

Director of Inc.'s Growth Strategy Consulting Group

SUCCESSFUL PLANNERS CAN EXPECT to address one of two scenarios likely to appear in maturing firms. One involves shifting the compensation structure from commission-only to fee and commission, and from fee and commission to fee-only. The second one involves converting an existing fee practice, in a related profession, such as accounting or law, to an advisory practice with asset management.

First, let's look at why some planners suggest that you may want to consider moving to fee-only. Ron Tamayo of Spraker, Fitzgerald and Tamayo in Orlando, Florida, has been a fee-only planner since 1992. He worked with a regional planning firm that accommodated not only fee planners, but also commission-only and fee and commission combination advisers. In 1998, Ron formed a new practice with two commission-based planners, Susan Spraker and Charlie Fitzgerald, with the expressed purpose of becoming a fee-only business. During eleven of fourteen years in practice, Susan was commission-only, then began to take larger clients on a fee basis. Charlie had been commission-only since the day he began. All three felt a commitment to change the way they did business.

"When Ron and Susan told me they wanted to go out on their own and invited me to join them, I did a lot of soul-searching," said Charlie. "Probably the defining moment was when I looked at my $1.5 million life insurance policy and asked myself who I would want to advise my wife and children if I died. Truthfully, I'd choose a fee-only planner. I'd want that guy to be on the line, responsible for helping her achieve her goals for the rest of her life." Charlie feels that the nature of commission business and the need to be a "perpetual marketing machine" may prevent the close counseling relationship necessary for working with the clients he wanted. "Commission work is like the quarterback suiting up for the football game, calling the first play, then walking off the field. I want that player to be in the game until the end. If I'm paying a fee, I am assured that he will be."

Because they were forming a new business entity as well as shifting to fees, Ron, Susan, and Charlie had a potpourri of complex issues to deal with. The business entity issues were discussed earlier in Chapter 2. The issues involved in converting to a fee practice included the following:

Potentials

◆ Create a dependable source of income

◆ Provide independence from a broker/dealer relationship

◆ Position the practice favorably in the eyes of the media

◆ Allow flexibility in selection of investment vehicles and reporting

Perils

◆ **Less income (at least initially).** Consider that in a commission practice an investment of $100,000 will generate a commission, paid up front, of about $4,000. In a fee-only practice with a base fee of 1 percent and a quarterly billing cycle, the initial income would be $250. That's a BIG difference when you're planning your cash flow. "There is no question, you can make more money on a transaction basis," said Susan, "but, with fees you develop different relationships and get paid for them over a longer period of time."

◆ **More accountability.** Clients are more aware of what is happening with their accounts. They receive statements from everyone, including you. You wave their performance under their noses every quarter. Fees are also much more obvious than commissions.

◆ **More service required of you.** You may be incorporating more offerings and amenities into your practice. You will probably be communicating more with your clients as well.

Register with the SEC

IF YOU PROVIDE ADVICE for a fee and you have not already registered with the Security and Exchange Commission, you will need to do this. There are new regulations in place, directing how you must file and whether you must file with your state. I recommend that you contact one of the organizations that specialize in filings, listed in the Resource chapter. The following are examples of the types of questions you will be expected to answer in completing your SEC application.

◆ **Advisory services:** how much of your activities are supervisory and whether or not you use market timing

◆ **Fees:** how they're calculated, when they're payable, and how a client may terminate and get a refund

◆ **Types of clients:** individuals, families, pension plans, endowments

◆ **Types of investments you will recommend and give advice about**

◆ **Methods of analysis:** fundamental, charting, cyclical

◆ **Sources of research information:** annual reports, newspapers, newsletters, on-line sites
◆ **Investment strategies used to implement advice**
◆ **Reviews:** how often you will provide reports and meet with clients

Fees and Minimums

YOU CAN CHARGE BY the hour, by the project, for assets under management, by some calculation of net worth, or any combination of those. Most fee advisers use a combination of a project fee for the initial planning work, then a percentage of the assets they manage.

If you elect to use an asset-based fee, you will need to be clear about the minimum dollar investment you will accept under your fee arrangement. As I did earlier, do the math. If your client has $100,000 to invest and you use load funds, your commission may be four or five percent. If you are charging fees, let's say one percent, you make $1,000 annually. If you charge on a quarterly basis, that is $250 per quarter. How much work can you afford to do for your client?

As I mentioned in earlier chapters, we originally set our minimums at $100,000 investable assets, with no rationale whatsoever. Later, when we decided to analyze our client base, it was with the declared purpose of establishing minimums based upon intelligent thinking. I decided on a cost analysis first. I determined that in consideration of our space, reporting costs, operating costs, including reasonable owner salaries, we needed $3,000 per year to maintain a client relationship. A 1 percent annual fee would suggest a $300,000 minimum.

In the calculation, it is important to include reasonable owner salaries, representing the time you need to spend on the client relationship on an ongoing basis. A few years ago I attended a business-planning seminar for the IAFP presented by Mark Tibergien. As a requirement for the session, attendees had to complete a questionnaire about our businesses. One section asked about overhead costs. Almost everyone in the room wrote down staff salaries, but neglected to include salaries for the owners. When Mark asked how we got paid, we admitted that we thought owner salaries were a function of the profit the company generated. "My God," Tibergien barked at us, "isn't your time worth anything?"

There is controversy about how practices set their fees. Our practice determines fees by the amount of the assets that we manage. I consider the fees paid a retainer and refer to it that way in our practice.

Some advisers charge based on net worth. Planners who have done this admit that there is often resistance from clients who have a significant net worth. These clients balk at paying a fee based on a net worth that the adviser had no role in creating. On the other hand, it does focus the adviser's services away from performance. Joe Kopczynski admits that when he began to charge based on net worth, he had some clients who did not feel comfortable with the arrangement, but eventually, they agreed. "Now it's not hard for my clients to see our value, separate and apart from the asset management, when I charge this way."

When I presented my partners with the $3,000 minimum fee proposal, both froze at the thought of turning business away. Harold stuttered and Peter said he simply could not do it. I persisted. It was a necessity to our business plan. To make it easier, we redesigned our brochure, screened prospects more carefully, and wrote a letter to existing clients outlining our minimums for new clients. We all took a leap of faith and actually declined business, and as you'll recall from Chapter 10, we started getting more business.

Investment Selection

THE COMMON BELIEF is that becoming an independent fee adviser will give you more investment flexibility. In fact, although your selections will be different, you will have fewer options, not more. There is greater flexibility to a portfolio designed around no-load funds, in that you can rebalance when necessary with little concern for penalties or loads. On the other hand, there are limited annuity and insurance choices in the no-load area, particularly if you are intent on becoming totally fee-only and will not maintain licenses to sell product.

Investment Planning

DESIGNING YOUR INVESTMENT POLICY, optimizing portfolios, devising investment criteria, and selecting funds are clearly outside the scope of this book. Nearly every adviser I interviewed suggested four books for advice and support in this area: Roger Gibson's *Asset Allocation,* Harold Evensky's *Wealth Management,* Charles Ellis' *Investment Policy: How to Win the Loser's Game,* and Don Trone's *Management of Investment Decisions.* These are all listed in the Resource chapter.

Select a Custodial Partner

YOU WILL NEED to select a custodian to handle client assets on a fee basis. The three largest players are Schwab, Fidelity, and Jack White (now Waterhouse). Schwab has been supporting independent advisers for ten years, and commands a whopping 80 percent of the marketplace.

Think carefully before you make a decision. Poor back-office operations can destroy a client's trust in you and your organization. Before you make your choice, you will want to consider these issues.

◆ **How easy is it to open accounts?** How long does it take? Can you get forms and supplies online?

◆ **How well do they manage distributions?** If your client needs a check, how difficult is if for you to get it to him?

◆ **What are the procedures for transferring assets?** Do they estimate the time and work involved and keep you well informed of the progress?

◆ **How is data transferred to you?** Most of these companies have their own proprietary software that links to some of the major portfolio management software. Does it tie into what you are currently using? Is it reliable and easy to use?

◆ **How are trades executed?** Can you do the bulk of them electronically?

◆ **What are the fees and transaction costs?**

◆ **What other support systems do they have available?** Some have referral programs and significant soft dollar arrangements (benefits to your company in the way of services or equipment that you may be entitled to when you reach different production levels).

◆ **Do they carry all the investments in your recommended universe?** Ask them what their policy is for adding new funds.

◆ **If you use individual securities, what is the background and education of their staff at the trading desks?**

◆ **How effectively do they protect their institutional clients from the retail market?** (Are they farming your market or are they likely to farm your clients?)

◆ **How do you fit in their target institutional market?** Do they want you for a client?

Manage Client Conversion

ANTICIPATE SOME ATTRITION in your client base once you have made the decision to shift to fees. Some of your clients will not be appropriate for conversion, while others will just be uncomfortable with the new fee program.

When I was in the real estate business in Chicago, if we wanted to rehabilitate a building, we devised a progressive program. We allowed one-third of the leases to lapse and began our work on that one-third of the building. The other two-thirds generated some income so we could eat. When the first third was complete, we leased that space, then began working on the second third. This is the approach I recommend for your own conversion to fees.

Susan Spraker started meeting with her larger clients individually, reviewing their goals, objectives, and portfolio, then explained that henceforth she would be working on a different compensation arrangement. "This seemed to work well," she says. "Clients usually end the conversation with, 'What do I have to do to stay with you?'" Meanwhile, the clients she still worked with on a commission basis were undisturbed.

If you plan to migrate to entirely fee-only, during this period you should identify which clients will be inappropriate for the transition. You will need to decide if you will be able to maintain the relationship on an hourly or project fee basis. In any case, have a list of advisers you'd recommend who you know would take them as new clients.

JERRY NEILL'S STORY

"WHEN I DECIDED TO GO TO FEES, I sat down with one of my biggest clients, explained that I had elected to change my compensation structure, and told him what the new fees would be," says Jerry Neill. "He blanched at the $16,000 fee, when with the commission arrangement, he felt like he was paying nothing. It was the toughest sale I'd ever made. Next time I sat down to convert a client, I first told him of my decision to add services to my practice and outlined them in detail. I explained how these new services would benefit my client. I then calculated the commissions I had reaped and compared that to the fee I would be charging. That went over much better. One thing I learned though, not every client will want to make the change. Just be prepared to let them go."

Straddling the Fence

YOU NEED TO BE AWARE that if you elect to maintain relationships with both a broker-dealer and an institutional custodial partner, you will need to discuss the arrangement with the broker-dealer. There are regulatory constraints. For example, your broker-dealer may want a percentage of your fee business since they are still responsible for you whether you work for commissions or fees. Be sure that you understand the requirements before you get too far in your planning.

Invest in You

USE THE OPPORTUNITY to create a new corporate image or consider a new name, with new brochures and stationery. Like it or not, many of your clients have seen you in a salesman's role, rather than that of counselor or planner. New marketing material and letterhead will help to reposition you in their minds.

Related Professional Practice Changes

THE DISCUSSION SO FAR has been about an existing financial advisory firm's moving to a different business style and compensation method. Plenty of other professionals with overlapping skills are eyeing planning these days. It is reported that thousands of CPAs will be entering the financial planning and asset management business within the next few years. In a 1996 survey completed by *Accounting Today*, 58 percent of the respondents indicated they were already involved in personal financial planning. Not surprisingly, CPAs generally have strong relationships with the clients for whom they provide tax-planning advice. It seemed appropriate that they would gravitate to financial planning and investment advisory. CPAs have their own designation to identify planners, the PFS, although many have embraced the CFP mark.

"The accounting profession is changing," reports Randi Grant, CPA, PFS,CFP at Morrison Brown Argiz in Miami, Florida. "CPAs are looking for new sources of revenue. Many want to provide more support to their current clients. CPAs have the public trust."

Many states have made it easier for CPAs to work in the investment world. In Florida, for example, the CPA membership organization, the FICPA, has formed the CPA Service Corporation to hold securities licenses and provide product sales support. After a career of taking fees, many CPAs are scrambling into the commission business. Randi and her firm have elected to stay fee-only. "Our partners were already concerned about liability. Our clients are used to paying fees to us, and we believe they are more comfortable continuing to do that for investment advice."

One of the biggest hurdles is making the commitment. "This is not a part-time job," says Mark Ritter of Maxwell, Locke, & Ritter, a CPA firm in Austin, Texas. "We assigned two of our partners to the financial planning and investment advisory division. They are no longer responsible for conventional accounting activities." Randi Grant agrees. "The planning CPAs must be relieved from preparing 1040s, for example. We not only need the time to spend with financial planning clients, but we need time to educate our own partners so they are comfortable with the work we are capable of handling now as well."

That's great advice if you have a big practice behind you. You can parcel out the responsibilities and still handle all the accounting activities as well. If you are a sole practitioner, warns Ben Tobias of

Tobias Financial Advisors in Plantation, Florida, you will have to decide what hat you will wear. "I always did a limited amount of financial planning with my clients. If you are doing individual tax returns, you generally do. When I began to offer investment advice to my current clients, it worked for a while, but it's not easy to keep up with both worlds."

Many CPAs see this kind of functional shifting of their practices as a slam-dunk. "Farming our current clients can keep us busy virtually forever," said Randi. "But," she cautions, "you need to handle this with care. There's a lot on the line if you don't handle the relationship well; you not only lose the investment business, but the tax business too."

If you're planning to make this jump, here are some valuable tips from folks who've done it:

◆ Investigate your options carefully. CPAs are in big demand now. Every broker-dealer and asset manager would like your business.

◆ Decide what form of compensation will be most comfortable for you. If you have been charging fees for your entire professional life, you may be uncomfortable positioning yourself with your clients once you begin charging commissions.

◆ Educate your partners. A lack of knowledge and fear of the unknown may prevent them from committing to the change.

◆ Restructure current relationships and delegate work to colleagues, so that you will be able to handle the time commitment.

◆ If you do not have education and training in financial planning, work with someone who does. You cannot be an expert in everything. (The AICPA offers a professional designation for planning, the CPA/PFS [Personal Financial Specialist].)

When you're restructuring your practice, use local resources as much as possible. Roger Smothers, a Certified Financial Planner from Binghamton, New York, who is also a practicing psychologist, has found his local study group extremely helpful as a source of information, as well as a good sounding board. "We are at all different levels of transition. We really can offer substantive advice to each other." Whether you have an existing practice in planning or any other professionally related field, the best advice is to network. Go to the planning industry conferences and conventions and ask questions. The planning and investment community is quite generous with time and information.

THE
CLIENT

I'VE SPOKEN WITH ADVISERS all over the world who tell me that attracting and retaining good clients is a major challenge. This is an issue that potentially presents many heartaches.

This section is concerned with building your clients' trust by understanding their needs, and by managing expectations through superior service and continual communication, increasing solid value for clients.

CHAPTER 13

HIRING, FIRING, & REFUSING CLIENTS

If you give a mouse a cookie,
he's going to ask for a glass of milk.

—LAURA JOFFE NUMEROFF

SOMETIMES WE EITHER DON'T SEE or don't want to see

the obvious, that our client base includes inappropriate

clients. This failure may drag down a practice's ability to

grow. Recently, in a special section in *Fortune (Fortune*

Magazine, Vol. 138, No. 5, September 1998), it was reported

that a radical shift is taking hold in how one thinks about

a customer. Serve a customer at any cost? No. The article

notes that research indicates "… it can be ten times more expensive to acquire a new customer than to keep a current one; yet *more than 50 percent of existing relationships are not profitable*" [my emphasis]. The solution often requires that you fire those inappropriate clients.

One day David Bugen, of Bugen, Stuart, Korn & Cardero in Chatham, New Jersey, was having a particularly rough day. His most difficult client arrived unannounced to bark about recent market performance. David had always been patient with the guy, who seemed to go ballistic without warning and rarely for any good reason. At the start of their relationship he threw a fit because a transfer of funds was delayed by the sending institution. He'd miss appointments, but show up days later expecting to be seen. At the end of this altercation, David wandered into his partner's office, visibly shaken. "Just what am I going to do with this guy?" His partner said, "David, you train people by your behavior. You have trained this guy to treat you miserably. Treating him like a child will elicit childlike behavior. He just had another tantrum."

A friend once told me that a wise investor repurchases his portfolio every day. The same could be said for your client base. Why would you want to throw time, resources and money at a relationship that clearly is not working? At some point in our professional lives, we find it necessary to fire a client. From talking with others in practice, it's safe for me to say that most of us put up with a great deal more than we should before hollering "uncle." We usually have had enough long before we actually find the words and recognize the moment to end it.

I asked thirty top advisers what, in their minds, would necessitate firing a client. Every adviser told me they would instantly sever a relationship with someone who was disrespectful to staff. That's an easy one. We all agreed that we have taken clients over the years that we absolutely shouldn't have. Jerry Neill, a planner in Kansas City, suggests that he would consider firing a client "if I can't educate him, I find I don't like working with him, or he's a lawsuit waiting to happen. Many times you don't see this going into the relationship, but as time goes by, you need to do something about it." Of course, most of us would not have had the courage to do this early in our practices. As Paul Brady from Sydney, Australia says, "The ability to fire a client is one of the benefits of a mature business."

The ability to fire does allow you great freedom. You know that you can terminate a relationship if it's not working, or you can attempt to salvage it. Sometimes it's hard to tell which path you should be taking. Here are some early warning signs for troubled relationships:

◆ You get a sinking feeling each time that client calls.

◆ Each time he is up for review, you hope he won't want an appointment.

◆ There is an increase in the frequency of the times your staff appears in your office to tell you about yet another unpleasant call with Mr. Client.

◆ Each time you meet with him you find yourself going over the same issues.

◆ After a meeting with him, you'd like to put your hand or his head through a wall.

Eleanor explains that she and her partners assign a "hassle factor" to their clients. How difficult or unpleasant is this person? How many times does the client call with the same questions? The higher the factor, the more likely the fees for additional services are charged, or the client is released. Eleanor explains that she does not want to work with any client who seems to be using money in a destructive, greedy, or fraudulent way. She feels that she and her clients must share the same basic values in order for the work to be productive.

There are several issues to consider before you actually decide to release a client:

◆ Do you really want to work with the person? Eleanor says her gut "is never wrong." If she is not feeling good about this relationship, it has to go.

◆ Does your client have unrealistic expectations that can be handled over time, but over the long haul will consume more effort than they repay?

◆ Does having this relationship prevent you from spending more time with other clients? "There's only so much time," says Paul Brady. "I can spend it trying to make this one guy comfortable, or

I can spend it providing ongoing services to several clients who are already comfortable."

◆ Can you or do you want to diffuse this situation with humor? In 1997 Richard Busillo of RTD Advisors received a call from a client unhappy with his mediocre returns from a well-diversified portfolio at a time when the domestic stock market was reaching new highs. "I could've put my money in a shoebox and done better," he barked at Rich. That afternoon, Rich visited the client's office, shoebox under his arm. "What'll it be?" he asked his client. The client broke into a hearty laugh, and Rich talked with him about his short-term time horizon.

◆ Has the relationship broken down? Sometimes relationships that appear to be good at the beginning deteriorate. Ross Levin considers severing the relationship if the client is not forthcoming about information or if there is a "value disconnect," when Ross and the client do not continue to share the same priorities and outlook.

◆ If communication has broken down, is this a control issue or an economic one? Dave Diesslin maintains that conflicts with clients generally stem from one or the other. It's helpful for you to be clear in your mind on how and why the relationship is broken. Mark Ralphs explains that he will never quibble over a fee. If his price tag becomes an issue, he gives the fee back to the client and refuses the engagement.

Ross Levin mentioned that not long ago, he and his partner decided to end a relationship with two of their biggest and most difficult clients. "Anticipating the break was terrible, but it's very liberating once you've done it. The hard part is convincing yourself that you will be able to replace those clients with other, more rewarding relationships." Ross did, we did, and you can too.

But, What Do You Say?

LET'S ASSUME THAT you've gone through the checklists and determined that you need to release a client. What do you say? David Norton of Norton Partners, in Bristol, Great Britain, says he takes his cue from the health care industry. When a family member was too much of a problem to keep in the long-term care facility, the administrator called in the family and told them, "We simply cannot meet Mr. Baker's needs any longer." That's just what David says to clients who can't seem to get comfortable with the relationship.

In our office, we keep copious notes on all conversations with clients. When a relationship has broken down, we can usually tell by the number of times we've referred to the notes. Once a year we review those notes with staff and decide which client we are going to set free. Staff is very much a part of this decision because they are usually the ones who have been abused more than the partners.

We are honest and straightforward. We just tell them that the relationship is not working and we don't think we can help any longer. We usually follow that statement with some examples from our notes. As much as possible, we prefer to do this in person, rather than on the phone. We then recommend that the client seek advice elsewhere and offer a list of advisers who may be more suitable.

For clients who just can't seem to get comfortable taking any advice, we review these situations and point out that it is unnecessary for them to be paying for advice when they only want to follow their own. To them, we suggest they seek a discount brokerage arrangement.

David Diesslin looks at all his client relationships once a year in terms of the economics and pleasure, rating each aspect positively or negatively. If both are negative, David "graduates" them. "The key is to make them feel good about graduating, not upset about being fired." David feels that most advisers stay with their relationships longer than they should. "It's like a bad marriage; we're more afraid of the unknown, so we do nothing until it gets so bad that we can't ignore it any longer." Dave maintains that two percent of the client base is responsible for 98 percent of the headaches.

Here are some good suggestions from experienced practitioners for severing that two percent:

◆ Mark Ralphs, Financial Planning Corporation, in the UK, also graduates his clients. "You don't really need me anymore; you can handle this yourself." Be firm, though—sometimes they need a little push from the nest.

◆ Ron Tamayo, Certified Financial Group in Longwood, Florida, has used "There is just not a chemistry for this relationship to work."

◆ Roy Diliberto describes the communication that is failing between himself and the client. He then explains, "I really don't think I can provide value for the fees you are paying."

◆ Eleanor Blayney says she prefers to position it in such a way that it appears the client is releasing her firm. "We are unable to do what you want," she says.

◆ In some cases, Jerry Neill explains that he is "slowing down," looking toward semi-retirement, and offers to let them work with another person in the firm or move on.

◆ David Norton suggests you "engineer it so they will fire you. That way, you can at least try to keep good relationships, even if you are not working together any longer. I certainly don't refer them to anyone else, particularly if they are a problem. Who wants to wish that on anybody?"

What If They Fire You?

SO FAR THIS CHAPTER has dealt with your decision to part with a client. What if they want to dump you? A couple of years ago, Ross Levin of Accredited Investors in Minneapolis called to talk. "I just lost a client and I feel terrible about it. I looked back over the three years this guy has been a client. I feel I did everything right. When he left, he told me he wanted to do it himself, but I keep thinking, 'What did I do wrong?'" We all lose clients, and it is not unusual to look to yourself when a relationship is broken. It's helpful to take Dave Diesslin's suggestion and ask yourself, "Is it economic, or is it control?"

Ross has spent some time trying to think this though. When you lose a client you want to keep, there are two alternatives, in hindsight: you either had control over the relationship, or you didn't. "The one you agonize about is the one you had control over, but just blew it." Ross admits that systematizing your practice can help you keep clients. He also points out that no matter how hard you try, there will once in a while be that "black cloud" client. "Every mistake possible happens with that guy. There's just not much you can do about it."

"Losing a client may be evidence that you are doing a good job with your business," offers Eleanor Blayney. It means that you have defined your business well and some people just won't fit. If you don't lose a client, you lose yourself." Eleanor also suggests that for some clients there may be a point at which you have done everything you can do for them. An ongoing relationship is just not practical for either of you. Often times, we just don't want to admit it.

Harry Beckwith, in his remarkable little book, *Selling the Invisible*, says that when service fails, everyone takes it personally. "So rarely we take product failures personally. The services we use, by contrast, usually are provided by people we have met or at least spoken with. When that person fails to do what she promised, we often take it personally. We ask, 'How could she do this to me?'" (New York: Warner Books 1997; pp. xix-xx.)

As I've spoken to many senior advisers that I admire around the country, it was very comforting to hear them admit to losing clients that they really wanted to keep. How enlightening! Even the best advisers can lose clients! Because this business is highly personal, it is very difficult to ignore the hurt when a client with whom you have enjoyed a good relationship summarily dismisses you. I used to try to talk clients out of this decision. In fact, I vividly remember speaking with the daughter of one of my clients who had called to tell me that her mother was moving her account to another firm in town. I expressed my concern that her mother needed a great deal of handholding and attention that she may not get with a different firm. I discussed our personal relationship that spanned several years, including the tumultuous period after the death of her husband. "Look," said the daughter, "I've got a guy who can get Mom a 15 percent return with low risk. Can you do that?" I confessed I couldn't, nor did I have any confidence that any one else could either. That conversation taught me that it is not necessarily my personal failure that encourages a client to change advisers. I also learned that occasionally people outgrow you. Although the client needed my attention and mothering during her personally challenging times, she was now declaring her independence.

If a client wishes to release us today, I no longer use rhetoric to convince them to stay. I recognize how hard it must be for them to say this to me, so I make it easy. I express my regret that we could not meet their needs and I tell them we will always be available should they wish to reconsider. We follow it up with a nice cordial letter, reconfirming that we are releasing their account. We also offer to assist with the transition to a new adviser.

Refusing a Client

IT IS BETTER TO REFUSE an inappropriate relationship at the outset than to try to figure out creative ways to sever it when it's not working. When a prospect's profile is not appropriate for us, we apologize for being too narrowly specialized to give him or her the best service. We say that we're sorry we are so focused that we can't accommodate them, rather than indicating they don't have enough money or in some way are lacking. It's bad for business to make people feel embarrassed or uncomfortable about their money, or lack of it.

We make it clear to a prospect that even though we are unable to help, our commitment is to find them a more appropriate adviser relationship. We keep a list of people we know and trust and share it with them, adding that if the recommendations don't work out, they may check back and we will be happy to suggest others. It's our commitment to them for their confidence in calling us initially. Most of the time, people take us up on it. It is, nevertheless, a challenge to refuse a relationship, especially when the prospect somehow made it through your screening process and is sitting across from you. Eleanor admits she uses her "gut" much more than she used to. "I have my own comfort level. When that's disturbed, I try to find a pleasant way to say no. I might say, 'I don't think we can help you' or 'clearly, this isn't a good fit.'"

David Norton confides that he frequently refuses relationships based on his estimation of the situation as he talks with them. David will refuse a relationship if he doesn't like or trust someone, or if the prospect appears to be a "messer" (someone who can't make decisions). He will also refuse if he perceives that his services are not a good value for the client.

Paul Brady tends to be more blunt. He recommends being honest and frank about it. "I simply tell them this is not a good match." Jerry Neill prefers a less direct approach. "I usually price my service out of the market or explain we can't take on that project now, but perhaps in a few months...." Jerry also points out that if you have bundled services, you can use that as an excuse as well. A client who only wants you to manage money will probably not want to do a comprehensive plan with you. Roy Diliberto will simply not take a new client unless they agree to a comprehensive plan.

David Bugen looks for compatibility. "If a prospect's expectations do not mesh with ours, we say, no, sorry. Sure, we love to take new clients, but we don't want today's solution to be tomorrow's problem."

Many advisers screen heavily prior to the first meeting. David Bugen sends out a questionnaire for the prospect to complete prior to that session. We do, too. If someone balks at this, we explain that "when you visit a new doctor, he needs information to make an assessment of your medical situation. This information will help us determine if we can help you. We don't want to waste your time or ours. We believe that if you are not prepared to commit your time to providing the information we consider critical, we are not likely to be the right firm for your needs." This really discourages "tire kickers."

Just Say "No"

AS HARD AS IT MIGHT BE to fire clients or refuse new relationships, it is necessary for developing your practice. Remember, part of Pareto's Law states that roughly 20 percent of your income in ten years will come from your current client base. You'll want to weed out, then concentrate on retention. Managing your client base effectively will make your business more efficient, and better yet, more fun.

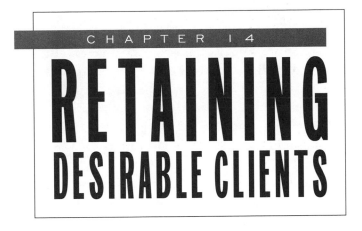

CHAPTER 14

RETAINING
DESIRABLE CLIENTS

Do less than customers expect and service is seen as bad.
Do exactly what customers expect and service is seen
as good. But do more that customers anticipate
and service is seen to be superior.

— PAUL DORRIAN, Intensive Customer Care

I WANTED TO DEVOTE an entire chapter to client

retention. It is easy to lose sight of its importance while

your business is experiencing extraordinary growth.

Research suggests that it's five times more expensive

to acquire a new customer than to keep an existing

client (Deloitte and Touche, Relationship Marketing Report, 1997). Corporate America has recognized this and made a buzzword of CRM, or customer relationship management. As John Bermudez, group director of AMR Research, recently noted, "Stronger customer loyalty, increased competitive edge, improved profitability...these are the dividends of customer relationship management. The secret, according to *Fortune* magazine, is that we need to touch customers the way they want to be touched."

For our firm, the core of client retention is communication and management of client expectations. The comedian Danny Thomas told a wonderful story about expectations. A guy is driving down an old country road at midnight when his car breaks down. He discovers that his tire has blown out and he reaches in the trunk for a jack so that he can change it. While he's opening the trunk, a hard rain begins. He then discovers there is no jack in the trunk. Standing in the muddy road, drenched and forlorn, he spots a light in a farmhouse in the distance and heads toward it. While walking, he speculates about his encounter with the farmer. "Well, it's pretty late," he mutters, "the farmer will have been asleep. Yet, farmers are nice fellows as a general rule, so if I give him five bucks, he probably won't mind loaning me a jack." He walks on, still talking with himself. "Of course, farmers probably go to bed very early, even so, he's had a few hours of sleep anyway, but he probably will be aggravated that I woke him up at midnight. So, what could he want, twenty, thirty bucks?" As he knocks at the door he realizes it's raining harder and getting colder. "That farmer will probably be very angry. He's got to get up at 3:00 A.M. to milk the cows. It's rainy and cold. He'll probably want a hundred bucks for that jack! A hundred bucks! That's highway robbery!" Just then, the farmer raises a second story window and calls out, "Yeah? What do you want?" The man looks up at the farmer and yells, "Keep your damn jack!"

It is human nature to build a "jack story" when no one is available to put things in proper perspective. Our job as advisers is to help our clients keep their perspective, and in essence, to manage their expectations. We don't want the client to have to come to us when the markets are volatile or down. We contact them first, and we tell them how to assess what's happening.

Behavioral Finance

IT'S DIFFICULT TO TALK about managing client expectations without discussing behavioral finance. It's important to understand and to apply psychological as well as economic principles to improve financial decision-making. Most of us learned in economics classes that humans are rational investors. We developed investing strategies based on classical influences until the mid-1980s, when Amos Tversky and Daniel Kahneman identified behavioral finance principles, which included the heuristics, or mental shortcuts that investors use to process information. Tversky and Kahneman demonstrated that although investors are not rational, they are predicable. They maintained that the more we understand how investors process information, the better they can make decisions. With this knowledge, we can be more effective advisers.

One of the best known Tversky and Kahneman studies demonstrates that the average investor is loss averse, not risk averse. A study group was offered two choices, both with the same expected value. The difference was in how the question was framed. Participants were asked to choose A or B in a two-part question as follows:

Part One

A. You win $800

B. You have an 80 percent chance of winning $1000

Part Two

A. You lose $800

B. You have an 80 percent chance of losing $1000

Ninety-five percent of the participants choose A in part one and B in part two. Tversky and Kahneman concluded that people would not take a chance to win more, but were willing to take a chance not to lose. In other words, investors are loss averse, not risk averse. We use a modified version of this question as part of our risk coaching questionnaire to help our clients understand the importance of investing some funds in what they perceive as risky investments so they will not lose their standard of living during retirement.

Although I believe the principles of behavioral finance should be the foundation for managing client expectations, a detailed discussion is clearly outside the scope of this book. However, here are a few traits of typical investors that you may want to investigate further:

◆ **Availability information.** Making decisions based on recent information rather than taking the time to research and analyze

◆ **Anchoring.** "Anchoring" decisions to the last 'guesstimate,' rather than evaluating them independently

◆ **Confirmation bias.** Crediting information that confirms the original judgment and ignoring or discounting that which does not

◆ **Contagious enthusiasm.** Following the crowd. Buying when an investment story is "hot"

◆ **Mental accounting (adding and subtracting).** Placing a higher psychological value on losses than on gains, which results in the reluctance to cut losses

◆ **Mental accounting (multiple accounts).** Mentally creating multiple accounts based on the nature of the account, such as IRA and personal, or on how the funds were received, such as through salary or bonus

◆ **Overconfidence.** Tendency to believe that one can consistently produce superior returns or hire somebody to produce such returns

◆ **Regret, pride, and shame.** Assigning personal characteristics or social commentary to investments. "I won't buy that stock, it's a dog."

◆ **Representativeness.** Predicting the future from the past. A stock will be up tomorrow because it was up yesterday.

Nurturing

OUR CONCEPT OF CLIENT SERVICE originated with my observation of my mother's actions in my childhood home in Michigan. The concept grew as I observed occasions of unique service over the years, and coalesced when I visited a top hotel in New York about five years ago.

When I was nine years old, my family had the luxury of a guest bedroom. One evening, my mother announced that she was going to spend the night in that room. We all thought she was a little nuts. The next morning mom rearranged the furniture, added an extra washcloth in the bathtub area, and brought in a lamp for the bedside table. "Deena," she said, "you can never tell how your guests feel until you spend a night in your own guest room."

Taking mom's advice, we put a critical eye to our practice from the client's perspective, and began to develop a new approach to client service and support. While working on this process, my husband and I spent a weekend in a New York hotel renowned for its fine service. During our stay, I was waiting in the lobby one morning when a woman approached the concierge desk, railing about various things wrong in her room. She continued venting her frustration, yelling about a charge to her account that she didn't think should be there. Before she was finished, she had rattled off half a dozen problems she demanded be rectified immediately. The concierge, rather than referring her to the housekeeper, cashier, and assistant manager, picked up his pen, made notes, then assured her he would call her by three o'clock in the afternoon to report how things had been handled to her satisfaction. Not once did he indicate these problems were someone else's responsibility. He simply told her he would take care of them and report back to her at a specific time. What emerged from my mother's guestroom idea, coupled with my observations in New York, was our Concierge Service, and a complete shift in client support.

Taking Responsibility—
The Elements of Concierge Service

OUR FIRST TENET IS "You pick up the phone, you own the problem." That doesn't mean that the staff person is solely responsible for resolving the problem. He is expected to solicit help. It simply means that the client sees seamless service. Our policy is that the original person to take the call will report back to the client. I am sure the woman at the New York hotel did not care which employees made things right for her, just that everything was made right, period. One of the conclusions we reached from "spending the night in our guest room" was the realization that a receptionist without authority or responsibility is merely a barrier to our clients. A traditional receptionist, by the very nature of her job, can *only* pass the client on to someone else. We no longer have a "warm body" receptionist. The person greeting our clients and prospects when they call or enter the office is a full-fledged member of our concierge team. Depending upon the nature of the call and the request from the client, she either handles it herself or finds the person who can.

Phone Etiquette

OUR CONCIERGE PHILOSOPHY strengthens the loyalty of both our clients and our employees. We know that people want to be treated in a special way. Our concierge service is a tangible demonstration that we appreciate and want to keep our most valuable asset—our clients. Our special attention starts with phone calls. Think about how important that first phone call is. It sets the tone for your entire office.

One evening I arrived home to find that our television cable service was out. I called the cable service number. A recorded voice told me to press number one if I have no picture, press number two if the picture is distorted, press number three if there is no picture but audio, and so on. I pressed number one. A recorded voice told me to press number one if only one television was out, or number two if all of the televisions were out. I pressed two. Then a recorded voice informed me that no problems with the service had been reported in our neighborhood and to hold for the next available service representative. I'm not sure which was more irritating after that—the elevator music, or the intermittent commercial extolling the praises of the cable company. After twenty minutes, no human voice picked up the line. After thirty minutes I felt like a damn fool and hung up. These barriers can just give the wrong impression to our clients. We have neither a traditional receptionist, nor an automated answering machine.

Anyone answering the phone in our office will be familiar with all of our clients and with the basics of the client's personal circumstances (e.g., spouse's name, recent trips, new grandchildren) or will be able to quickly access this information. Consequently, they can answer in a less formal and more personal way. As a fail-safe backup, we have voice mail, but only if the caller asks to leave someone a voice mail message.

Uncommon Courtesy

THIS IS GOING TO SOUND SIMPLE, but did you ever notice that some people can smile right through a phone? You can hear instantly that they are in a good mood and are happy to talk with you. I love that, because even if I am having a bad day, it's pretty hard not to respond positively to someone who has been trained to smile through the phone.

A friendly smile does not mean a casual or inappropriately familiar attitude. I am constantly amazed at the number of companies whose receptionists, whom I've never met nor am ever likely to, address me casually as "Deena." It is a rule in our office that no one, especially clients, are called by their first names unless they have invited us to do so. A flip side to this is that our staff always gives their full name when asked. There is nothing more unprofessional than telling the caller who asks, "I'm Candy."

Tell Them How You Feel

BEING TOO FORMAL in our relationships with others can be a barrier too. When I moved from Chicago to Miami, I needed to find a new doctor. Using recommendations from clients and friends, I visited several doctors' offices. Most of the visits were the same. The offices were attractive, the staff competent and the doctors, professional. The visit with the last doctor proved to be the best, and the one that gave me an insight that I incorporated in the way I run my practice.

Prior to the physical exam, I sat in the doctor's office while he took an extensive health history. After the exam, I sat again with him while he went over his findings. Then he said something very unusual. "I would like to be your doctor. I would value you as a patient, and I believe that together we can keep you healthy." I almost fell out of my chair. No doctor has ever expressed his willingness, let alone eagerness to have me as a patient. It's a simple thing, but since then, we always tell our prospective clients that we want to be their adviser and that we will value them as clients. They like to hear this, and potential barriers melt right away.

Greetings

WHEN AVAILABLE, our Concierge Director personally greets prospective clients and introduces them to the assigned adviser. Together, the clients and the adviser meet the partner for the initial interview. We try to have the prospects meet as many of our partners and staff as possible on the first visit. We want to demonstrate our depth of knowledge and expertise, as well as encourage them to embrace the team approach.

This seems like good sense to me, but how many times have you sat in some waiting room while people scurried around, not acknowledging your presence? Let's face it, how many people do we have descending on us at one time? Our practices are not based on walk-in traffic. We pretty much know who's supposed to show up and when. It doesn't take much effort for a staff member to greet our visitors, welcome them by name, and make them feel wanted. Our database keeps a list of their beverage preferences, so we can offer them what they like when they visit. Once the initial greeting has taken place, one of the staff sits with them, engaging them in conversation until their meeting begins. Rarely do we leave clients or prospects sitting in the waiting area by themselves.

Be Indispensable

ROY DILIBERTO SAYS the key to retention is becoming indispensable to his clients. Roy maintains that the stronger the relationship, the more clients tend to rely on you for everything. "One of my clients died last year. Of course I went to the funeral. It was amazing. I had never met my client's kids, but every one of them knew me by name. Obviously, I had been an important part of his life."

Roy tells another story of a client who inherited a huge sum of money. The client decided that for diversification, he would invest some of it with Sanford Bernstein and the rest with Roy's firm. He called to tell Roy of his decision and to make an appointment to bring in the Bernstein application so Roy could help him complete it.

Cater to Their Egos

MANY YEARS AGO I visited Stan Corey of Great Falls Financial Services. Stan's practice at the time comprised many physician clients. While we were talking, his receptionist interrupted with a call from, "Dr. Holloway, an Eagle client." When he got off the phone I asked Stan what an Eagle client was. "Oh, that," he said. "Doctor's egos arrive three weeks before they do. So I've devised a little program to make them feel special. It's called Eagle clients. I tell them when we start working together that they will be Eagle clients. That means when they call, if I am not on the phone, I will take their call immediately. If I am on the phone, their call will be the next one I return. I tell them that they will receive special treatment, but they must identify themselves as an Eagle client when they call."

"The truth is," he added, "I treat all my clients special. I take their calls right away or I call them back as soon as I am free. It works, though. These doctors all identify themselves as Eagle clients." Stan has redefined his Eagle clients in recent years, based on revenue to the firm. Clients are not informed that they are Eagle clients until they become one. The premise hasn't changed, however. Stan explains, "It is more of a mental benefit for the clients, but it's tangible. They appreciate knowing that you recognize their importance to the business."

Are You Providing a Hotel or a Bed?

ONE OF THE MAJOR REASONS for our company's thrust toward superior, intensive client care is our philosophy regarding portfolio performance. We tell our clients from day one: we don't provide performance; we report it. We do not maximize return; we don't have to, and neither do they. Our clients need portfolio performance sufficient to achieve their objectives. We don't believe in market timing either; our clients are fully invested in the market, good times and bad.

A client's expectation that you can consistently provide superior performance for them is attributed to the heuristic "overconfidence." In order to challenge this behavioral characteristic, we must emphasize something other than performance. For us, that has been continual support and extraordinary service.

One of my clients is a nationally known consultant to the hospitality industry. He has written textbooks used at the Cornell University Hospitality School, one of the finest in the world. When I described our concierge idea as a philosophy and a commitment, he immediately fell in love with it and agreed that it was an appropriate model for our profession. When I related my experience with the concierge in New York, he told me that the Ritz Carlton hotel chain far exceeds what I had witnessed. Not only the concierge is charged with completely seamless service; it is required of every staff member. If, for example, I ask a maid where to find a certain room, she is instructed to stop what she is doing and walk me to the place I'd requested.

My client went on to tell me of an incident at the Hyatt Hotel in Coral Gables, Florida. The Hyatt is a posh hotel, with a beautiful marble and brass lobby. One evening at 10:00 P.M., a man appeared at the check-in desk in his pajamas. He was irate. It seemed he'd just returned from dinner to get ready for bed and found that his bed had not been turned down. "For two hundred and ninety bucks a night," he argued, "I deserve a turn-down." The hotel manager told my client, the consultant, that she has thought about this incident quite often since then. "People walk into this lovely hotel, see this beautiful lobby, and immediately have certain expectations. What we must to do," she added, "is to make reality exceed their expectations." She recognized that the Hyatt is not just in the business of providing a room and a bed; they are providing a *hotel*. This is the essence of our concierge service. In the financial advisory business, providing asset management is merely providing the bed. To be successful we have to provide far more. Our "hotel" is the planning and peace of mind we provide our clients, through good markets and bad.

Lifestyle Consultant

PAUL BRADY, in Australia, calls himself a lifestyle consultant. Paul told me there are three pictures on his office wall. One is a map of the world, and two are pictures of Portofino, Italy, his favorite place. On the opposite wall are masks he's collected. "I am in the business of helping people dial up their lifestyle." He always talks with his clients in terms of an annual travel budget for arriving at their financial destination. If they tell him they need a $40,000 income at retirement, he says, "Let's see, that's about a $5,000 travel budget. Is that enough?" All his important discussions revolve around clients' travels. He points to the wall, telling his clients, "I practice what I preach. I love to travel. I've collected my masks from all over the world. When we work together, we'll help you reach your goals. You tell me one of those goals is having the money and flexibility to travel, so when you're out and about, I hope you will keep me in mind when you see an interesting mask." Try to find a metaphor that replaces a client's preconceptions with something useful, illuminating, and distinctly yours.

In our office, we have a lifestyle collage. This is a compilation of pictures of our clients doing the activities they like best. Some are playing golf; some are gardening, carving wooden pens, or horseback riding. If anyone asks to see our "track record," we point to the collage. The collage is an elegant testimony to the fact that our clients accomplish their goals.

Judgmental Overlay

THE PRIMARY RESPONSIBILITY of our Director of Concierge Services is to heighten the client sensitivity of our practice. She provides the "judgmental overlay" to our other activities. For example, if we are preparing letters, newsletters, or any other communications for our clients, her job is to look at them from the client's viewpoint. In addition, she has her own small advisory group composed of a number of our long-term clients. The participants, all thoughtful and perceptive, are carefully selected to ensure that they vary in age, status (self-employed, retired, married, or widowed), and interests. We explain to them that we are asking for their honest feedback. Our single goal is to continuously improve our service. We look to this advisory group to help us exceed expectations. They quite often beta test changes in our forms or documents. They offer substantive input, and we listen. This is critical, as our concierge service is a major element of our client retention strategy.

Concierge Levels of Service

IN NICE AMERICAN HOTELS, if you pay for a concierge level room, you receive a key that will take you to a special floor. Extra amenities such as thick terry cloth robes and French milled soaps are placed in your room. A hospitality is open for continental breakfasts and afternoon cocktail hours. If you don't pay for the concierge level, you still have a very nice room and basic services. Although we provide all of our clients with a basic level of concierge service, not all of our clients provide the same revenue to the firm. Therefore, in 1990, when we decided to analyze the demographics of our clients, we devised a system of client levels for service, based upon revenues.

Analyzing the Client Base

IT BECAME CLEAR after reviewing our client list that we'd grown like Topsy, with no rhyme or reason. We had, more or less, a microcosm of society, and we were delivering services developed more out of client request than our own philosophy and capabilities. To analyze our client base, I divided the clients into ages, assets under management, needs of services, and types (e.g., widows, divorced, couples). I discovered that most of our clients were over age 50 and came to us in preparation for retirement. A significant portion had sold a business, retired with a substantial pension, inherited, or in some other way experienced a windfall that they felt was too overwhelming to manage. I then looked at the quality of our relationships with every client. Some were entirely rewarding. I looked forward to talking with Mrs. Nathan. I found Mr. Zachery's questions challenging. I noted how often staff came in to my office to vent about how rude Mrs. Logan was. I tracked my own behavior as well. Why did I feel like ducking calls when any of the Tylers called? Eleanor Blayney said she went through much the same activity. When she discovered that she picked up her phone calls and voice mails from a particular client with dread, she recognized that it was time to re-evaluate the relationship.

The next thing I realized was that as we had increased our minimums over the years, our newer clients had less and less in common with our early clients. The newer ones were more concerned with estate preservation and multi-generational issues than with strategies to make their money last a lifetime. My partner Harold commented that these newer clients could reach their goals by stuffing cash in a mattress, or for diversification, three mattresses. We needed to make a decision about how we wanted to be serving our clients' needs into the future, and then envision what types of clients they would be. We also needed to know what types of relationships were profitable, rewarding, or both.

Judy Shine caters to mostly small business owners and corporate executives as clients. "One day I recognized a common personality trait in these clients. They were highly intelligent, used to being in control, and wanted to be involved, but did not want to manage their investments. I began to see myself as a facilitator. They would come to me with some ideas, ask me to research them, and give them my professional opinion on them." Judy has developed a way to keep these control people interested and involved in their portfolios by buying some individual lots of blue chip stock for them. "These are corporate people, they hear things, they get information, and they love to talk about stocks." Judy's philosophy is, "I always want to control the part of the portfolio that interests my clients. If stock excites them, I don't want them to take that excitement to a broker."

Determining Profitability

IN 1995, I RECOGNIZED that our practice was growing at an even faster pace than it had in the prior five years. We were hiring more staff, working harder, and making less. I felt we needed direction if we were ever to be profitable. I decided it was time to re-analyze our client base. First, I determined the reasonable number of clients that each of the three partners could handle with existing staff and facilities. At the time we averaged 40 clients each, or a total of 120. Our average client size was approximately $300,000. That was also our minimum account at the time. I estimated that we could comfortably add another twenty clients per partner without adding staff or facilities. If I added sixty clients at our minimum size, each would generate $3000 in new fees. Our additional income would be $180, 000.

I thought about this and realized that if we left our minimums at $300,000, at the rate we were acquiring new clients, we would very soon reach capacity. I recognized that the only commodity we have that cannot expand is our time, so if we wished to grow we needed clients with more assets. I also recognized that if we raised our minimum to $500,000 it might take a little longer to reach capacity but the profit would be larger because we would have significantly greater revenues without having to add new staff. So I raised the minimums to $500,000. As I mentioned before, this was not a slam-dunk choice. Our voices cracked the first few times we turned away $300,000 clients. We had continually to remind ourselves that at the higher minimum we could be increasing our annual revenue stream by an additional $300,000, not $180,000. Once we increased the minimums, an amazing thing happened. The pace of new clients increased! It seemed that the higher the minimum, the more professional we looked to prospects. Subsequently we've revisited and modified our minimums many times. Our current minimum is $2 million. Of course, we have clients in all ranges, which we regularly review in terms of the cost in partner time. Our challenge is how to deliver the extraordinary service our new larger clients expect, while continuing to work with smaller clients who have helped us grow.

Eileen Sharkey, of Sharkey, Howes, Wagner & Javer, Inc., points out the dilemma presented by a desire to adequately serve small clients while maintaining, as she does, that nearly every client relationship should be profitable. "If not all your clients are profitable, let's just call it therapy and forget it." She also echoes the results of the Bain study (*Fortune*, Vol. 138, No. 5, September 7, 1998, pp. 162–63.) and notes that it costs more to develop a new client relationship than it does to maintain an old one. Our commitment was to provide good basic services to all clients. However, we admitted that all clients did not necessarily want to receive the same services. As with our other efforts at triage, we determined appropriate levels of service by categorizing our client base by fees to the firm.

Service Level	Annual Fees
Copper	Fees below $7,500
Silver	Fees of $7,500 to $10,000
Gold	Fees of $10,000 to $25,000
Platinum	Fees of $25,000 to $35,000
Diamond	Fees of $35,000 and above

We then elaborated the types of service that would be provided for each category. Through the years we have refined that list and the services many times, and we understand it to be a starting point, not a straitjacket. The types of service and the way we deliver that service is unique to each client. One of our platinum clients told me that she thought it was odd that we sent her a birthday card. "Birthday cards to me are very personal. Only my closest friends and family send them." Our concierge told me that we will stop sending cards until she considers us close friends. The following list is our current division of clients. This list only captures the number of contacts we have with clients, not the level or types of service, since each is so unique.

Levels	Services
Copper	Semiannual Review
	Newsletter
Silver	Quarterly Review
	Newsletter
	Periodic Flash Reports
Gold	Quarterly Reviews
	Newsletter
	Flash Reports
	One Other Contact per Month
	Two Principal Contacts per Quarter
Platinum	Quarterly Reviews
	Newsletter
	Flash Reports

<table>
<tr><td></td><td>Two Other Contacts per Month</td></tr>
<tr><td></td><td>Two Principal Contacts per Quarter</td></tr>
<tr><td>Diamond</td><td>Quarterly Reviews</td></tr>
<tr><td></td><td>Newsletter</td></tr>
<tr><td></td><td>Flash Reports</td></tr>
<tr><td></td><td>Two Other Contacts Per Month</td></tr>
<tr><td></td><td>Principal Contact 1 per Month</td></tr>
<tr><td></td><td>Dinner or Special Event–Quarterly.</td></tr>
</table>

The levels, as you can see, are based upon revenue. However, our management consultant client pointed out that in luxury hotels, if you are willing to pay the up-charge for the concierge level, you can have access to it. Our original method did not encourage this. We now make it clear, that if a client *wants* platinum concierge service, even if he does not have the assets, he can pay the minimum fee for that category and be a platinum client.

Customized Gifts

CLIENTS OF OURS who are Gold Level and above receive customized birthday cards, holiday cards, gifts, and an anniversary card commemorating their years with us. We send gifts for special events, such as the birth of a grandchild, as well as specialty items at holidays. All of our cards are created with our Hallmark or American Greetings software and printed on our color printers. That way, we can customize them with names and events and even pictures. If we need to be a bit more formal, the cards are handwritten on our company card stock.

Many of our clients were becoming grandparents. To acknowledge this event, we did the obvious. We did the obvious very well. We'd send a lovely silver rattle to the new grandchild. One day our Director of Concierge Services challenged this tradition. "What message are we giving our client by sending a gift to the grandchild? Many times we don't even know the child's parents. Alternatively, if we sent a grandparent's package with a picture frame and a journal for our client to chronicle his or her life for the family, we are sharing the event with our client. And the gift is for him or her, to share with the newcomer." This one idea has brought us wonderful responses from our clients. One grandmother-client told me, "This birth brings us mixed feelings. Our daughter now has a daughter. So it was so nice to get little gifts just for us to share with our grandchild. It makes us feel special, too."

When we take an extended trip, we take some address labels for all the gold, platinum, and diamond clients. It usually takes us two or three days to personally hand write a short note to everyone, affix a stamp, and mail them back home, but the clients love them. They also love that we thought of them while we were on the road.

It's important to note that although the quantity of our services may vary by account size, the quality of our financial planning and investment advice is consistent and uniform throughout. All clients are invited to contact us with questions or issues, and we are prepared to provide any additional planning or counsel as part of their retainer fee. Our staff provides *concierge level* service and are prepared to do what it takes to satisfy the client, regardless of asset size. If at any time, we think a client is abusing our time, we talk with them about it. Rarely do we find it necessary to charge additional fees to reflect the extra time we are spending.

Each year my partners and I, along with our advisory staff, write down a description of our "perfect client" in personality, temperament, net worth, and complexity of issues. We then compare our client base to our descriptions and attempt to weed-out those relationships that are personally and emotionally unrewarding. (See Chapter 13 for more on this.)

Peppering the Client

OVERLAYING OUR BASIC concierge services we also add a bit of extra spice. We use every opportunity to "pepper" clients with articles, notes or other items of interest. Using our resource system (see the section under Keywording in Chapter 9), as well as Internet resources, we have many articles on hand to pique their interests. Because we have some high-profile clients, our concierge scans the papers daily, looking for articles with client names in them. She sends these along with little notes of congratulations.

Managing Client Expectations with Communications

COMMUNICATIONS ARE ESSENTIAL to maintaining the best relationship with our clients. We use it to reinforce our philosophy and manage our clients' expectations. Our communications strategy has changed drastically over the years. What's interesting is that while originally our communications appeared highly structured to clients, now it is highly structured for us, but appears to be more fluid, comfortable, and natural for our clients.

"Crisis" Conversations

RICHARD BUSILLO OF RTD ADVISORS in Philadelphia maintains that it is vitally important to control your clients' expectations from the beginning of the relationship, and especially when people panic during market volatility. "One of my clients is a high-powered attorney, used to getting his own way." After significant planning, Rich determined that the client had a long-term time horizon. The investment policy called for the client to invest $700,000 in the domestic market in February 1994. In March, the portfolio was down more than 10 percent and the client called. Coincidentally, Philadelphia was having a major winter storm, with a foot of snow on the ground and more coming. The client, clearly agitated, yelled, "I just got my statement. Just what are you advising your clients, considering what's going on out there?" "Well," said Rich, "I'm telling them, when you shovel, just make sure you use your legs and not your back." The client laughed and Rich notes that this client has not been overwrought about short-term volatility since.

Right after the 500-point drop on October 19, 1987, my partner Harold called all his clients. "It's not the end of the world," he explained. "AT&T must still be in business because we're on the phone. People are still taking pictures at Disney World, so Disney and Kodak are still around. That's what you own, AT&T, Disney, Kodak."

"Five years," he told them. "Remember, you have at least a five-year time horizon."

Reviews to Manage Client Expectations

ALMOST EVERYONE in our industry prepares quarterly performance reviews. In the past few years, we have all struggled with what information to include in these reviews. Many advisers I interviewed expressed concern about finding the right balance between customization and standardization. I briefly discussed our reports and standardized review appointments in Chapter 9; now I'll address the review documents in more detail.

Each quarter our client receives a copy of our standard reviews for their first quarter. These were designed specifically to manage client expectations. Further, they are deliberately assembled in a way to reinforce our own philosophy of investing.

◆ **Page one—market highlights.** My partner Peter writes an overview of the various markets and the general economic climate over the past quarter. It gives the client a point of reference when he compares it to his personal portfolio on page three.

◆ **Page two—asset allocation.** We developed a document in Excel that grabs data from our portfolio management software and produces two multi-color pie charts on one page. The first is the current allocation. The second is the investment policy allocation. We use this page to discuss whether or not we need to rebalance the portfolio to the policy allocation. By placing it at the beginning of the report, we are emphasizing the importance of asset allocation.

◆ **Page three—portfolio positions.** This is a list of the client's current positions and current values. We do not include cash invested or tax basis. We think this encourages short-term comparisons.

◆ **Page four—manager reviews.** We include a written narrative about each of our portfolio managers, describing important aspects of the management style, composition of the fund, and so on. We review one-fourth of the managers each quarter or when changes dictate. The narrative is dated, so our client knows the last time we were in contact with this manager.

◆ **Page five—performance chart.** This chart, generated in Excel, graphically illustrates three returns: inflation as indicated by the Consumer Price Index (CPI), the policy target return, and the actual return. We designed this chart to help the client focus on how well the portfolio is staying ahead of inflation, which is exactly where we want the emphasis to be.

◆ **Page six—performance.** This page lists time and dollar-weighted returns from inception and annually. We do not provide quarterly or year-to-date returns to discourage clients from thinking short-term. This page is not included for any client review under one year.

◆ **Page seven—manager statistics.** This page, written in Excel format, provides details on the managers, such as standard deviation, alphas, betas, and five- and ten-year returns. We specifically include expense ratios to remind our clients that we take the expenses seriously, and monitor them closely.

Each month I write a letter that accompanies the review. It is usually casual and conversational. If the markets are down, it is a positive letter, putting short-term performance in perspective. If markets are up, it is a dampening letter, designed to control ebullient enthusiasm. Although computer generated, the letters are warm and personal. My partners and I sign each one, adding a handwritten note at the bottom.

As I mentioned in Chapter 9, we use the opportunity of a review to discuss financial planning issues. Each meeting is dedicated to one of four subject areas: estate planning, retirement planning, tax planning, and risk management.

Flash Reports

AT THE BEGINNING of our relationship with clients, we ask how they would like to receive intermittent information from us. We offer them e-mail, fax, and snail mail. Periodically, when we want to explain the economic climate, transmit interesting material from a portfolio manager, or just stay in touch, we issue a Flash Report. If we have information that we think will need some discussion, we always supplement the flash with a phone call. We have a special form for this communication so the client will know that it is something important enough to read. We only send these a few times a year.

Newsletters

NORM BOONE spends significant time designing and writing his own newsletter. Most of the advisers I know write their own. "My newsletter is a reflection of me, my company, and our philosophy. It is our opportunity to show our personality and reinforce ideas," said Norm. "I have a section in each newsletter that talks about my family. I get more reaction to that than nearly anything else."

You can create and reinforce your image through your newsletter. Powers & Phillips, a law firm specializing in securities law, consists of three partners: a husband and wife team and one other woman partner. They position themselves as "two bitches from hell and a short fat guy." Their newsletter, *The Bitches from Hell Reporter*, has a unique format, with columns like "Dear Flabby," advice for men working with professional women; and "The Dragon Lady Speaks," stories about firm clients. They believe that lawyers are viewed as stuffy and intimidating, so they've elected to use their newsletter to inject humor and single themselves out in a professional world where everyone seems the same. They report that this has not tarnished their image, but it does attract a great deal of attention. They now send over 4000 copies of their newsletter to people all over the country.

To add interest and depth, we have asked some of our clients to contribute articles for our newsletter. They enjoy it. In fact, our clients have written some of our best newsletters. Retired clients have useful perspectives to share with others contemplating retirement. Our clients have written articles on Elder Hostel, local adult education programs, the value of personal medical checkups, and the emotional aspects of retiring. No one can tell it better than someone with experience. Our clients tell us they love writing for us and reading first-hand accounts.

If you don't feel comfortable writing your own newsletter, contact a local college or university and outsource it to a student. You don't have to produce them monthly, or even regularly. Our first newsletter included the words "Published Intermittently" in the masthead. In any case, most advisers believe it is better to have no newsletter than use a service where you just slap your name and/or picture on the top.

Client Advisory Boards

ROY DILIBERTO DEVELOPED his client advisory board a few years ago. His board is very structured, with clients serving three-year staggered terms. Roy says the development of the board was a practical decision. He and his partners would argue about what services and reports to provide to the clients. Now, "we just ask them what they want." The board has vetted every report, correcting grammar and making them more user-friendly.

One year Roy asked his board, "Why did you hire us?" "We had the most revealing responses. 'Trust, integrity, clarity, understanding, continuity, and reasonable rates of return.' Notice, they didn't say, performance, performance, or performance." Roy admits his board is handpicked, but he says he and his partners try to choose an adequate mix by age, sex, and asset size. "Advisory boards are wonderful," Roy adds. "Clients buy the dream, now they can claim ownership of it, too." Karen Spero has had an advisory board for years. She recommends treating the board professionally and compensating them for their participation.

Client Surveys

A FEW YEARS AGO we developed a survey and sent it to clients. We received two criticisms. One client remarked that he did not like the Schwab statements, and he gets too much paper when we trade. That was it. Everyone else thought we were wonderful and did everything to perfection. I learned a valuable lesson. If you are going to conduct surveys, let a third party handle them. Clients are not going to jeopardize a good relationship with you by telling you that your reports are ugly and your response time for phone calls could be improved. The next time we contracted with a local secretarial service that conducted our survey. The results were much more helpful, because the clients were not responding directly to us. It *does* make a difference. The box on the following page is a sample of a survey we prepared for use by our third-party consultants.

Evensky, Brown & Katz Client Survey

PLEASE RATE EBK's PERFORMANCE IN THE FOLLOWING AREAS:

	EXCELLENT	GOOD	NEEDS IMPROVE-MENT	NOT APPLI-CABLE
1. Overall staff rating				
PERSONNEL				
2. Courtesy of staff				
3. Knowledge of staff members				
4. Promptness answering phones				
5. Timeliness of follow-up calls				
TIMELINESS				
6. Setting up new accounts				
7. Follow up on account transfers				
8. Processing disbursements				
ACCURACY				
9. Setting up account transfers				
10. Processing disbursements				

Do you have any suggestions to improve EBK's service to you?

_____

_____

What is your opinion of how Schwab is handling your account (e.g., statements, accuracy, and timeliness)?_____

_____

_____

Just *What* Are You Saying?

LAST YEAR, the Hershey Corporation had a great ad, titled, "Change is Bad," picturing a paper coffee cup with the following notice printed on its side:

> WARNING. PLEASE TAKE NOTICE that by accepting the hot beverage in this container, the recipient of the aforementioned beverage agrees to waive any liability that might arise, including, but not limited to, any burning, scalding, marring or any other physical and/or mental damage to the aforementioned recipient. Enjoy.

Hershey is right. Who are these container people kidding? It's a good lesson for us. I know that the financial advisory business is highly regulated. I know that we must have certain documents in place to protect our clients and ourselves. But, I don't believe that these documents need to be mired down in legalese. They must be straightforward and easy to understand. Any document that creates a barrier between our clients and us or that can serve as the basis for misunderstanding is detrimental to our relationship with them. Take a good long look at your engagement letters, contracts, and initial communication with your clients. Spend the night in your guest room. Just what message are you communicating to them? I wouldn't even attempt to suggest how you should have your legal documents written. However, I firmly believe that you can ensure that your contracts protect you without being formal and unfriendly.

Train Your Clients, Don't Let Them Train You

THE CONCIERGE at the Beverly Wilshire in the movie *Pretty Woman* does everything from arranging for a young prostitute to buy a dress, to teaching her which utensils to use for dinner. The concierge at our office does everything from monitoring quarterly reviews to selecting gifts for special occasions. We refer to her as our concierge because she is our resident problem solver. Clients know that when they ask Tammi, it's done. As I've said before, she also looks relentlessly at each of our activities from the client's viewpoint. She informally polls her client advisory board before she makes decisions about changing a form or a service.

Despite this high level of service and interaction, we never confuse providing exceptional service with agreeing to provide some information or design reports that we don't believe are appropriate or in the client's best interest. We've been asked, for example, to include numerous benchmarks on our performance reports. We will not. We have been asked to calculate estimated tax payments, complete real estate appraisals, and hire maids. We do not have expertise in those areas and we won't do it. We will help them find the appropriate person, however.

A few months ago I hired a new landscaper. While we were looking around the property I pointed out that the sprinkler system wasn't working very well and the lights around the plants needed replacing. I asked him if he did that. He replied, "Ma'am, I want this job. If that's what it requires to get it, I'll do it." I then asked him if he knew any good outdoor lighting and sprinkler people. He quickly rattled off a few names of people he'd worked with before. "If you don't normally provide this service and you know good people who do it, why did you offer to do it anyway?" I asked. "Some people like one-stop shopping. I try to be accommodating because I want the work," he replied. "It usually doesn't work though," he went on. "I'm a great landscaper but only fair at sprinklers and lights." I hired him. The lawn looks great, and whenever there is a problem with lights or sprinklers, I pay him to find the right people to fix them.

Our Biggest Challenge

YOU'LL THINK IT'S ODD, but the biggest impediment to growth is not lack of new clients, it's poor client retention. It is immeasurably more time consuming and costly to find the next client than it is to take good care of the current ones. Increased competition and volatile markets can only be managed with proactive, consistent initiatives.

CHAPTER 15

GOTTA-HAVE-IT RESOURCES

You can't build a house without a hammer.

—TYLER WELLS, six years old

THIS LAST SECTION is really one big chapter of recommendations from the sixty-three advisers that I've listed in the Acknowledgments. Successful planners have, at the tip of their tongues, a *Gotta Have* list of resources that put them in business, helped them grow, or had a lasting effect on their professional lives. They were all pleased to share their great finds.

To make finding what you need easier, I have categorized the resources by subject matter; for example, the top ten books on practice management, or the top Web sites. As you read through these and you find something that you'd like to share, please send your suggestions to me at **pepper@evensky.com**. I keep a current list of the *Gotta's* on our Web site at **www.evensky.com.**

Gotta-Have-It Resources

THERE'S NOTHING I LIKE better than to get a recommendation for a good book from a close friend. I used that concept to provide you with a list of articles, books, Internet Web sites, software—anything in fact, that top advisers worldwide told me they would recommend to a good friend in the business. As far as I'm concerned, these are "gotta haves."

TOP 9 BOOKS FOR AND ABOUT YOUR PRACTICE

1 *The E Myth Revisited*, Michael Gerber, HarperBusiness, 1995. Turn your entrepreneurial practice into a viable and successful business. A number one pick.

2 *Wealth Management*, Harold R. Evensky, McGraw-Hill, 1997. A good blend of solid investment theory and practical application.

3 *Wealth Management Index*, Ross Levin, McGraw-Hill, 1997. An innovative strategy for quantifying a client's success in financial planning.

4 *Best Practices for Financial Advisors*, Mary Rowland, Bloomberg Press, 1997. One of the nation's best personal financial writers has distilled the experience of an elite group of fifty-five financial advisers.

5 *Protecting Your Practice*, Katherine Vessenes in cooperation with the IAFP, Bloomberg Press, 1997. Katherine is the expert's expert when it comes to questions of compliance.

6 *Creating Equity*, John Bowen, Securities Data Publishing, 1977. Detailed strategies for building a successful practice of your own.

7 *Taking the Mystery Out of TQM*, Peter Capezio and Debra Morehouse, Career Press, 1995. Great strategies for using Total Quality Management in your office for team building.

8 Make It So, Wess Roberts, Ph.D. and Bill Ross, Pocket Books, 1995. Leadership skills, team-building strategies, all delivered entertainingly using vignettes of Captain Jean Luc Picard and the *Star Ship Enterprise.*

9 *Money and the Meaning of Life*, Jacob Needleman, Currency/ Doubleday 1994. This one is Ross Levin's pick: "While I think that it is helpful for planners to read many books on psychology and why people make decisions, Jacob Needleman's *Money and the Meaning of Life* best answers the question, "How do we walk the line between the material and the metaphysical?""

TOP 3 BEHAVIORAL FINANCE BOOKS

1 *Advances in Behavioral Finance*, Edited by Richard H. Thaler, Russell Sage Foundation, 1993. A compilation of behavioral finance papers, presented in a real-world context.

2 *The Winner's Curse: Paradoxes & Anomalies of Economic Life*, Richard H. Thaler, Princeton University Press, 1994. Some of Thaler's best views on heuristics and behavioral finance principles.

3 *Judgement and Choice*, Robert Hogarth, John Wiley & Sons, 1994. Serious treatment of the subject for serious advisers.

TOP 8 TECHNICAL/PROFESSIONAL BOOKS

1 *Asset Allocation: Balancing Financial Risk*, Roger C. Gibson, Irwin Professional Publishing, 1996. Roger reviews asset allocation in light of the capital market theory, including a practical approach to developing your own allocation techniques.

2 *The Financial Advisor's Analytical Toolbox*, Ed McCarthy/International Association for Financial Planning/ McGraw-Hill, 1997. All the analytical tools you'll ever need packed between two covers. If this is not on your bookshelf, go get it.

3 *Stocks, Bonds, Bills and Inflation,* Ibbotson & Associates. Published yearly with market results back to 1926.

4 *The Prudent Investor's Guide to Beating the Market*, Reinhardt, Werba, Bowen, Richard D. Irwin, a Times Mirror Higher Education Group, Inc. Company, 1996. Thoughtful comments on passive investing.

5 *Management of Investment Decisions*, **Donald B. Trone, William R. Allbright, Philip Taylor (Contributor), McGraw-Hill, 1996.** One of the best references on the development of investment policies.

6 *The Third Restatement of Trust.* A legal treatise published by the American Law Institute and the basis for the Uniform Prudent Investor Act.

7 *Investment Policy: How to Win the Loser's Game*, **Charles D. Ellis, Irwin, 1992.** Eighty pages packed with common sense approaches to investment planning. Give it to your clients, too.

8 *Against the Gods: The Remarkable Story of Risk*, **Peter L. Bernstein, Wiley & Sons, 1996.** A fascinating read to put the concept of risk in historical perspective.

TOP 4 MARKETING BOOKS

1 *Selling the Invisible*, **Harry Beckwith, Warner Books, 1997.** Readable, valuable marketing advice to change your marketing efforts permanently.

2 *The One to One Future: Building Relationships One Customer at a Time*, **Martha Rogers, Ph.D. and Don Peppers, Doubleday, 1997.** See Chapter 11 for more information on this book.

3 *Customer Satisfaction Is Worthless—Customer Loyalty Is Priceless*, **Jeffrey Gitomer, Bard Press, 1998.** How to get—and keep—customers forever.

4 Nick Murray—Anything you can get your hands on. Here are a few of his books:

◆ *The Excellent Investment Advisor*, The Nick Murray Company, November 1996.

◆ *Gathering Assets: The Best of Nick Murray*, 1995.

◆ *Serious Money: The Art of Marketing Mutual Funds*, 1991.

TOP 7 JOURNALS

ALL OF THESE JOURNALS provide timely, substantive research and analysis on various financial issues. Expect the articles to continuously challenge your thinking.

1 Journal of Private/Investment Portfolio

Institutional Investor, Inc.
488 Madison Avenue
New York, NY 10022
(212) 224-3300

This journal is designed to provide a forum to explore investment issues relevant to individual investors. It covers subjects such as behavioral finance, investment policy, tax-aware investing, and performance measurement.

2 The Journal of Investing (Institutional Investor Inc.) is designed to be useful and readable; the journal has a number of unique author guidelines, such as to keep in mind that writing is for the readers; write to express, not to impress; write the way you talk. Subject matter includes issues such as asset allocation, global investing, risk management, technology, and mutual funds.

3 The Journal of Portfolio Management (Institutional Investor Inc.) is an equally reader-friendly publication. Its guidelines to authors say "We publish this journal so that its subscribers will read the articles we select....We agree with Polonius that brevity is the soul of wit." Recent coverage includes articles on indexing, equity duration, tactical allocation, and bond portfolio management. Peter Bernstein is consulting editor. That alone is reason enough to subscribe.

4 Financial Analyst Journal

Association for Investment Management and Research
P.O. Box 3668
Charlottesville, VA 22903
(804) 980-9775
www.aimr.org

The *Financial Analyst Journal,* Association for Investment Management and Research, is the official journal of AIMR. Its articles cover the landscape of investment theory and practice, reflecting the best thinking of leading academics and practitioners in the investment profession.

5 Journal of Financial Planning

Institute of Certified Financial Planners

3801 E. Florida Ave.

Suite 708

Denver, CO 80210

(303) 759-4900

www.icfp.org/journal/jfpindex.htm

The *Journal of Financial Planning* is published by the ICFP for the free exchange of ideas, facts, and information relevant to the financial planning profession.

6 Journal of Retirement Planning

CCH Incorporated

4025 W. Peterson Avenue

Chicago, IL 60646

7 AAII Journal

625 North Michigan Avenue

Chicago, IL 60611

(312) 280-0170

www.aaii.com

Although this is for the public, Eleanor Blayney recommends it as an excellent source for articles on financial planning issues that are practical and written at a level that clients can understand.

TOP 5 PROFESSIONAL MAGAZINES

WHAT BETTER WAY to find out what's going on in our industry than to read articles written by thoughtful, well-informed reporters and practitioners. All these periodicals offer practical and technical advice as well.

1 Financial Planning Magazine

Securities Data Publishing

40 West 57th Street

11th Floor

New York, NY 10019

(212) 765-5311

www.financial-planning.com

2 Investment Adviser Magazine
170 Avenue at the Common
Shrewsbury, NJ 07702
(732) 389-8700
www.djfpc.com

3 Bloomberg Wealth Manager Magazine
P.O. Box 99670
Collingswood, NJ 08108-9877
(609) 279-4635
www.bloomberg.com

4 Financial Advisory Practice
RIA Group
31 St. James Avenue
Boston, MA 02116-4112
(800) 950-1216

5 Personal Financial Planning
RIA Group
31 St. James Avenue
Boston, MA 02116-4112
(800) 950-1216

TOP INDUSTRY NEWSLETTER
◆ **Inside Information**
P.O. Box 820
Mars Hill, NC 28754
(828) 689-4560

Anything financial writer Bob Veres puts on paper is worth reading. Practical tips, industry gossip, and technical strategies make this an absolute must.

TOP 5 BUSINESS ASSISTANCE SOFTWARE PROGRAMS

THE FIRST TWO are step-by-step preparation software for employee reviews.

1 Employee Appraiser

Austin-Hayne Corporation
2000 Alameda de las Pulgas
Suite 242
San Mateo, CA 94403
(888) 850-3566
(415) 655-3800 (fax)
www.austin-hayne.com

2 Performance Now!

Knowledge Point
1129 Industrial Avenue
Petaluma, CA 94952
(800) 727-1133
www.knowledgepoint.com

Standard, boilerplate, but good for getting started on your own manual.

3 Employee Manual Maker

JIAN Tools For Sale, Inc.
1975 W. El Camino Real
Suite 301
Mountain View, CA 94040-2218
(415) 254-5600
(415) 254-5640 (fax)

Either of the following easy-to-use programs will handle company books, including payroll and a general ledger.

4 Peachtree Complete Accounting

Peachtree Software
1505 Pavilion Place
Norcross, GA 30093
(800) 247-3224
www.peachtree.com

5 Quickbooks Pro
2650 E. Elvira, Suite 100
Tucson, AZ 85706
(888) 246-8848
www.quicken.com

TOP 4 PORTFOLIO MANAGEMENT SOFTWARE PROGRAMS

THE SELECTION OF YOUR portfolio management software is another one of the more critical software decisions you must make. If a significant part of your practice is based on investment management, the software will provide the basis for much of the written material you provide your clients. Flexibility, dependability, and speed should be your major selection criteria. Cost should be a secondary consideration. I received recommendations for all four of the following, although by far the majority was for Centerpiece and Advent.

1 Centerpiece
Performance Technologies, Inc.
1008 Bullard Court
Suite 100
Raleigh, NC 27615
(919) 876-3555
(800) 528-9595
(919) 876-2187 (fax)
www.centerpiece.com

2 Advent Software, Inc.
301 Brannan Street, 6th floor
San Francisco, CA 94107
(415) 543-7696
(800) 523-4708
(415) 543-5070 (fax)
www.advent.inter.com

3 Captools Co.
P.O. Box 9
Issaquah, WA 98027
www.captools.com

4 dbCAMS+
FCSI
14 Commerce Drive
Oakland, MD 21550
(301) 334-1800 (tel)
(301) 334-1896 (fax)
info@dbcams.com
www.dbcams.com

TOP 5 MUTUAL FUND ANALYSIS PROGRAMS

1 Morningstar Principia Plus
225 West Wacker Dr.
Chicago, IL 60606-1228
(800) 735-0700
www.morningstar.com
Hands down the single most frequent "gotta have." This is the primary reference tool for mutual fund data in our office. To say it is invaluable would be a gross understatement. Ten years ago my partner Harold said that anyone who did not have Morningstar in their office should not be in this business. The same statement is true today.

2 CDA Investment Technologies
1455 Research Blvd.
Rockville, MD 20850
(800) 232-2285
A complementary mutual database that also serves as an integral part of our office analytical tools. Two particularly useful components are the excellent scattergrams and the style analyses.

3 Value Line
220 East 42nd Street
New York, NY 10017
(800) 654-0508
(212) 907-1913 (fax)
vlsoft@valueline.com
www.valueline.com
Value Line provides both stock and mutual fund data reports in an easy-to-read format.

4 Overlap

(800) 683-7527

www.overlap.cpm

This software compares the overlap in portfolio holdings among most mutual funds.

5 Ibbotson Associates

Fund Analyst

225 North Michigan Ave

Suite 700

Chicago, IL 60601-767

(312) 616-1620

www.ibbotson.com

Good analytical software for attribution reporting.

TOP 4 FINANCIAL PLANNING SOFTWARE PRODUCTS

EVEN THOUGH MANY senior planners don't use comprehensive planning software, my friends tell me these few are worth a look.

1 Money Tree Software

1753 Wooded Knolls Drive, Suite 200

Philomath, OR 97370-9023

(541) 929-2140 (tech support)

(541) 929-2787 (fax)

www.moneytree.com

2 Execplan; Sawhney Systems, Inc.

777 Alexander Road, Suite 204

Princeton, NJ 08540

(609) 987-5000

(609) 987-0707 (fax)

1-888-SAWHNEY (1-888-729-4639)

www.sawhney.com

3 Financial Profiles, Inc.
The Financial Planning Building
2507 North Verity Parkway
P.O. Box 42430
Middletown, OH 45042-0430
(800) 666-1656 (sales)
(513) 424-1656 (bus off)
(513) 424-5752 (fax)
www.financialsoftware.com

4 CCH Financial Planning (on disk); CCH Canadian Limited
90 Sheppard Avenue East
Suite 300
North York, ON
Canada
M2N 6X1
(800) 268-4522
(800) 461-4131 (fax)
www.ca.cch.com

TOP 3 RETIREMENT PLANNING SOFTWARE PROGRAMS

SENIOR ADVISERS ADMIT to using one of these three programs for capital needs analysis.

1 CCH and BNA's financial planning modules
CCH Incorporated
4025 W. Peterson Avenue
Chicago, IL 60646
(800) 344-3734
www.cch.com

2 M PREPS
Mobius Group, Inc.
World Headquarters
120 Old Post Road
Rye, NY 10580
(914) 921-7200
(914) 921-1360 (fax)
info@mobius-inc.com
www.mobius-inc.com

3 Golden Years Retirement Resource Manager
Money Tree Software
1753 Wooded Knolls Drive, Suite 200
Philomath, OR 97370-9023
(541) 929-2140 (tech support)
(541) 929-2787 (fax)
Sales@moneytree.com
www.moneytree.com

TOP 2 OPTIMIZERS-PORTFOLIO ANALYZERS
THE TWO LISTED BELOW are the major vendors for financial planning practitioners. We use both; you can't go wrong with either one.

1 Ibbotson Associates
225 N. Michigan Avenue, Suite 700
Chicago, IL 60601
(800) 758-3557
(312) 616-1620
(312) 616-0404 (fax)
www.ibbotson.com

2 Wilson Associates International
17128 Rancho Street.
Encino, CA 91316
(818) 999-0015
(800) 480-3888 (sales)
(818) 905-5340 (fax)
info@wilsonintl.com
www.wilsonintl.com

TOP 2 CONTACT MANAGER SOFTWARE PROGRAMS
1 ACT!
Symantec Corporation
175 West Broadway
Eugene, OR 97401
(800) 441-7234
(541) 334-6054
(541) 984-8020 (fax)
www.symantec.com

2 GoldMine Software Corporation
17383 Sunset Boulevard, Suite 301
Pacific Palisades, CA 90272
(800) 654-3526
(310) 454-4848 (fax)
www.goldminesw.com

TOP 2 PERSONAL INFORMATION MANAGERS

BOTH HAVE GOOD personal address and schedule features. Franklin Covey follows Stephen Covey's book, *The Seven Habits of Highly Effective People.*

1 Day-Timers, Inc.
One Day-Timer Plaza
Allentown, PA 18195-1551
(800) 225-5005
(800) 452-7398 (fax)
www.daytimer.com

2 Franklin Covey
2200 West Parkway Blvd.
Salt Lake City, Utah 84119
(801) 975-1776
(800) 655-1492
www.franklincovey.com

TOP 3 DATABASE OR RELATIONSHIP MANAGERS

THESE FIRST TWO ARE NOT SIMILAR, but both offer useful features for maintaining client data.

1 Protracker Software, Inc.
31 Forest Drive
Hampton, NH 03842-1920
(603) 926-8085
(603) 926-1249 (fax)
www.protracker.com   <http://www.protracker.com>

2 Financial Planning Consultants, Inc.
Financial Planning Building
2507 N. Verity Parkway
P.O. Box 42430
Middletown, OH 45042-0430
www.financialsoftware.com   <http://www.financialsoftware.com>

3 Ken Golding Software
BAM (Basically A Monkey) Database
4316 Holly Drive
Palm Beach Gardens, FL 33410
(561) 776-5685
www.kengolding.com   <http://www.kengolding.com>

TOP 3 INSTITUTIONAL PARTNERS (CUSTODIANS)

ALTHOUGH MANY SENIOR ADVISERS have a bias toward Schwab because they've been at it the longest, all three of the following provide institutional services for the independent planner.

1 Charles Schwab & Co., Inc.
101 Montgomery Street
28th Floor
San Francisco, CA 94104
www.schwab.com

2 Fidelity Distributors Corporation
Fidelity Investments Institutional Services Company, Inc.
82 Devonshire Street, Boston, MA 02109
(800) 854-4772
www.fidelity.com

3 Jack White (now owned by Waterhouse Securities)
La Jolla Gateway Building, Suite 220
9191 Town Centre Drive
San Diego, CA 92122
(619) 587-2000
(800) 233-3411
www.waterhouse.com

TOP 2 COMPLIANCE SERVICES

EVEN WITH KATHERINE VESSENES'S book, you'll probably want to maintain your own ADV.

1 National Regulatory Service
   323 A Main Street
   Lakeville, CT 06039
   (860) 435-2541 x25
   (860) 435-0031 (fax)
   www.nrs-inc.com

2 ProFormWare, Inc.
   3900 N.W. 2nd Court
   Boca Raton, FL 33431
   (800) 800-3204
   (561) 447-6686 (fax)
   www.proformware.com

TOP 2 RIA (SERIES 65) REGISTRATION COURSES

NEED TO PASS THE RIA EXAM? Try these helpful crash courses.

1 Investment Training Institute
   3569 Habersham at Northlake
   Tucker, GA 30084
   (800) 241-9095
   (770) 491-0299 (fax)
   www.iti-training.com

2 Pass Perfect Associates
   176 Bedford Road
   Greenwich, CT 06831
   (800) 349-3396
   www.passperfect.com

TOP 3 LICENSING ORGANIZATIONS

1 CFP Board
   1700 Broadway, Suite 2100
   Denver, CO 80290-2101
   (800) 433-4292
   www.CFP-Board.org

The CFP Board controls the CFP mark, not only in the United States, but internationally as well.

2 Securities and Exchange Commission

450 Fifth St. NW

Washington, DC 20549

(202) 942-7040

www.sec.gov

The SEC doesn't really license, but as an independent RIA you will need to file an ADV with them if you manage $25 million and above. Under $25 million, the individual states have jurisdiction.

3 NASD

NASD Institute for Professional Development

80 Merritt Boulevard

Trumbull, CT 06611

(212) 858-4241

www.nasdr.com

If you're taking commission or securities, you'll be governed by the rules of the NASD.

TOP 2 CFP PROFESSIONAL EDUCATIONAL PROGRAMS

1 College for Financial Planning

6161 S. Syracuse Way

Greenwood Village, CO 80111-4707

(303) 220-1200

www.fp.edu

Owned by Phoenix University, the college provides home-study CFP programs.

2 American College

270 S. Bryn Mawr Ave.

Bryn Mawr, PA 19010-2196

(888) AMER-COL

(610) 526-1465 (fax)

www.amercol.edu

American College provides classes for professional insurance credentials, such as CLU, ChFC, as well as the CFP program.

TOP 3 WEB-SITE DESIGN FIRMS

I'VE DISCUSSED THESE firms in Chapter 7.

1 Advisorsquare, d/b/a Manhattan Analytics
2615 Pacific Coast Highway
Suite 329
Hermosa Beach, CA 90254
(800) 251-3863
www.advisorsquare.com

2 Lightport Advisors, Inc.
6234 Grand Boulevard
Suite 212
New Port Richey, FL 34652
(888) 800-0188
(813) 815-8005
www.lightport.com

3 Web Dynamics, Inc.
476 Heritage Park Boulevard, Suite 215
Layton, UT 84041
(801) 927-1008
www.myfrontdoor.com

TOP 2 PLACES TO GO FOR INTERNS

IT'S HARD TO BELIEVE it's a secret, but it seems that one of the best sources for extraordinary staff talent is still unknown to many practitioners, namely the graduates from some of the preeminent CFP educational programs.

1 Jerry Mason
Texas Tech
Merchandising, Environmental Design
& Consumer Economics
P.O. Box 41162
Lubbock, TX 79409-1162
(806) 742-2067

2 Bruce Brunson, Ph.D.
Virginia Tech
101 Wallace Hall
Blacksburg, VA 24060-0410
(540) 231-6178

TOP 8 PERSONAL DEVELOPMENT PROGRAMS

1 Voice-Pro
4000 Executive Parkway
San Ramon, CA 94583
(925) 866-8866
www.voicepro.com
This firm, recommended by Karen Spero, was one of the more intriguing recommendations. Voice-Pro, Inc. provides workshops to assist professionals to become better communicators.

2 Strategic Coach
33 Fraser Avenue, Suite 201
Toronto, ON
M6K 3J9 Canada
(800) 387-3206
(416) 531-1135 (fax)
www.strategiccoach.com
Strategic Coach is a great program for entrepreneurs wanting to reach their full potential.

3 Focus 4
Richard Zalack
4178 Center Road
Brunswick, OH 44212
(330) 225-0707
(330) 273-6703 (fax)
Focus 4 is similar to Strategic Coach, helping entrepreneurs put their business and personal lives in perspective.

4 Dale Carnegie Training
780 Third Avenue, 22nd Floor
New York, NY 10017
(800) 231-5800
www.dale-carnegie.com

Fred Pryor and Career Track below provide management and business seminar for professional improvement.

5 Fred Pryor Seminars

P.O. Box 2951

Shawnee Mission, KS 66201

(800) 255-6139

6 Career Track Programs

3085 Center Green Drive

Boulder, CO 80301-5408

(800) 488-0929

www.careertrack.com

7 Myers Briggs Type Indicator

Consulting Psychologists Press, Inc.

3803 East Bayshore Road

Palo Alto, CA 94303

(800) 624-1765

www.mbti.com

See Chapter 6 on retreats for more details on the Myers-Briggs or Personal Style Inventory.

8 Personal Style Inventory

PAR- Psychological Assessment Resources, Inc.

P.O. Box 998

Odessa, FL 33556

(800) 331-TEST

TOP 2 DICTATION SOFTWARE PROGRAMS

1 Dragon Systems, Inc.

320 Nevada Street

Newton, MA 02160 USA

(800) TALK-TYP or (617) 965-5200

(617) 527-0372 (fax)

My partner Harold and I use Dragon in the office—it's quite amazing!

2 IBM ViaVoice

IBM North America,
1133 Westchester Avenue,
White Plains NY 10604
(800) IBM-4YOU
(770) 863-3030 (fax)

TOP 7 WEB-SITES

AS WE ALL KNOW, these grow exponentially by the second. There were, however, a few that were mentioned frequently enough to warrant your consideration.

1 CFP Board   www.cfp-board.org   Among other information, you can find out who has a current CFP license.

2 IAFP   www.iafp.org   Get current industry information, discussion rooms, keep up with their various conferences and conventions.

3 ICFP BIZ   www.icfpbiz.net   The ICFP Web site has good industry information, but the *ICFP BIZ* section is a comprehensive guide to the world of practice management.

4 Bloomberg   www.bloomberg.com   This site offers financial information, latest stock reports, and more.

5 Financial Planning Magazine   www.fponline.com   In addition to a comprehensive and searchable archive of past articles, this site includes a number of very active professional discussion rooms on subjects such as practice management and compliance.

6 The White House   www.whitehouse.gov   Complain here.

7 Letterman's Top 10   www.cbs.com   Have a laugh here.

Final Note: As the International Association for Financial Planning (IAFP) and the Institute of Certified Financial Planners (ICFP) have unified to form the Financial Planning Association (FPA), some Web sites listed above will, in time, be converted to a new FPA site.

POTPOURRI

THE FOLLOWING ARE MORE free association "gotta haves" suggested by some of my respondents. Although they don't fit particularly well into neat categories I thought they were worth including.

1 Dave Diesslin, Diesslin & Associates, Fort Worth, Texas
Sense of Humor
Involvement with organizations like ICFP, IAFP, NAPFA
2 Eleanor Blayney
A love seat, coffee table, and two side chairs

PERMISSIONS CREDITS

GRATEFUL ACKNOWLEDGMENT is made to the following for permission to reprint material copyrighted or controlled by them. This constitutes a continuation of the copyright page.

◆ Staff Self-Assessment Form. Reprinted by permission of Karen Spero, Spero-Smith Investment Advisers, Cleveland, OH.

◆ Personal experience: partner disability. Reprinted by permission of John W. Ueleke, CFP, Legacy Wealth Management, Memphis, TN.

◆ Firm's Mission Statement. Reprinted by permission of Eleanor Blayney and Greg D. Sullivan, Sullivan Bruyette Speros & Blayney, Inc., McLean, VA.

◆ Personal experience: loss of a partner. Reprinted by permission of William B. Howard, ChFC, CFP, William Howard & Co., Financial Advisors, Inc., Memphis, TN.

◆ Firm's Philosophy Statement. Reprinted by permission of Ross Levin, CFP, Accredited Investors, Inc., Edina, MN.

◆ Firm's Core Values. Reprinted by permission of Roy T. Diliberto, CLU, ChFC, CFP, RTD Financial Advisors, Inc., Philadelphia, PA.

◆ Firm's Mission Statement. Reprinted by permission of John Blankinship, Jr., CFP, Blankinship & Foster, Del Mar, CA.

◆ Firm's Core Values. Reprinted by permission of David H. Bugen, Bugen Stuart Korn & Cordaro, Inc., Chatham, NJ.

◆ "Dos & Don'ts" List. Reprinted by permission of Mark Tibergien, Moss Adams Advisory Services, Seattle, WA.

◆ Firm's Mission Statement. Reprinted by permission of David S. Norton, Norton Partners, Bristol, United Kingdom.

About Bloomberg

Bloomberg L.P., founded in 1981, is a global information services, news, and media company. Headquartered in New York, the company has nine sales offices, two data centers, and 85 news bureaus worldwide.

Bloomberg, serving customers in 126 countries around the world, holds a unique position within the financial services industry by providing an unparalleled range of features in a single package known as the BLOOMBERG PROFESSIONAL™ service. By addressing the demand for investment performance and efficiency through an exceptional combination of information, analytic, electronic trading, and Straight Through Processing tools, Bloomberg has built a worldwide customer base of corporations, issuers, financial intermediaries, and institutional investors.

BLOOMBERG NEWS℠, founded in 1990, provides stories and columns on business, general news, politics, and sports to leading newspapers and magazines throughout the world. BLOOMBERG TELEVISION®, a 24-hour business and financial news network, is produced and distributed globally in seven different languages. BLOOMBERG RADIO™ is an international radio network anchored by flagship station BLOOMBERG® WBBR 1130AM in New York.

In addition to the BLOOMBERG PRESS® line of books, Bloomberg publishes *BLOOMBERG® MARKETS, BLOOMBERG PERSONAL FINANCE™,* and *BLOOMBERG® WEALTH MANAGER.* To learn more about Bloomberg, call a sales representative at:

Frankfurt:	49-69-92041-200	São Paulo:	5511-3048-4500
Hong Kong:	85-2-2977-6600	Singapore:	65-212-1200
London:	44-20-7330-7500	Sydney:	61-2-9777-8601
New York:	1-212-318-2200	Tokyo:	81-3-3201-8950
San Francisco:	1-415-912-2980		

FOR IN-DEPTH MARKET INFORMATION and news, visit the Bloomberg website at **www.bloomberg.com,** which draws from the news and power of the BLOOMBERG PROFESSIONAL™ service and Bloomberg's host of media products to provide high-quality news and information in multiple languages on stocks, bonds, currencies, and commodities.

About the Author

Deena B. Katz, CFP, has shared her expertise on *Good Morning America* and *CBS This Morning* and was the authority selected by *Consumer Reports* to evaluate the work of other planners. She is the editor-in-chief of the *Journal of Retirement Planning* and has published extensively for other magazines such as *Financial Planning* and *Financial Advisor*. In the January 2001 issue of *Financial Planning*, she was named by her peers as one of the five most influential people in the planning profession. She was among the top 250 planners selected by *Worth* magazine in September 2001 and was listed in the top 100 by *Mutual Funds* magazine. Ms. Katz is an internationally sought-after speaker for national and international legal, accounting, and financial organizations and the author of the acclaimed book with CD-ROM, *Deena Katz's Tools and Templates for Your Practice.*

FOR MORE INFORMATION go to www.evensky.com or contact the author directly at DeenaKatz@evensky.com with questions or comments.